The RHS Encyclopedia of Practical Gardening

GROWING FRUIT

HARRY BAKER

Editor-in-chief Christopher Brickell
Technical Editor Kenneth A. Beckett

Harry Baker has recently retired as Fruit Officer of the RHS Garden at Wisley, Surrey. He is a leading world authority on cool temperature fruits, and the author of the classic work *The Fruit Garden Displayed.*

D0493497

MITCHELL BEAZLEY

The Royal Horticultural Society's Encyclopedia of Practical Gardening © Octopus Publishing Group Ltd 1979, 1992

The Royal Horticultural Society's Encyclopedia of Practical Gardening: Growing Fruit © Octopus Publishing Group Ltd 1980, 1999
First published as The Royal Horticultural Society's Encyclopedia of Practical Gardening: Fruit
All rights reserved
Reproduction of any kind in part or in whole in any part of the world reserved by the publishers

First published 1980
Herbicidal and pesticidal sections revised 1989, 1992
First published in this edition 1992
Reprinted 1993, 1994, 1995
New edition 1999 Reprinted 2000, 2002, 2003, 2004, 2005, 2006

ISBN-13: 978 1 84000 153 2
ISBN-10: 1 84000153 4

Edited and designed by Mitchell Beazley, an imprint of Octopus Publishing Group Ltd
2-4 Heron Quays, London E14 4JP
Produced by Toppan Printing Co (HK) Ltd.
Printed and bound in China

Contents

Introduction 1

Few gardeners will deny that one of the most rewarding aspects of gardening is growing and tasting freshly picked sun-warmed fruits. They are far superior to shop fruit because they are picked when they are at their best and their subtle flavours and textures have not been marred by handling and packing. Add to this the delight of a garden decked each spring with colourful blossom, the perennial beauty of mature, shapely trees, and the pride in a well-stocked freezer or storehouse through the winter and you can really appreciate the joy of fruit growing.

How to use this book
Fruit is divided into four major sections. The first deals with the practical aspects of fruit growing, from tools and equipment to planning the fruit garden. The second section concerns all soft fruits from strawberries to melons, which are the quickest to bear fruit and which are suitable for even a small garden. In the third section of the book tree fruits, which are slow to bear fruit but have a longer fruiting season, are discussed in detail and information is given about renovation of neglected trees, growing fruit in containers, and fruit storage. There are also comprehensive pollination tables. The fourth section covers warm temperate fruits, such as citrus fruits and the less well known but equally easy to grow Chinese gooseberries (kiwi fruits).

Climate and local conditions
Climate is important whether the gardener wishes to grow and ripen exotic fruits such as figs, peaches and grapes or cool temperate fruits such as apples and pears. Using climate zone maps of Europe and the United States (devised by the Arnold Arboretum), each fruit is keyed in to its ideal growing area.

Fruit has been written mainly for gardeners in the cool temperate regions, with timings based on the comparatively mild southern area of Britain. For gardeners in more northern areas, timings may be two or three weeks later. Where applicable, there are details of cultivation of fruits under glass or in the greenhouse, which can extend the season.

Because fruit is susceptible to frost damage, the fruit gardener must also take note of local climate conditions, the microclimate. The dangers of frost pockets and wind turbulence are discussed in terms of the choice of site, with suggestions on how to overcome them.

Once the site has been chosen the gardener needs to know how to get maximum benefit from it. The planning pages outline the possible yields and spacings of most fruits and fruit forms.

Fruits are usually long-term projects; some trees can berar fruit for a lifetime if given good care, and so it is particularly important to prepare the ground thoroughly before planting. A two-page section gives the essentials of soil content, soil depth, drainage, soil acidity (or alkalinity), fertilizers and digging.

Pests and diseases
To spray or not to spray is a question most gardeners are divided about. In *Fruit* the emphasis has been placed upon correct cultivation procedures and the selection of certified disease-free plants whenever possible. If the cultural instructions are followed, pests and diseases should be kept in check. If, despite this, the garden is seriously invaded by pests and diseases, or they are inherited in a new garden, a detailed spray guide has been included in the month-by-month guide. A list of the most common pests and diseases and their treatments is in the front section of the book and each fruit page outlines those to which it is prone. A companion volume in this series, *Garden Pests and Diseases*, gives more comprehensive information on this subject.

Chemical control of weeds is another area of controversy. The policy of this book is to give full information on the various chemicals approved for garden use and their correct use, for those who wish to use them. For those who do not, hand weeding, hoeing or mulching with black plastic are suggested as alternatives. **Remember: keep all chemicals in their properly labelled containers and safely out of the reach of children.**
Read the product label before buying, and mix and apply strictly according to the manufacturer's recommendations accompanying the product.

There is also a month-by-month guide to remind the gardener of the tasks in the garden and their timings during the year.

Glossary

Adventitious buds Normally growth buds develop between leaf and stem in a definite order. Adventitious buds are growth buds· that arise without any relation to the leaves, usually in response to a wound.

Annual A plant that completes its life-cycle within one growing season.

Apex The tip of a stem, hence apical bud, the uppermost bud on the stem, and apical shoot, the uppermost stem on a system of branches.

Axil The angle between leaf and stem; hence axillary bud and axillary shoot, the bud or shoot arising between leaf and stem.

Bark-ringing The removal of a ring of bark from the trunk of an unfruitful tree to check shoot growth and encourage fruiting.

Biennial A plant with a life-cycle spread over two growing seasons.

Biennial bearer A tree bearing a good crop of blossom or fruit only in alternate years.

Branched head A branch system on a tree in which there is no central-leader shoot.

Break The development of lateral shoots as a result of pruning a shoot to an axillary bud.

Breastwood Shoots growing forward from plants trained against support structures.

Bush tree A tree pruned to give a dwarf form with about 2–2½ ft of clear stem.

Central leader The central, vertical, dominant stem of a tree.

Chelated compound An organic compound containing a metal such as manganese or iron which is slowly released into the soil.

Clone A plant propagated asexually, with identical characteristics to its parent.

Cordon A tree pruned to form a main stem bearing spurs. It may be planted obliquely, at an acute angle to the ground or vertically.

Cultivar A named, cultivated form of a plant.

Current year's growth/wood Shoots that have grown from buds in the present growing season.

Deblossoming The removal of individual flowers or flower trusses.

Defoliation The removal of leaves.

Dehorning The severe cutting back of main branches.

Disbudding The removal of surplus buds or shoots that are just beginning to grow.

Dormant buds Buds which, although formed normally, do not become active unless there is some injury to the shoot or branch system.

Dormant period The time in the life-cycle of a plant when no new growth is produced, usually in the winter.

Double working A way of overcoming the incompatibility between certain varieties of fruit and the desired rootstocks by grafting the former on to a compatible variety which is in turn grafted on to the rootstock.

Dwarf pyramid A tree pruned to form a pyramid-shaped central-leader tree about 7 ft high.

Espalier A tree trained with a vertical main stem and tiers of horizontal branches.

Extension growth Shoots that develop from the apical or terminal bud of a stem.

Eye A growth bud, especially of vines.

Fan A tree or shrub with the main branches trained like the ribs of a fan against a wall, fence or other support system.

Feathers The lateral shoots on a one-year-old (maiden) tree.

Flushes Irregular successive crops of flowers and fruit, as on perpetual strawberries.

Framework The "skeleton" of main branches.

Friable Describes a fine and crumbly soil with no hard or wet lumps.

Fruit buds Large, round prominent buds which produce flowers and fruit.

Germination The development of a seed into a seedling.

Grafting Propagation by uniting a shoot or single bud of one plant – the scion – with the root system and stem of another – the stock or rootstock.

Growth or wood bud A small narrow bud that gives rise to a shoot.

Half-hardy A plant that cannot survive the winter without protection.

Half-standard A tree or shrub grown with about 3½–4½ ft of clear stem.

Harden off To acclimatize plants raised in warm conditions to colder conditions.

Hardy A plant that can survive winter conditions in the open.

Heading back The first tipping of the central-leader stem of a maiden tree.

Heel in To store stems, cuttings or plants in an upright or inclined position in a trench, which is then filled with earth and firmed.

Humus Fertile, decomposed organic matter.

Hybrid A plant produced by cross-pollinating two or more species or forms of a species.

Lateral A side growth that develops at an angle from the main stem of the tree.

Leader The terminal shoot of a tree or branch that determines the main direction of growth.

Maiden A one-year-old tree or shrub.

Maiden lateral A one-year-old lateral shoot.

Microclimate The climatic conditions in a particular small area.

Mulch A layer of material, such as straw or plastic sheeting, put on the soil surface to conserve moisture and to suppress weeds.

Offset A young plant that develops close to or at the base of the parent plant.

Pan A hard layer of soil beneath the surface.

Perennial A plant that lives for more than three seasons.

pH The scale used to measure the acidity or alkalinity of the soil: 7.0 is neutral, above 7.0 is alkaline and below 7.0 is acid.

Pinching back or stopping To cut or nip out with fingers the growing tip of a shoot.

Plunge outside To bury container-grown plants up to their rims in an ash, peat or sand bed to protect the roots from frost in winter.

Prick out To transfer seedlings from a seed tray to another container or the open ground.

Primary branches The branches that are formed first, arising from the main stem.

Propagation The production of a new plant from an existing one, either sexually by seeds or asexually, for example by grafting.

Regulatory pruning Pruning to remove crossing, crowded and weak shoots and branches.

Renewal pruning Pruning to maintain a constant supply of young shoots.

Rod The main, woody stem of a vine.

Root cutting A piece of the root of a plant used for propagation.

Rooted tips The shoot tips of plants such as blackberries that have been buried in the soil and taken root to form a new plant.

Root-pruning Severing some or all of the main roots of a tree to reduce vigour.

Rootstock *See* **Grafting.**

Runner A rooting stem that grows along the surface of the soil, as in strawberries.

Scion *see* **Grafting.**

Secondary branches The branches that develop later from the primary branches.

Self-compatible or self-fertile A plant that can produce seed after fertilization with pollen from the same flower or from other flowers on that plant or on a plant of the same clone.

Snag A short stump of a branch left after incorrect pruning.

Soakaway A pit into which water drains.

Spit depth The depth of a blade on a normal digging spade; about 10 in.

Sport or mutant A plant that differs genetically from the typical growth of the plant that produced it.

Spur A slow-growing short branch system that usually carries clusters of flower buds.

Spur-bearer A fruit tree that bears most of its fruit on spurs.

Standard A tree or shrub grown with 5–7 ft of clear stem.

Stock *See* **Grafting.**

Stopping *See* **Pinching back.**

Stub-back To cut back a lateral after it has fruited, leaving a 1 in stub.

Sub-lateral A side-shoot growing from a maiden lateral.

Sucker A shoot growing from a stem or root at or below ground level.

Systemic compound A pesticide or fungicide that totally or partially permeates the plant including the internal tissues.

Terminal bud A growth or fruit bud at the end of an unpruned one-year-old shoot.

Thin To reduce the number of seedlings, buds, flowers, fruitlets or branches.

Tilth The structure of the soil surface. A good tilth is fine and crumbly.

Tip-bearer A tree that bears most of its fruits at the tips of one-year-old shoots.

Tipping The removal of the apical part of a shoot by pruning.

Trace elements Substances necessary for plant growth which are usually present in the soil in minute quantities.

True leaves Leaves typical of the mature plant as opposed to simpler seed leaves.

Truss A cluster of flowers or fruit.

Union The junction between rootstock and scion or between two scions grafted together.

Vegetative growth Leaf and stem growth as opposed to flowers or fruit.

Water shoot A vigorous, sappy shoot growing from an adventitious or dormant bud on the trunk or older branches of a tree.

Wind-rock The loosening of the roots of plants by the force of the wind.

Wood bud *See* **Growth bud.**

Climate 1

The most important aspects of climate the fruit gardener must consider when planning a fruit garden are temperature, rainfall and wind. Of these, temperature is the most crucial. Fruit plants can survive drought conditions and gales but they may fail to produce crops or even be killed by untimely low or high temperatures.

Broad climatic divisions are a useful basis for judging the general viability of a specific crop but local conditions must also be carefully considered (see pages 10–13).

Zones of hardiness

The map of hardiness in North America (below) was devised by the Arnold Arboretum of Harvard University in the USA. It defines zones of consistent average, annual, minimum temperatures. The map of Europe is based on the same principles.

Throughout this book, the information on individual fruits includes the zones in which they are hardy. For example, figs are generally hardy in zones 9 and 10 and half-hardy in zone 8. However, some cultivars, such as 'Brown Turkey', will survive even up to zone 5 with winter protection and several cultivars are hardy in zone 8.

The Mediterranean climate of zones 9 and 10 seems ideal for fruit growing, with mild

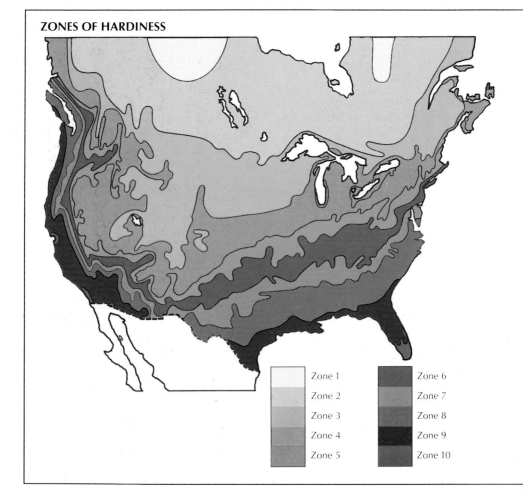

ZONES OF HARDINESS

Zone 1
Zone 2
Zone 3
Zone 4
Zone 5
Zone 6
Zone 7
Zone 8
Zone 9
Zone 10

Temperature ranges

Zone 1
Below −45°C/−50°F
Zone 2
−45° to −37°C/
−50° to −35°F
Zone 3
−37° to −29°C/
−35° to −20°F

Zone 4
−29° to −23°C/
−20° to −10°F
Zone 5
−23° to −21°C/
−10° to −5°F
Zone 6
−21° to −15°C/−5° to 5°F

Zone 7
−15° to −12°C/5° to 10°F
Zone 8
−12° to −7°C/10° to 20°F
Zone 9
−7° to −1°C/20° to 30°F
Zone 10
−1° to 4°C/30° to 40°F

winters and little frost to damage blossom or setting fruitlets; the growing season is long and there are many hours of sunshine for ripening. Although it is ideal for the typical Mediterranean fruits (such as peaches, figs and apricots), which are adapted to this climate and need long hot summers and mild winters, it is not suitable for all fruits. Deciduous trees such as apples, pears, plums and cherries require a dormant period in each year and this is brought about by colder weather. In zone 10, not all cultivars are able to become truly dormant in the winter, because the temperature is too high. The trees usually become spindly with sparse, poor crops. These fruits, as well as gooseberries, currants and cane fruits, are adapted to more temperate conditions and are happiest in zones 6–8.

It is not difficult to grow fruits in zones in which they are half-hardy. Peaches, nectarines and apricots, for example, grow well in zone 8 provided they are planted in a sunny position and protected against low temperatures and frost. Alternatively, fruits can be planted in containers and moved under cover when conditions become unfavourable. Also, the conditions of a warmer zone can be artificially reproduced in a greenhouse, although this is expensive.

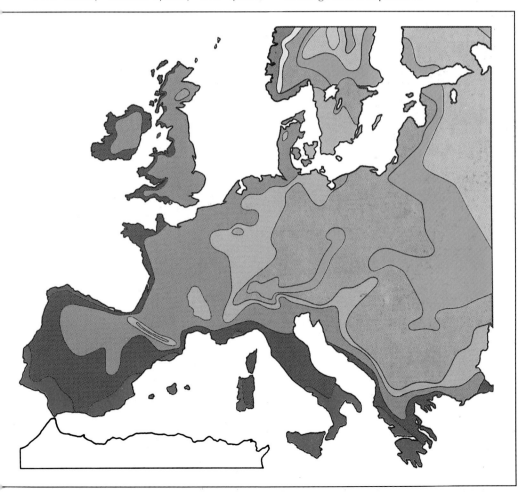

Climate 2

Coastal and lakeside fruit gardens

A large body of water, whether a freshwater lake or the sea, exerts a strong, modifying influence on a region's climate. Water takes longer to heat up and to cool down than land, so winter temperatures are usually higher and there is less risk of frost. As a result, it is possible to grow earlier-flowering cultivars of plants that are hardy to the zone and to grow half-hardy plants more easily.

Conversely, areas away from the sea's modifying influence are exposed to extremes of temperature.

Ocean currents also affect temperature. For example, the warm Gulf Stream affects the climates of Britain and western Norway to the extent that these coastal regions fall into a higher zone than that of other areas in the same northerly latitudes.

A large body of water can also have unfavourable effects on coastal areas. Winds tend to be strong because the uninterrupted expanse of water offers no resistance to slow them down. This can cause considerable damage to blossom, leaves, branches and fruit. In addition, winds blowing in from the sea are salt-laden and can burn leaves, young shoots and fruits. It is essential to provide shelter with wind-breaks in the form of fences or hedges (see pages 10–11). However, windy conditions do decrease the risk of radiation frosts.

High humidity and heavy rainfall can also cause problems in lakeside and coastal gardens as well as on high ground (see below).

Rainfall

The right amount of moisture is essential to the healthy growth of fruit crops, and both drought and excessive rainfall can be serious problems. Drought can be overcome to a considerable extent by regular watering and mulching, but excessive rain is difficult to combat.

Frequent rain and high humidity cause leaves to remain wet for prolonged periods, rendering them more prone to fungal infections. Fruits may fail to ripen and excessive rain may cause them to rot. If the soil becomes waterlogged, the roots may also rot. For example, it is difficult to obtain a good crop of disease-free apples in an area with an average rainfall of more than 35 in because of scab and canker, unless there is a very rigorous spraying programme. Certain cultivars of fruit withstand these conditions better than others; for example, cooking apples, in which appearance and flavour are not so important, tolerate heavy rainfall better than do dessert varieties of apples.

Temperature

The temperature at which grass usually begins to grow is about 6°C/43°F and this is regarded as the beginning of the growing season. The number of days per year at or above this temperature and, therefore, the length of the growing season, increases zone by zone the shortest season being in zone 1 and the longest in zone 10.

The length of the growing season should be taken into consideration when deciding what fruits to grow. Some fruits, such as grapes, require a long season to ripen, whereas others, such as strawberries, require a short period. For practical purposes, the growing season can be thought of as the number of frost-free days from spring to autumn. Grapes, for example, require about 180 frost-free days.

Although, as mentioned above, the minimum temperature for the growing season is about 6°C/43°F, some plants require consistently higher temperatures. For example, for melons, the ideal is a minimum night-time temperature of 24°C/75°F and a minimum daytime temperature of 30°C/86°F throughout their growing season although an average of 24°C/75°F is satisfactory. Citrus fruits are also very sensitive to temperature. Seville oranges and mandarins, for example, require a minimum daytime temperature of 16°C/60°F throughout their growing season and do not reach their full flavour if temperatures are below 18°C/65°F while the fruit is ripening.

Frost

Frost in the spring can be more damaging to fruit plants than consistent low winter temperatures. Plants may survive low temperatures when they are dormant, but a sudden spring frost can kill new buds, shoots and sometimes flowers.

The degree of vulnerability depends upon the stage of bud development; the more advanced the fruit buds are, the greater the danger. Taking the apple as an example, frost damage can occur at green cluster stage at −3.5°C/26°F; at pink bud stage at −3°C/27°F; at full bloom stage at −2°C/28°F; at petal fall stage at −1.5°C-29°F; and at fruitlet stage at −1°C/30°F.

In areas susceptible to frost, choose, where possible, late-flowering cultivars, those with long flowering seasons or those with a reputation for blossom hardiness. Suitable cultivars of apples, for example, would be the late-flowering 'Edward VII', 'Crawley Beauty' and 'Royal Jubilee', or the frost-resistant flowered 'Lane's Prince Albert' and 'Worcester Pearmain'. 'Cox's Orange Pippin' and 'Bramley's Seedling', however, are particularly susceptible to frost damage. Raspberries, blackberries and loganberries flower fairly late and are not likely to be much damaged by frost. Black currants are very susceptible to frost damage and red currants and gooseberries are also at risk. Strawberries can be damaged by ground frost but have such a long flowering season that it is rare to lose an entire year's crop.

Altitude

Altitude is also an important factor in that the higher it is, the cooler the climate and the shorter the growing season. There is also an increased risk of frost, and rainfall tends to be higher. Dessert fruits are usually grown commercially at altitudes of less than 400 ft, although this is a counsel of perfection and fruit can be grown at much higher altitudes. There are warmer microclimates in certain positions at higher levels, such as on south-facing slopes or between the folds of hills. In hotter climates, fruits that grow best at cooler temperatures can be planted on mountain slopes at comparatively high altitudes.

The slope of the land is also a consideration. A steep slope is a handicap to essential cultivation and picking operations, and it usually means soil erosion and poor soil conditions are present. A gentle slope is preferable because it can help soil drainage.

FROST DAMAGE

Strawberry flowers damaged by frost have developed black "eyes" (a). The ovaries have been killed and cannot develop into fruit. Apples scarred by frost develop russet patches and cracking (b). Fruits with this scarring may continue to grow if the ovaries have been only slightly damaged. Although frost-damaged pears can become distorted (c) as they grow, they are still edible.

Choice of site 1

If there is any choice within the garden, choose the sunniest site possible for fruit (see pages 15–16). Light and warmth are necessary to ripen the fruits and the wood and to promote the development of fruit buds for the next year's crop. Most fruits tolerate some shade but crop yields may be affected, particularly with warm temperate fruits such as apricots, peaches, nectarines, figs and grapes that must be in full sun. Other fruits grow reasonably well as long as they receive sunlight for at least half the day throughout the growing season. Dessert fruits, in which colour and flavour is important, require more light than do culinary fruits. Bush and cane fruits, such as blackberries, will tolerate some shade provided the soil is not dry and the plants do not suffer from rain dripping from overhanging branches.

Wind protection

The fruit plot should be sheltered from strong winds which inhibit the movement of pollinating insects, damage growth and cause fruits to fall prematurely. In an exposed site, the gardener should provide a wind-break.

Wind turbulence

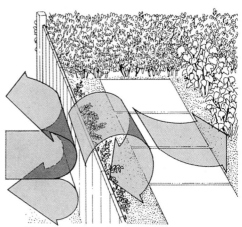

Avoid evergreen hedges and solid fences which may block the wind and cause severe turbulence among the plants next to them.

An open wind-break

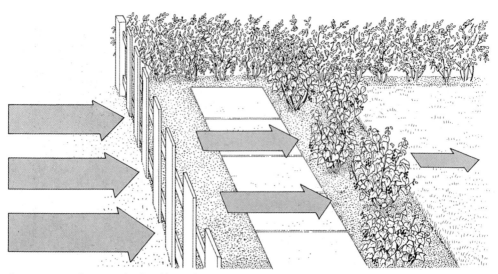

A more open fence or hedge filters the wind, reducing the wind's force by letting it flow through. Locate wind-breaks on the western and eastern sides of the garden where the wind is usually strongest and coldest and most damaging.

The type of wind-break depends upon the scale of planting; for example, a large orchard is best protected by a living wind-break such as a row of trees. For this, plant deciduous, fast-growing, upright trees which leaf early in the spring, in preference to the more solid evergreens which block rather than filter the wind, creating turbulence among, and possibly damage to, the fruit they are supposed to protect. The most widely used are the alder, willow and poplar.

On a smaller scale there are many hedge plants that make a good screen if the smaller fruit tree forms are to be planted. Hedges such as beech and hornbeam can form attractive features in their own right. Nevertheless, the living wind-breaks compete with the fruit trees for light, water and nutrients and can be hosts to pests, diseases and birds. Also, where every bit of land is valuable, it is best to erect an artificial one.

The usual surround for a small suburban garden is a wall or lapboard fence against which fruit plants can be trained. These reduce the wind just beyond the structure but may cause turbulence farther away.

The height of the wind-break also affects the area sheltered because the sheltered zone to leeward of a moderately solid wind-break may extend to about 30 times the height of the structure, although the effect beyond 20 times its height is slight.

Wind-breaks made of coir or plastic netting erected on poles and wires are suitable for use in both large orchards and gardens because they can be placed where they are most needed to protect maturing crops or newly planted trees. They are preferable to a solid wall because they filter rather than block the air and prevent local turbulence.

To protect newly planted trees, drive 7½ ft long supporting posts, about 3–4 in in diameter, 2 ft into the ground, spaced at 9–12 ft intervals. Place struts at an angle to the posts to ensure that they are strong enough to withstand the force of the wind. Stretch two strands of gauge 8 galvanized wire between the posts, one about 1 in above soil level and one 5 in below the tops. Fasten 5 ft deep plastic netting between the wires by folding the edges over and interlacing them with hop or plastic string.

Erecting a wind-break

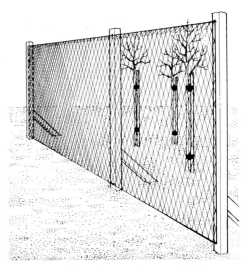

Drive 7½ ft long supporting posts, about 3–4 in in dia., 2 ft into the ground, at about 9–12 ft intervals. Place struts on the lee side of the wind-break. Stretch gauge 8 wire between the posts. Tie plastic netting to the wires with string.

Choice of site 2

Frost protection

Avoid planting in a frost pocket if possible because all fruits are sensitive to cold during the growing season, particularly at blossom time, when a few degrees of frost can ruin the potential crop (see pages 6–9). Frost pockets are formed because cold air is denser than warm air and naturally flows downwards on sloping ground. The areas where this cold air collects, or is impeded, are most prone to severe radiation frosts and so are called frost pockets.

When planting a wind-break be careful not to create a frost hazard and, where such an obstruction already exists, it should be examined to see whether it can be removed or modified so that air drainage is improved. With a hedge, for example, it may be possible to create a gap or remove some of the lower growth to allow the cold air to flow away. If there is no alternative to planting in a frost pocket, plant the larger fruit trees at the bottom and the smaller ones on the higher ground. Also consider planting late-flowering cultivars or those that are the most frost-tolerant (see pages 8–9).

It is impractical to try to protect large fruit trees in the garden but it is certainly worth while providing protection for the smaller fruit trees. The simplest way is to provide some kind of cover over the plants whenever frosts are anticipated. The cover should be removed once the danger of frost is over to allow access for pollinating insects and to let in light and air. Rows of cordons or espaliers can be draped with hessian, horticultural fleece, or with two or three layers of the type of netting used for bird protection. Insert canes around the plants to prevent the cover rubbing against the blossoms. Wall-trained fruit trees can be protected in a similar way. Branches of black and red currants and cane fruits can be tied together in loose bundles for protection. Untie them once the buds break to avoid etiolation of the young growth. Strawberries in the open and the smaller fruit bushes can be covered with fleece, netting, straw or even two or three sheets of newspaper. Plants under cloches or frames are safe against mild frosts but the glass should be covered with sacking in the event of severe cold. Remove the covering during the day.

Frost pockets

Avoid planting fruit trees and bushes in a frost pocket but if there is no alternative, improve the air drainage by creating a gap to allow the cold air to flow away. Plant larger fruit trees and later-flowering cultivars of bush fruit.

The provision of artificial heat by oil or paraffin burners is perhaps best reserved for crops under glass because of the cost. Burners in the open are ineffective unless used on a large scale. It may sometimes be worth while to cover bushes or wall-trained trees with a polythene tent and then put the burner inside. Make sure that the burner is working efficiently, and that there is no danger of the polythene catching fire.

Water as a means of frost protection is used commercially. This could be adapted to the garden provided permission is obtained, where necessary, from the water authorities. As water freezes, latent heat is liberated and this protects the buds and flowers. It is important to keep them sprinkled more or less continuously throughout the period of frost with droplets of water about the size of raindrops. In long periods the branches become covered in ice and it is advisable, therefore, to prop up weak branches beforehand. Soil drainage must be efficient or the soil may become waterlogged which could seriously harm the roots (see pages 18–21).

Frost protection for large trees

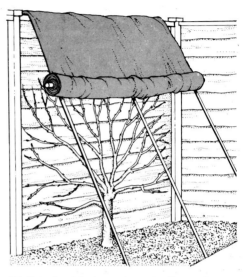

Wall-trained fruits such as the fig can be protected from frost by draping them with hessian or packing them with straw.

FROST PROTECTION FOR SMALL PLANTS

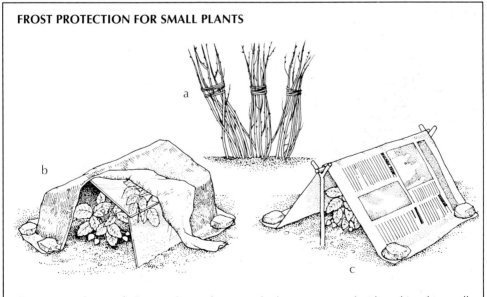

Currants and cane fruits can be tied together in loose bundles (a); fruit under cloches are covered with sacking (b); small plants are protected with paper (c).

Planning 1

The planting of tree, bush and cane fruits represents a long-term investment. Once planted there should be no need to move them until the cropping life of that particular plant is over. This could range from 20 to 50 years and more for tree fruits, and about 10–15 years for soft fruits. It is worth while, therefore, before planting to draw up a scale plan so that the plants are correctly sited.

The planner needs to take into account the approximate yield from each fruit to meet the family's requirements in relation to the amount of land available; the correct spacing; and the right aspect.

Yield
The yield depends upon many factors, such as the fertility of the soil, the climate, and the cultivar and the size of the plant. As a guide, the table below lists approximate yields from reasonably mature plants of the fruits commonly grown outside.

Spacing
The eventual size and yield of a mature fruit plant are influenced by the environment, the variety and, with many tree fruits, the rootstock on which it is grafted. Trees grafted on vigorous rootstocks in time grow larger than trees grafted on dwarfing stocks, even though they may be the same variety. Nowadays, most trees are cultivated for small gardens and are usually grafted on non-vigorous stocks, except for the half-standard or the

YIELDS AND SPACING TABLE

APPLES AND PEARS

Tree form	Apples	Pears	In rows	Rows apart
		Yield	**Spacing**	
Bush	60–120 lb	40–100 lb	12–18 ft	12–18 ft
Dwarf bush	30–50 lb	20–40 lb	8–15 ft	8–15 ft
Dwarf pyramid	10–15 lb	8–12 lb	5–6 ft	6 ft
Espalier (2-tier)	20–25 lb	15–20 lb	10–18 ft	6 ft
Fan	12–30 lb	12–30 lb	12–18 ft	—
Single cordon	5–8 lb	4–6 lb	2½–3 ft	6 ft
Standard	100–400 lb	80–240 lb	18–30 ft	18–30 ft

OTHER TREE FRUITS

Tree form			In rows	Rows apart
Bush (Morello cherry)		30–40 lb	12–18 ft	12–18 ft
Bush (plum and peach)		30–60 lb	12–18 ft	12–20 ft
Bush, half-standard and standard (sweet cherry)		30–120 lb	15–40 ft	15–40 ft
Bush or small tree (fig)		15–20 lb	18–20 ft	18–20 ft
Fan (all stone fruits)		12–30 lb	12–18 ft	—
Fan (fig)		15–20 lb	12–15 ft	—
Fan (sweet cherry)		12–30 lb	18–25 ft	—
Pyramid (plum)		30–50 lb	10–12 ft	10–12 ft
Standard (plum, peach and apricot)		30–120 lb	18–25 ft	18–25 ft

SOFT FRUIT

			In rows	Rows apart
Bush (black currant)		10–12 lb	5–6 ft	6 ft
Bush (gooseberry)		6–8 lb	4–5 ft	5 ft
Bush (red and white currant)		8–10 lb	5 ft	5 ft
Cordon (gooseberry, red and white currant)		1–3 lb	12–15 in	5 ft
Blackberry or hybrid berry		10–30 lb	8–15 ft	6–7 ft
Raspberry		1½ lb per ft of row	15–18 in	6 ft
Strawberry		8–10 oz per plant	12–15 in	2½–3 ft

standard forms. Soft fruits are grown on their own roots.

The spacings given in the table below are intended only as a guide for the planner. For more detail, refer to the relevant fruit pages. Allow a wider spacing on very fertile soils.

Fruit against walls and fences

While in many gardens the bulk of the fruit crop comes from a plot of land specially set aside for this purpose, the use of walls, fences and trellises should not be neglected, particularly where space is limited. Their structure provides support for the plants and also for netting as protection against birds or frosts. Walls and solid fences have the added advantages of giving shelter and, where the aspect is sunny, extra warmth and light is reflected from the masonry or wood. The added warmth improves the quality of the fruits, promotes fruit bud development and makes it possible to grow the more exotic fruits such as peaches, nectarines and figs where otherwise it might not be worth while.

Because wall and fence space is usually limited, use the restricted forms that are kept in shape and contained by summer pruning.

Apples and pears can be grown as cordons, espaliers or fans but stone fruits, such as apricots, peaches and cherries, do not respond to the cordon and espalier methods of training and are therefore grown only in fan-trained form. The climbing fruits, such as blackberries, hybrid berries and grapes, grow well against walls and fences. The grape vine in particular is perhaps the most versatile of all the trained fruits, being amenable to many forms of training against walls, fences or on pergolas but, of course, the aspect must be sunny.

The height of the supporting structure decides the shape or form in which the fruit is best trained.

Walls and fences up to 6 ft high are suitable for the low-trained tree forms such as the espalier, and for cordon and fan-trained gooseberries, red and white currants as well as blackberry and raspberry canes.

With walls and fences 6–8 ft high, it is possible to grow apples and pears (on dwarfing or semi-dwarfing stock) as cordons, fans or multiple-tiered espaliers, the number of tiers depending upon the height of the structure.

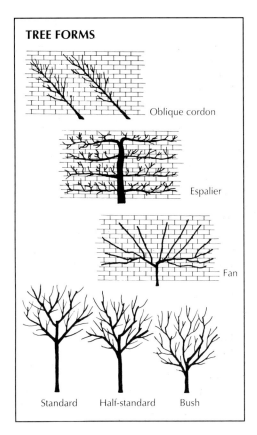

TREE FORMS

Oblique cordon

Espalier

Fan

Standard   Half-standard   Bush

There is no really dwarfing stock as yet developed for stone fruits, although it is anticipated there will be in the next five years, so the minimum height required for fan-trained apricots, peaches, nectarines, plums, gages and Morello cherries is 7 ft. There are successful peaches on semi-vigorous stocks grown on lower structures than this but they need regular pruning and tying down. The sweet cherry is a vigorous plant and needs a wall or fence of at least 8 ft. Structures can be given extra height by the use of trellis-work.

Aspect

The aspect of the wall, fence or trellis decides the kind of fruit that can be grown. In the northern hemisphere the warmest and sunniest aspect is the south-facing and the coldest and shadiest is the north, with the west and east somewhere between the two.

Planning 2

South The southern, south-eastern and south-western aspects are best reserved for the sun-loving fruits, although most fruits would thrive in this situation. The soil at the base of a south-facing wall can become very dry, so ensure there is adequate moisture during the growing season by mulching and watering. This aspects is suitable for figs, peaches, nectarines, apricots, grapes, gages, pears, plums, cherries and apples.

West The western aspect receives the afternoon sun but it is exposed to south-westerly winds and usually receives more rain than do other aspects. It is suitable for peaches, nectarines, apricots, sweet and sour cherries, grapes, gages, pears, plums, apples, raspberries, hybrid and blackberries, gooseberries, red and white currants.

East The eastern aspect is a dry situation receiving the morning sun but shaded in the afternoon. It is open to cold easterly winds. Suitable fruits include the early pears, apples, plums, sweet and sour cherries, currants, gooseberries, hybrid berries, blackberries and raspberries.

North The northern aspect is restricted to those fruits that are able to grow and ripen in cold situations. Suitable fruits are fan-trained acid cherries and damsons, early culinary apples, cordon currants and gooseberries and blackberries. They will ripen later than those in full sun.

Wiring walls and fences

Horizontal wires firmly attached to the wall or fence are necessary to support the framework branches and for tying in the new growth. Use gauge 14 galvanized fencing wire for espaliers and cordons, and gauge 16 for fan-trained trees.

WIRING WALLS AND FENCES

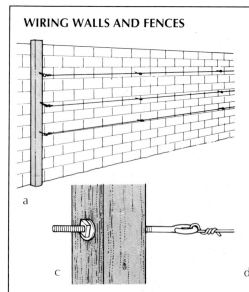

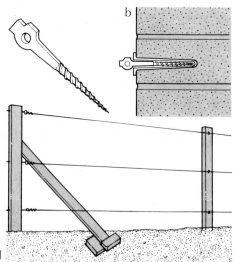

Wires must be held 1½–4 in away from walls by fixing 2 in square wooden battens (or 1½ in × 1½ in angle irons) to the masonry to hold the straining bolts and the ends of the wires (a). Screw or drive in 4 in galvanized or lead wall nails with eyes, or vine eyes (b) every 5 ft to hold the wires between the battens. With the screw type, drill and plug the wall first. Wires should be kept taut by attaching straining bolts (c) to one end post. Use wire staples (d) to hold the wires on the intermediate and other end posts. Tighten the wires with the straining bolts before driving the staples home. A diagonal post is needed to brace the main post.

For espaliers, fix the wires so that they coincide with the height of the arms (tiers). Generally the tiers are 15–18 in apart but plant the espaliers first to see where the wires should be placed. The wires for oblique cordons are usually fixed every 2 ft, the highest wire being 6 in below the top of the wall or fence.

Fan-trained trees require horizontal wires every 6 in or two brick courses apart, starting at 15 in from the ground and continuing to the top of the wall or fence. Straining bolts are not necessary on wires for fan-trained trees because the wires are placed closer together, so wire staples will suffice on wooden fences and lead wall eyes on walls.

Buying fruit plants

To ensure healthy new plants, it is best to buy fruit stock from a specialist fruit nursery.

Apart from having a better selection, the specialist is likely to stock cultivars of a guaranteed high standard of purity, health and vigour.

In many countries now, there are government-operated schemes for certain fruits, such as those in Britain for apples, pears, plums, black currants, raspberries, strawberries and cherries, whereby each cultivar is inspected and, if healthy, certified as such.

Healthy, certified stock also has the advantage of being guaranteed true to name.

Also, before choosing any fruit plant check its pollination requirements. Some fruits such as sweet cherries, apples, pears, certain plums and gages must be grown in compatible pairs or they will not produce fruit (see pages 94–7). Select the best cultivars from the lists of recommended cultivars and descriptions which head each fruit page.

Planning a small fruit garden

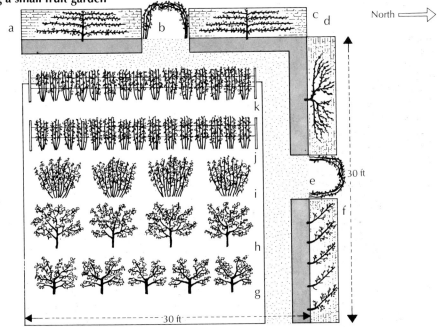

The above plot is a guide for planning a small intensively cultivated fruit garden. It can be modified to suit individual requirements. It contains: espalier pear (a); loganberry arch (b); espalier pear (c); fan peach (d); grape arch (e); cordon apples (f); gooseberries (g); red currants (h); black currants (i); summer-fruiting raspberries (j); autumn-fruiting raspberries (k).

Soil and soil drainage 1

Soil depth

Most soils will grow fruit of some kind, provided the land is reasonably well drained. The larger the fruit plant the greater the depth of workable, fertile, well-drained soil required. Strawberries need a minimum depth of 12 in, cane fruits, currants and gooseberries need 18 in, and tree fruits 24 in, with the exception of sweet cherries which require at least 30 in. Some fruits such as currants, gooseberries, blackberries, plums, damsons, pears and culinary apples will tolerate a little impeded drainage below 18 in, as will dessert apples, gages and sour cherries but to a lesser extent. For raspberries, peaches and sweet cherries good drainage is essential throughout. A thin soil over chalk is unsuitable for all but the smallest fruits such as strawberries. Raspberries do not thrive in chalky soils unless plenty of organic matter is added.

Soil drainage

A basic idea of the natural drainage conditions of the garden can be discovered by a few simple observations. If the soil is heavy to dig and close-textured, with pools of standing water after rainfall, the soil or sub-soil probably has a high clay content and water drains into and away from it very slowly. This type of soil can be improved by digging in bulky organics such as strawy compost, manure or peat and by improving the drainage.

Soils that are waterlogged for long periods must be drained, otherwise root death can occur, leading to extensive die-back or perhaps the total loss of the plant. For small plantings a simple soakaway can be constructed, but for larger plots a line of drains or even a herringbone system of plastic, concrete or tile drains may be necessary. Where it is impossible to drain the soil, the trees and bushes may be planted on mounds and the raspberries and strawberries on ridges.

If the soil is light and dries out fast, it probably has a low nutrient and high sand or gravel content, or it may be a shallow soil over chalk. Such soils can be improved by digging in plenty of bulky organics to help the soil retain moisture and nutrients. The ideal soil contains coarse sand, fine sand, clay and silt in roughly equal proportions. It is moist, not too sticky, but has a good crumbly texture, breaking up easily when squeezed by the fingers.

The pH level of the soil

The ideal soil for fruit should be slightly acid (about pH 6.5). The soil's acidity or alkalinity level, known as the pH, can be measured with a pH soil-testing kit, which is available from garden shops or nurseries.

Lime is not needed for growing fruits unless the soil is very acid; for example, soils with a pH lower than 5.8 should be limed. Garden lime is usually carbonate of lime. Lime does exist in other forms but the carbonate (or ground limestone) is generally used. Rates of application vary from 2 oz to 1 lb per square yard according to the acidity of the soil. Do not apply lime directly to recently fertilized or manured soil, because the two substances react chemically together. Lime is best applied at least a month before or after other fertilizers. Preferably, apply the lime in the autumn and the fertilizer in the spring.

Fruits grown in very alkaline or chalky soils may suffer from iron and manganese deficiencies resulting in chlorosis, which is a yellowing at the tips of shoots and between the veins on leaves, and in die-back of branches. To remedy these deficiencies apply iron and manganese in chelated (sequestered) form to the soil in January/February. In the long term the pH of alkaline soils should be reduced by using flowers of sulphur annually for several years. It is safe even among growing plants but is slow-acting, particularly in cold weather. The quantity of sulphur required varies according to texture, type of soil and, of course, by how much the pH is to be reduced. As a general guide, a sandy loam will need about half (4 oz) that for heavy loams (8 oz per square yard). If it is not certain which type of soil predominates, apply a small quantity, say 2 oz per square yard, then after a few months test again and repeat the application until the required pH is reached. On naturally chalky soils, the pH level will revert to its natural high pH and further treatments will be necessary.

Soil preparation

Bush, cane and tree fruits are relatively long lived so it is important to prepare the ground thoroughly. The first essential is to free the site from perennial weeds. Where there are a few only, fork them out and burn them, but if the ground is infested with them, apply weed-killers (see pages 32–3).

If the gardener is reluctant to use these chemicals, or it is the wrong time of year, then double digging is necessary. Double digging is also essential where the sub-soil is hard or impervious and needs breaking up. For very large areas, if possible, borrow or hire a tractor equipped with a sub-soiler to break up compacted ground and a plough to turn the ground over. For widely spaced trees, provided the gardener is satisfied that there is no hard soil pan to be broken up, it is sufficient to prepare a 3 ft square at each planting site. For closely planted trees or a soft fruit plantation, single digging is all that is needed if the ground is reasonably clean.

Single digging
Before digging mark out the plot. Stretch a line down the plot to divide it lengthwise into two. Using a spade, nick out a shallow furrow along the line. Remove the line.

CONSTRUCTING A DRAINAGE SYSTEM

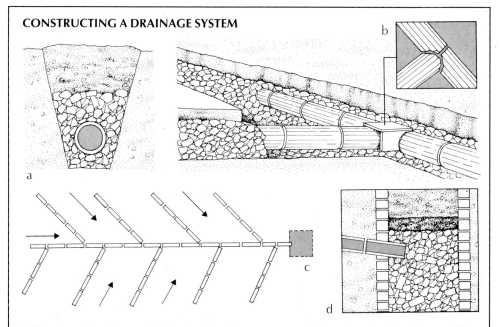

Following the slope of the land, dig V-shaped trenches (a) at the same level as the sub-soil, up to 3 ft deep and wide enough to take a 4 in dia. main pipe. At the same time dig side trenches for 3 in dia. drains. Cover the bottom with a 2 in layer of gravel. Lay the pipes on it.

The pipes (b) are butted, not joined, and the side drains lead into the main drain by breaking the pipes to fit together and covering them with tiles. Excess moisture soaks through the gaps between the lengths of piping. Cover all the pipes with coarse rubble or stones, then finer rubble, finishing with a layer of top-soil.

In the herringbone system (c), the side drains meet the main drain at an angle of 60 degrees. The drains must run towards a ditch or soakaway at a gradient of at least 1 in 40.

For the soakaway (d), dig a hole 3–6 ft in dia. and at least 6 ft deep. The sides should be loosely bricked to allow water to seep through. Leave space for the main pipe to enter. Fill the soakaway with coarse clinker or brick rubble. Finish with the top-soil.

Soil and soil drainage 2

Dig out the first 12 in wide trench to a spade's depth (known as a spit deep) across half the plot. Pile the soil removed from this first trench at the same end but on the other side of the plot, just outside the marked-off area. Work backwards down the first half of the plot, filling in each trench with the broken-up earth from the trench being dug. If bulky organics are necessary spread them over the soil at the recommended rate before beginning to dig, then dig them into the bottom of the trench before filling it in. Use the soil from the beginning of the second half to fill in the last trench of the first. When the end of the second half is reached, use the heaped soil from the very first trench to fill in this last trench.

The key to successful deep digging is to work with a vertical spade. A slanting thrust achieves less depth and makes the work take longer. It is also good technique to drive the spade in at right angles across the trench to free the clod of earth to be lifted.

Double digging

Double digging is similar to single digging, except that the width of each trench dug is 24 in (instead of 12 in), or roughly three spade widths. It is advisable to mark each trench out with sticks and a garden line. This ensures that the surface of the dug soil remains even because a measured amount of soil is moved each time. Work from left to right across each trench width, starting with the spit farthest away from the preceding trench.

Break up the sub-soil at the bottom of the trench with a fork to a further spit depth. Break up the soil all around the bottom of the trench and not just the area in the middle.

Fork manure or compost into the broken-up sub-soil at this stage. Fill in the trench with the soil from the next trench as for single digging, and so on.

Double digging grassland

Mark out the plot as described for double digging. Skim off the turf of the first trench to a depth of 2 in with a spade and place it at the same end but on the other side of the plot, just outside the marked-off area. Dig a 2 ft wide trench to a spade's depth and place the soil in a separate heap near the skimmed turf. Break up the bottom of the trench with a fork to a 12 in depth.

Put the skimmed-off turf from the second trench grass downwards on to the loosened soil in the first trench and chop it up. Place the soil from the second trench on top and so on. The turf and soil from the first trench are used to fill in the last trench in the second half of the plot.

Soil nutrition

Digging is the opportune time to incorporate the bulky organics such as well-rotted manure or compost which are necessary for healthy growth and longevity of fruit. Bulky organics are also invaluable for improving the soil structure, making heavy clays more amenable to cultivation and light soils more moisture-retentive. The amount to apply depends upon the soil texture and fertility, and the manurial requirements of the crop. Fertile soils with a high humus content need very little, whereas light, "hungry" soils need heavy applications. A good average rate is one barrowload per 25 square feet.

The basic nutrients supplied by fertilizers are nitrogen, phosphates and potash, although some may contain small amounts of other nutrients. All three are important: potash for colour, flavour and hardiness; phosphates for general health; and nitrogen for growth.

A balanced compound fertilizer, such as a proprietary brand of Growmore, is recommended because it supplies equal amounts of nitrogen (N), phosphate (P) and potash (K). Plums, pears and black currants require heavy dressings of nitrogen, but apples, raspberries and strawberries produce too much leaf and too little, poor quality fruit if given large amounts of nitrogen.

Do not use fertilizers containing chloride salts, such as muriate of potash, on soft fruits, particularly red currants, and use it with caution on tree fruits because chloride salts are toxic in large amounts.

Just before planting, apply the recommended rate of fertilizers for individual fruits, as specified on the following pages. Apply the fertilizer as a top dressing and then fork it into the soil, working the soil down to a good crumbly tilth.

CIRCULATING THE SOIL

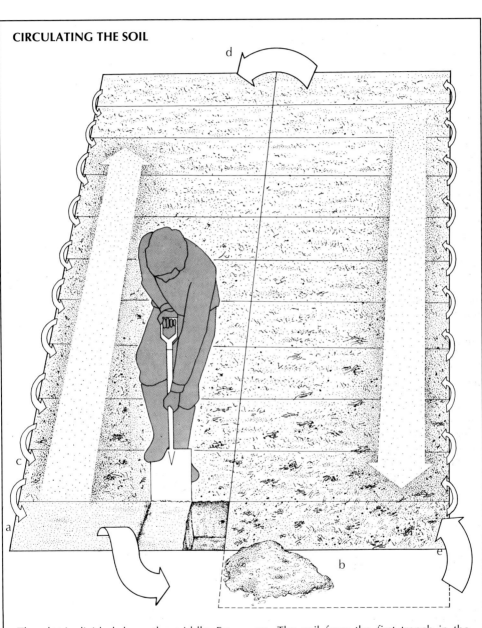

The plot is divided down the middle. Excavated soil from the first trench (a) is placed at the same end of the plot opposite the other half (b). The first trench is filled with soil from the second trench (c) and so on. The soil from the first trench in the second half fills in the last trench in the first half (d) and the last trench in the second half takes the soil removed from the first trench (e).

Tools and Equipment 1

The fruit grower needs a few special tools in addition to the basic ones used in other gardening activities. The illustrations on pages 24-5 show most of the tools and equipment needed for fruit growing.

Maintenance

Always clean garden tools and oil the metal parts as soon as possible after use. Store them in a dry place. Rusty tools mean harder work and they need replacement more quickly than tools that have been cared for.

Spade Choose good quality steel or stainless steel with a strong thin blade. Do not use a spade among established fruit plants because digging may damage the roots.

Fork Choose good quality steel or stainless steel with four well-spaced, rounded or square prongs for breaking up soil. Do not use around established fruit plants.

Dutch hoe (a) (see page 24). The easiest to use is a 4 in flat blade. It is ideal for shallow hoeing among established bush and cane fruits and strawberry rows.

Trowel and hand fork A trowel (b) is useful for making holes when planting strawberries, and a hand fork (c) is excellent for lifting rooted runners.

Garden line (d) A line of polypropylene string on a strong metal reel is used for marking out a plot and for spacing.

Irrigation equipment The equipment required depends upon the scale of planting. A one- or two-gallon watering can is sufficient for a small plot, but larger areas need a hose (e). Do not wet fruit or foliage (which encourages fungal diseases) but keep the spray from the hose low around the plants. Low-level sprinklers are also available or, better still, drip hoses that can be laid between the plants.

Labels Most fruit plants are long-lived, and so a permanent label is necessary. These can be made of wood, metal or plastic.

Gloves (f) A pair of leather or PVC gloves is essential for protecting the hands when pruning, particularly with thorny plants.

Secateurs Pruning established fruit trees needs a pair of heavy-duty secateurs with cutting blades about 2-2½ in long. The two main types of secateurs are the anvil (g) and the by-pass (h). The anvil type has a single cutting blade which moves against a fixed soft anvil made of brass or aluminium. The blade must be kept sharp and level with the anvil or it fails to cut cleanly and bruises the wood. By-pass secateurs have two blades; the lower blade supports the wood while the upper blade does the cutting. It has a scissor action and makes a clean cut without bruising the wood.

Points to note when buying secateurs are: a comfortable grip; a hardened steel blade; all parts replaceable; an easily sharpened and durable blade; a helper spring strong enough to return the blades to an open position after cutting; a safety-catch to lock the secateurs in the closed position.

Long-arm pruners (i) These are useful for people who do not want to climb ladders. One type has a 6-10 ft long metal pole with a blade attached by wire to a lever. This blade cuts with a slicing action, moving upwards against a fixed hook-shaped blade. Another type is basically a pair of secateurs on the end of a long rod.

Loppers (j) These are long-handled heavy-duty pruners, particularly useful for pruning well-established black currant bushes and for thinning out neglected trees. They are about 18 in long, with good leverage, able to cut branches up to 1½ in diameter.

Pruning saws These must be capable of cutting live green wood without the teeth clogging with wet sawdust. For this reason the teeth are widely spaced in the crosscut or fleam tooth pattern. There are three basic types: the one or two-sided straight blade (k); the Grecian curved blade (l) and the bow saw (m). The straight-bladed saw is good for light pruning, fast cutting and neat cuts. The Grecian curved saw grips the wood well, which makes it better for cutting awkwardly placed branches. The bow saw is used for heavy work, but sometimes the frame can get in the way.

The pole saw (n) is a pruning saw, usually the Grecian curved type, with a hollow handle into which a long metal pole can be inserted. It is useful for pruning branches that cannot be reached with an ordinary saw.

Knives (o) A 3½ in straight-bladed knife with a strong handle is useful for grafting work, cutting off unwanted shoots and suckers, and paring the edges of saw cuts before painting them. For propagation, a budding knife (p) is needed.

Ladders A ladder is useful for both pruning and fruit-picking. Tripod-style aluminium or galvanized steel steps (q) are a good choice for trees up to 15 ft high. They are stable, do not damage the tree by resting against it, and some have a knee-leaning rail which gives support and increases the height that can be reached. Some also have a platform on which to put a fruit container. Owners of larger trees need an ordinary extendable ladder. There are also long cherry-picking ladders, used mainly by professional growers. Always ensure that the branch is strong enough to bear the weight of both gardener and ladder.

Fruit-picking devices (r) These can be used by people who do not own a ladder or are unable to use one. They usually consist of a long metal pole with an attachment at the end which cuts off or gathers the fruit and catches it in a bag. These bags are also available as an attachment to long-arm pruners.

Tree ties There are three basic types of manufactured tree ties: the adjustable buckle type (s), the nail-on type (t), and the chain-lock type (u). The first two have a collar or spacer between the tree and the stake to prevent chafing. The chain-lock type, suitable for young trees, is tied in a figure-of-eight; the cross-over acts as a cushion. Manufactured ties are made of weather-resistant materials such as plastic or rubber.

Alternatively, the gardener can make ties from, for example, bicycle tyres, canvas, or strong sisal cord. To use cord, tie a knot (preferably a clove hitch) near the top of the stake. Wind the cord three or four times round both the tree and the stake about this knot. Then make a collar by winding the cord as tightly as possible around the loose strands between them.

All ties should be checked regularly and removed and re-tied each year in April, to allow the tree to expand.

Stakes Chestnut, oak and specially treated softwood are all suitable materials for tree stakes. Chestnut stakes can be bought already peeled, pointed and treated with a preservative. Untreated chestnut staks must be protected against rotting by applying a wood preservative to the bottom 2 ft of each stake. Oak stakes are comparable in price and durability to treated softwood. Pressurized or celcurized softwood is more expensive but has a much longer life because it is kiln-dried and then impregnated under pressure with a preservative. Stakes should be long enough to reach just below the lowest branches of a mature tree, allowing 18-24 in in the ground.

Sprayers These are used for applying pesticides, fungicides and sometimes weedkillers. There are various kinds: the double-action sprayer, in which the liquid is held in an open container; the pneumatic type (v), in which the container is pressurized; and a container with an external pump, which may be operated by hand or by motor.

Sprayers should be strong, light and able to take different nozzles. It is important to choose the size and type most suited to the job. For applying weedkillers use a low-pressure sprayer, preferably with a nozzle giving a fan-shaped spray. For trees, a high pressure sprayer is needed for fungicides and insecticides, using a hollow cone nozzle. A small hand sprayer (w) of about 1½-2 pints capacity is useful for short rows of strawberries, one or two bushes, or trees in pots. For a small garden of up to 30 ft × 30 ft, a free-standing sprayer with a flexible hose and lance and a capacity of ½-1 gal is adequate. Many of these have a shoulder strap to make them portable. A knapsack sprayer with a capacity of up to 4 gal is ideal for a larger garden of up to 100 ft × 60 ft. Extendable lances are necessary for tree fruit gardens. In plots larger than one acre, a motorized sprayer may be a worthwhile investment.

Remember to wash out the sprayer thoroughly after use, especially after using weedkillers. Ideally, use a separate sprayer for weedkillers.

Tree guards In areas where animal pests such as rabbits and hares are troublesome, tree guards are necessary. These can be either the manufactured plastic type or home-made ones of 1 in mesh galvanized wire netting.

Wire brush A stiff wire bush (x) is useful for cleaning up canker.

A tin of bituminous paint (y) **and brush** (z) These are essential for sealing large pruning cuts. The brush should have stiff bristles.

Tools and equipment 2

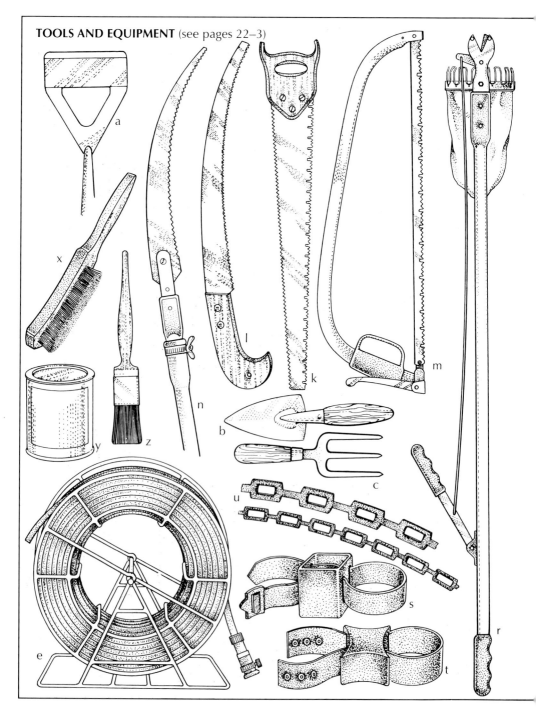

TOOLS AND EQUIPMENT (see pages 22–3)

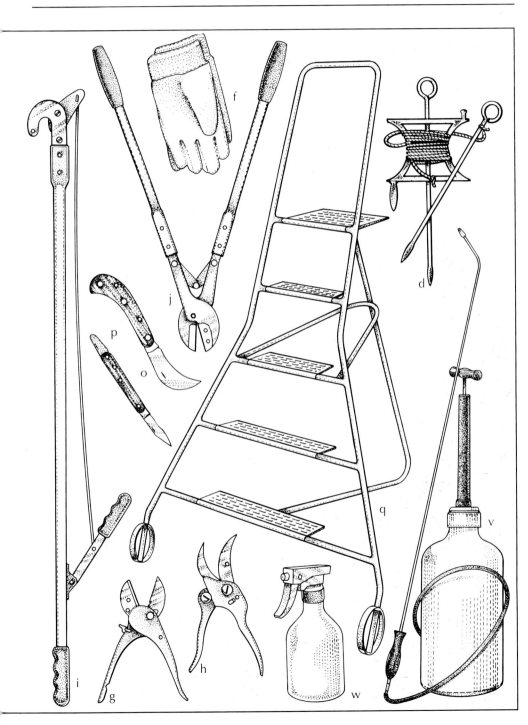

Pests and diseases 1

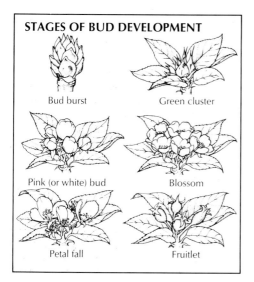

Bud burst

Green cluster

Pink (or white) bud

Blossom

Petal fall

Fruitlet

Correct cultivation and weed control help to prevent trouble with pests and diseases, although chemical control may be necessary.

Types of chemical control

Fungicides and pesticides are used to prevent, and sometimes control, infection or to treat infestation.

There are various kinds of pesticides and they act in different ways. A contact spray such as derris affects the insect itself. Ovicides such as tar oil washes kill the eggs. These take effect on contact, so it is important to cover all plant surfaces.

A third group, systemic insecticides such as heptenophos and dimethoate, are taken up through the roots and leaves of the plants into the sap. They are thus very effective against sap-sucking pests. Complete coverage is preferable but not essential because the chemical is transported within the leaf to a limited extent.

Most fungicides only check or prevent attacks so they should be applied before the disease first appears. The partly systemic fungicides such as benomyl and thiophanate-methyl are slightly absorbed into the plant's tissues only but are effective for a short period even after symptons are visible. However, resistant strains of the fungus may develop if systemic fungicides are used too frequently.

Precautions

Always follow the manufacturer's instructions when mixing and applying chemicals. Wash hands and equipment after using chemicals. Do not use the fungicide and pesticide sprayer for weedkillers.

Some chemicals must be treated with extra caution. HCH and malathion should not be used on fruit that is to be preserved. Thiram may irritate the eyes, nose and mouth; wear a mask and goggles if susceptible to allergic reactions. Do not use sulphur on sulphur-sensitive cultivars.

Do not use pesticides when the flowers are open because they kill bees and other pollinating insects.

DISEASES AND DISORDERS

American gooseberry mildew Affecting gooseberries and currants, it forms a white, powdery coating on young leaves, shoots and fruits, later turning brown and felted. The shoots may be distorted at the tips.
Treatment: Cut out and burn diseased shoots in late August or September. Spray with carbendazim, triforine with bupirimate or copper sulphate with ammonium hydroxide. Keep the bushes open by regular pruning and avoid excessive nitrogen feeding.

Apple canker It affects apples and pears. Sunken discoloured patches appear on the bark, becoming extended ellipses surrounded by concentric rings of shrunken bark. White fungus spores are visible on the sunken bark in summer. The branch becomes swollen above the canker and it may die.
Treatment: Cut out and burn diseased branches and spurs. On branches without die-back, cut out and burn diseased tissue. Paint the wounds with canker paint. Spray with bordeaux mixture after harvest but before leaf-fall. Repeat when half the leaves have fallen.

Apricot die-back The shoots and branches die back. It is usually caused by fungi but occasionally by adverse cultural conditions.
Treatment: Cut back all dead wood to healthy tissue and paint the wounds. Give adequate feeding, watering and mulching.

Bacterial canker Round brown spots appear on the leaves of apricots, cherries, peaches, plums, gages and damsons, later developing into holes. There are elongated, flattened, oozing cankers on the branches. The buds do not develop the following spring or they produce small, yellow leaves which curl, wither and die. The branches also die back.

Treatment: Remove badly cankered branches and dead wood. Paint the wounds with a wound paint. Spray with bordeaux mixture or copper oxychloride in mid-August, repeating one and two months later and again in the spring.

Bitter pit Affects apples, causing sunken pits on fruit skins, brown spots in the flesh and a bitter taste.

Treatment: Prevent it by watering and mulching the tree during dry weather. Spray with calcium nitrate at rates suggested by the manufacturer.

Boron deficiency The pear fruits on most branches are distorted and have brown spots in the flesh. The leaves are small and misshapen. There is some die-back of shoots and the bark is roughened and pimply.

Treatment: Apply 1 oz of borax (mixed with sand for even distribution) per 20 square yards.

Brown rot Affects apples, peaches, pears, plums, nectarines and quinces. The fruits are brown with soft, decaying flesh, later becoming covered with rings of greyish spores.

Treatment: Remove and burn affected fruit.

Cane blight: It affects only raspberries. A dark area can be seen on the canes just above ground level. The canes become very brittle and the leaves wither.

Treatment: Cut back diseased canes to below soil level and burn. Disinfect tools.

Cane spot It affects raspberries, loganberries, hybrid berries and, rarely, blackberries. Small purple spots appear on the canes in May to June, later enlarging and turning white with a purple border and then splitting to form pits or small cankers. The tips of shoots may die back, leaves may be spotted and the fruit may be distorted.

Treatment: Cut out and burn badly spotted canes in autumn. Spray raspberries with copper oxychloride (but not on fruit for preserving) at bud burst and just before flowering. Or spray with carbendazim at bud burst and repeat every two weeks until the

end of flowering. Spray loganberries with copper oxychloride (but not on fruit for preserving) just before flowering and when the fruit sets.

Coral spot Red currants are very susceptible, but other currants and figs are also affected. The branches die back and coral red pustules appear on the dead shoots.

Treatment: Cut out affected branches several inches below the diseased tissues. Paint the wounds. Burn infected shoots and any other woody debris in the garden.

Crown gall A walnut-size gall can be seen at ground level on cane fruits or there is a chain of small galls higher up.

Treatment: Destroy diseased canes.

Fireblight Affects pears and occasionally apples. The shoots die back and the leaves become brown and withered. Cankers form at the base of the diseased tissue and ooze in spring.

Treatment: Cut out diseased shoots to 2 feet below diseased tissues.

Grey mould (*Botrytis cinerea*) Strawberries, cane fruits, currants and grapes are among the many fruits affected. The berries rot and are covered with grey-brown fluff.

Treatment: Remove and destroy infected fruits if possible. Spray with carbendazim as soon as the flowers open, repeating two, four and six weeks later. For greenhouse crops fumigate with tecnazene smokes.

Honey fungus It affects all fruit crops. White, fan-shaped patches of fungus appear beneath the bark on roots and on the trunk just above ground level. There are blackish growths on the roots and honey-coloured toadstools grow at the base of the tree in autumn. Sudden death of the plant may occur.

Treatment: Dig out affected plants with as many roots as possible and burn them.

Leaf spot of currants and gooseberries Dark brown spots can be seen on the leaves, later coalescing and turning the leaves brown. Premature leaf-fall results.

Treatment: Collect and burn all diseased leaves. Spray with carbendazim or triforine with bupirimate, or mancozeb, or a copper fungicide. Feed the bushes well to help overcome the disease.

Lime-induced chlorosis All crops in chalky soils are affected but it is most serious on rasp-

Pests and diseases 2

berries. Yellow or white bands develop between the veins of leaves.

Treatment: Dig in humus and reduce the alkalinity of the soil. Apply a chelated compound or rake in fritted trace elements (see pages 18-20).

Magnesium deficiency Orange, red or brown bands develop between the leaf veins, especially of apples, grapes and raspberries.

Treatment: Spray at petal fall, or when the trouble shows, with magnesium sulphate at 8 oz per 2½ gal of water, plus a wetter. Repeat twice at 14-day intervals.

Peach leaf curl Reddish blisters appear on the leaves. Later, the leaves swell and have a powdery white covering of spores. Premature leaf-fall results.

Treatment: Spray with bordeaux mixture or copper oxychloride in January or February. Repeat 10-14 days later and just before leaf-fall. Alternatively, use polythene covering (see page 150).

Pear stony pit virus The fruit on some branches is pitted and deformed at maturity. Stony cells form in the tissue making the fruit difficult to cut and inedible.

Treatment: Destroy affected trees.

Plum rust Small, bright yellow spots can be seen on the upper surfaces of leaves, with pustules on the underscales containing brown or orange spores which later turn dark brown or blackish. Leaves may turn brown and fall prematurely. It only affects weak trees.

Treatment: Rake up and burn fallen leaves. Good feeding, watering and mulching should prevent a recurrence of the disease.

Powdery mildew Apple, grape, melon, peach and quince are affected. A white powdery coating of fungus spores appears on emerging shoots and young leaves. Apple and pear shoots are stunted, the fruits fail to set or develop brown patches, and the leaves fall. The skins of grapes become discoloured and shrivel and split.

Treatment: Remove silvered shoots at pruning. Cut off infected shoots of apples, peaches and quinces in spring and summer. Spray all crops at first signs of disease and repeat at least three times at fortnightly intervals, using sulphur, carbendazim (not grapes) or triforine with bupirimate (apple, blackcurrant and gooseberry only). Ventilate the greenhouse and avoid overcrowded conditions.

Quince leaf blight Dark red irregular spots appear on leaves, later becoming blackish. The leaves may turn brown or yellow and fall prematurely and the fruit may be spotted and deformed. Shoot tips die back.

Treatment: Rake up and burn fallen leaves. Cut out dead shoots in winter. Spray with bordeaux mixture as first leaves open in spring, and repeat in summer if necessary.

Raspberry virus diseases These are very troublesome; loganberries, blackberries susceptible to viruses and related organisms, and other cane fruits may also be affected. Yellow blotching or mottling is visible on the leaves. Poor growth and a reduced crop result.

Treatment: Remove and burn all affected plants at the same time. Plant new canes certified as healthy in a new site 50 ft away or change the soil on the old site to a depth of 1½ ft × 2 ft wide.

Reversion This affects only black currants and is spread by big bud mite. Mature leaves on the basal shoots are narrow with fewer than five pairs of veins on each main lobe. The flowers are bright magenta-coloured and there is a reduced fruit yield.

Treatment: Control big bud mite (see page 30). Destroy all diseased bushes at the same time. Plant new certified bushes on a fresh site.

Scab Affects apples and pears. Brown or black scabs are visible on the fruits which are sometimes misshapen and cracked. Olive green blotches develop on the leaves and they fall prematurely. There is a general loss of vigour and a reduced crop. Pimples on the young shoots later burst the bark and become cracks or scabs.

Treatment: Rake up and burn all leaves in autumn. Cut out cracked and scabby shoots at pruning. For both apples and pears, spray with carbendazim or mancozeb or triforine with bupirimate.

Shanking Grapes fail to ripen, become sour and watery due to shrivelling berry stalks.

Treatment: Good soil conditions and cultural treatment should prevent this trouble. Cut off affected berries.

Shothole Affects cherries, peaches and nectarines, plums and gages, causing brown spots on leaves which later become holes. Only weak trees are affected.
Treatment: Proper feeding should prevent a recurrence but if not, spray with a copper fungicide.

Silver leaf It can affect most tree fruits, currants and gooseberries, but it is most troublesome on plums, appearing as silvering leaves which may turn brown. There is progressive die-back of branches and a purplish fungus grows on the dead wood, later turning white or brown. Inner tissues are stained brown or purple.
Treatment: If there is fungus on the trunk, destroy the tree. Otherwise cut back dead branches to 6 in behind the staining of inner tissues. Paint the wounds. Sterilize all tools after use on diseased trees.

Soft rot (collar rot) of melons The stem rots at soil level causing the plant to collapse.
Treatment: Remove infected plants. Keep the stem dry.

Split stone Affects peaches and nectarines. Fruits crack at the stalk end producing a hole through which earwigs can enter. The stone is split and the kernel (if formed) rots.
Treatment: Hand pollinate the flowers. Lime the soil if necessary. Pay strict attention to watering.

Spur blight This affects raspberries and sometimes loganberries. Dark purple blotches appear around the nodes on canes. They enter enlarge, turn silver and become covered with minute black dots. Buds wither and die or produce shoots which die back in spring.
Treatment: Cut out and burn diseased canes. Spray with copper fungicide.

Strawberry leaf blotch Large brown blotches surrounded by purple and yellow may appear on the leaves. Stalks blacken and rot. The leaves die and the fruit withers.
Treatment: Remove and burn affected leaves. Spray the following season with mancozeb just after growth begins, repeating two weeks later.

Strawberry mildew Purple patches are visible on leaves, which curl upwards. Greyish fungal spores develop on the undersides and spread to flowers and berries.

Treament: Dust with sulphur. After harvest, cut off old leaves.

Strawberry virus diseases Various diseases cause stunting or death. The symptoms are most obvious from April to September. The leaves become dwarfed and puckered with yellow edges and yellow or purple mottling. A virus-related organism causes old leaves to turn red and young leaves yellow. The flowers have green petals and the fruits fail to ripen. Eventually the plant dies.
Treatment: Destroy all affected plants at the same time. Do not take runners. Plant certified strawberries in a fresh site or change the soil on the old site to a depth of 1 ft × 1½ wide.

Verticillium wilt It affects melons. Lower leaves turn yellow and wilt and then the whole plant wilts and collapses.
Treatment: Destroy diseased plants and sterilize the soil.

Walnut leaf blotch Irregular brown blotches appear on the leaves which wither and fall prematurely.
Treatment: Rake up and burn fallen leaves. Spray young trees with mancozeb, repeating two weeks later.

PESTS

Aphids (Greenfly, blackfly) Aphids suck sap from the leaves and shoots of most tree, bush, cane and other soft fruits, causing leaf curling and distortion, reddish discoloration, stunted growth and black sooty mould. They spread virus diseases.
Treatment: Spray with a tar oil wash in December (but not strawberries or myrobalan plum) to kill overwintering eggs. Use a systemic insecticide, such as pirimicarb, dimethoate or heptenophos, in the spring if aphids are present, repeating as necessary.

Apple sawfly Caterpillars tunnel into the fruitlets, causing them to fall in June. A ribbon-like scar forms on the skin of damaged fruits that remain.
Treatment: Spray with permethrin, pirimiphos-methyl or fenitrothion one week after petal-fall. Pick and burn affected fruitlets.

Big bud mite A pest of black currants. It lives inside buds, making them swollen and rounded (instead of narrow and pointed) and they fail to develop in spring. The mites spread reversion disease (see page 28).

Pests and diseases 3

Treatment: Pick off and burn big buds during the winter. Spray with carbendazim at the first open flower and again two and four weeks later. Destroy badly infested bushes and replant with virus-free stock in the autumn. The cultivars 'Foxendown' and 'Farleigh' are resistant to this pest.

Capsid bugs Affect currants, gooseberries and apples. Capsids stuck sap from shoot tips, leaves and fruits. Leaves at the shoot tips develop with tattered holes. Mature apple fruits have corky scabs or bumps on the skin.
Treatment: Spray with perimiphos-methyl, fenitrothion or dimethoate shortly after flowering has finished.

Caterpillars Caterpillars feed in the spring, causing damaged and ragged buds, leaves and blossoms.
Treatment: Pick off or spray with fenitrothion or permethrin as the young leaves appear. Place a sticky greaseband around the trunk in late October to trap emerging wingless female winter moths. Keep bands sticky and in position until late March.

Codling moth Caterpillars tunnel into the mature fruit of apples and sometimes pears.
Treatment: Spray with fenitrothion, pirimiphos-methyl or permethrin in mid-June, repeating three weeks later. Place bands of sacking around the trunk and larger branches in late July to trap over-wintering larvae. Remove and burn them in November. Pheromone traps placed in the tree in mid-May capture male codling moths and reduce the mating success of females, leading to fewer maggoty apples.

Fruit tree red spider mite A tiny, sap-feeding pest of apples and plums. It causes a yellowish mottling of the leaves, which can dry up and fall early.
Treatment: Spray thoroughly with an insecticide such as dimethoate, bifenthrin or pirimiphos-methyl in summer. Give two or three applications at 7-10 day intervals.

Glasshouse red spider mite These mites can attack all cane and bush fruits, strawberries, peaches and vines, especially plants grown under glass or against warm walls. They cause a fine mottled discoloration of the foliage and early defoliation.
Treatment: Spray three or four times at seven-day intervals with bifenthrin, pirimiphos-methyl or a systemic insecticide such as dimethoate. Alternatively, use biological control by introducing a predatory mite, *Phytoseiulus persimilis*. Maintain a high humidity for greenhouse plants.

Glasshouse whitefly Affects mainly greenhouse fruits such as vines, melons, Cape gooseberries and citrus fruits. Small, white, moth-like adults and their scale-like larvae suck sap and foul the foliage with honeydrew and sooty mould.
Treatment: Early treatment is necessary because heavy infestations are difficult to control. Spray with permethrin, pirimiphos-methyl or pyrethrum when adults are first seen, repeating at four-day intervals as necessary. Alternatively use biological control by introducing a parasitic wasp, *Encarsia formosa*.

Gooseberry sawfly These caterpillars are up to 1 in long, creamy-green with black dots. They can completely defoliate gooseberry and red currant plants.
Treatment: Pick off or spray with derris, bifenthrin, or permethrin as soon as caterpillars are seen, repeating as necessary, between late April and August.

Mealybugs Sap-feeding pests of greenhouse plants, especially vines and figs. The small white-pink insects can be seen in the leaf axils covered with a white fluffy wax.
Treatment: Scrape off loose bark from woody plants such as vines in December to expose the mealybugs. Then spray or paint the rods with a tar oil wash. Control summer infestations by spraying with an insecticidal soap two or three times at two-week intervals.

Pear leaf blister mite A minute pest causing pale green or pink blotches on the leaves in

May which later turn brown or black.

Treatment: No chemical controls are currently available to amateur gardeners but it is not a serious pest.

Pear midge Its grubs attack the fruitlets, causing them to blacken and fall in June.

Treatment: Spray with pirimiphos-methyl or fenitrothion at the white bud stage. Pick off and burn affected fruitlets. Keep the ground cultivated beneath the infested trees.

Plum sawfly Its grubs tunnel into the fruitlets and cause them to fall in June.

Treatment: Spray with fenitrothion or pirimiphos-methyl 7-10 days after petal-fall.

Raspberry beetle The maggot-like larvae damage the ripening fruits of raspberry, blackberry, loganberry and similar fruits.

Treatment: Prevent damage by spraying at dusk with derris or fenitrothion on raspberry when the first pink fruit is seen; on loganberry when flowering is almost over; and on blackberry when flowering starts.

Scale insects These are sap-feeding pests with shell-like coverings which are attached to the bark. Mussel scale attacks apples and brown scale attacks greenhouse fruits such as vines, peaches and figs.

Treatment: Control after leaf-fall with a tar oil wash in December or apply malathion in late May and again in late June for mussel scale; use insecticidal soap in early July for brown scale.

Slugs These damage fruits on strawberries.

Treatment: Scatter metaldehyde or methiocarb pellets among the plants when strawing down. Keep the garden clean and tidy in winter to reduce numbers.

Strawberry seed beetle A medium-sized, shiny black beetle that eats the seeds from the exterior of the fruits.

Treatment: Trap them in jam jars sunk up to their rims in the soil. Methiocarb pellets used against slugs gives incidental control of seed beetles. Keep the bed free of weeds because weed seeds feed the beetles at other times of the year.

Suckers These aphid-like sap-feeding pests attack the blossom and foliage of apples and pears and foul pear foliage with honeydew.

Treatment: Tar oil winter wash controls the overwintering eggs of apple sucker but pear suckers overwinter as adults and are less affected.

Apply fenitrothion, pirimiphos-methyl or dimethoate at the green cluster stage of bud development on apples or three weeks after petal-fall on pears.

Vine weevil Grubs feed on the roots of grapes and strawberries, sometimes destroying the plants. The adult beetles eat irregular-shaped notches from the leaf margins at night but this is less serious.

Treatment: Drench the root area with the pathogenic nematode, *Heterorhabditis megidis* in late summer.

Wasps These feed on the ripe fruit of apples, pears, plums and grapes.

Treatment: Enclose fruit trusses in bags made from muslin or old nylon tights. Destroy wasp nests by placing bendiocarb dust in the entrance at dusk.

Woolly aphid This aphid sucks sap from cracks in the bark and young shoots of apples. The colonies can be recognized by their fluffy white waxy coating.

Treatment: Spray or paint the colonies with a systemic insecticide such as pirimicarb, dimethoate or heptenophos when the aphid appears in April to June.

Weed Control/Fruit cages

Weed control

Weeds are basically any plants growing where they are not wanted. They compete with the cultivated plants for nutrients and moisture and may harbour pests and diseases.

Many gardeners find that digging before planting, removing all perennial roots at the same time, and regular hoeing help to control weeds. For those gardeners who prefer not to use weedkillers, these methods are sufficient. If there is a large garden, limited time or weeds are well established, herbicides may be more effective.

Herbicides (Weedkillers)

When buying weedkillers read the product label before buying, and mix and apply strictly according to the manufacturer's recommendations accompanying the product.

Weedkillers can be dangerous to humans, pets and fruit plants and so should always be handled with extreme care. Use separate sprayers for weedkillers and pesticides. Avoid spray drift, taking care not to contaminate any water source or pond.

Five chemicals, paraquat, diquat, simazine, dalapon and glyphosate, are suf-

---

HERBICIDES TABLE

Time of application	Weeds affected	Herbicide
APPLES AND PEARS		
Before weeds appear	Germinating seeds	Simazine
After weeds appear	Annuals; checks growth of perennials	Paraquat /diquat
Early spring or autumn	Actively growing grasses	Dalapon
End winter to late bud burst	Annuals, grasses, other perennials	Glyphosate
GOOSEBERRIES AND CURRANTS		
Before weeds appear	Germinating seeds	Simazine
After weeds appear	Annuals; checks growth of perennials	Paraquat /diquat
After leaf-fall to end of December	Grasses	Dalapon
CANE FRUITS		
Before weeds appear	Germinating seeds	Simazine
After weeds appear	Annuals; checks growth of perennials	Paraquat /diquat
STONE FRUITS		
March onwards, repeating as required	Annuals; checks growth of perennials	Paraquat /diquat
End winter to late bud burst	Annuals, grasses, other perennials	Glyphosate
STRAWBERRIES on plants established 12 months or more (not on sand)		
July/November, after harvest	Germinating weeds	Simazine
Between harvest and flowering as a directed spray avoiding the plants	Annuals, unwanted runners	Paraquat diquat

ficient for the amateur fruit grower. They are available under brand names but look for the active chemical constituents on the label.

Paraquat with diquat This kills all green tissue on contact by scorching so avoid spray drift. It kills annual and checks perennial weeds – but will only kill them by repeated use. On clay soils it is quickly inactivated on reaching the ground and fruit plants will not absorb it through their roots. The risk is greater on sandy soils so wet the soil as little as possible. It is most effective in cool weather.

Take care not to wet the foliage or green stems of any fruit plants. Avoid spraying the trunks of apple, pear, plum and cherry trees less than three years old.

Simazine Taken up by germinating weed seeds before their emergence, simazine will not kill established weeds or weed seedlings.

Incorrect dosage can render the soil sterile for some months, so carefully follow the manufacturer's instructions. Simazine persists in the soil so allow seven months to elapse after spraying before attempting to grow crops from seed. Use it to keep clean land weed-free among newly planted and established crops of apples, pears, black currants, gooseberries and cane fruits. Do not use near stone fruits or strawberries grown in a sandy soil.

Dalapon This kills grasses and some related plants by absorption through the leaves and distribution through the system. It is suitable for use against annual and perennial grasses around apple and pear trees that have been established at least four years. Check the manufacturer's instructions because some varieties are adversely affected. Do not use it among stone fruits. It is readily taken up by the roots of trees and bushes so use only enough to spray the grass foliage without excessive run-off. It remains effective in the soil for between six and eight weeks.

Glyphosate Applied to the foliage of weeds, this is most effective when they are in active growth. It destroys annual and perennial weeds, especially grasses, creeping thistle and docks. It is inactivated on contact with the soil and crops can be sown or planted three or four weeks after treatment, or as soon as all the weeds are dead and the dead foliage

has been removed.

Protection against birds
Ripening fruit grown in the open needs protection against such birds as blackbirds, thrushes and starlings, which can inflict considerable damage on the crop. Winter protection may be necessary against bullfinches who can destroy overwintering buds, particularly on plums, gages, cherries and bush fruit.

Commercial bird scarers are available but birds quickly become used to them. Bird repellants have a low success rate. In wet winters, the material washes off and in hard weather the birds eat the buds no matter what chemical is used.

Fruit cages Soft fruits, with the possible exception of strawberries, are usually grown in a group together and so can be surrounded by a single enclosure. Use $^1/_2$–$^3/_4$ in wire, polythene, nylon or plastic netting, 6–7 ft high, supported by wires stretched between the tops of posts, spaced 6 ft apart. Cover the top of the cage with $^3/_4$ in mesh netting. For very large cages, it may be necessary to drape the "roof" over battens nailed to the tops of the supporting posts. The roof netting can be polythene nylon or plastic. Wire mesh is not suitable because zinc toxicity may be caused by condensation drops from the galvanizing. The netting should be left on in winter, except in heavy snowfalls. Open the cage during the flowering period to allow access to pollinating insects because insects tend to avoid fruit bushes in an enclosed cage.

Netting Fruit trees and bushes can be protected by draping them with lightweight nylon or plastic netting. To protect strawberries, drape netting over the plants, supported on posts at least 18 in high.

Cotton Black cotton thread wound between branches will deter birds but it is a time-consuming task if the trees are large or numerous. Do not use nylon thread because it can strangle birds or trap their feet.

Bags and sleeving Individual fruits can be protected by securing paper, muslin or perforated polythene bags or sleeving around them provided the tree or crop is small.

Collars Cardboard collars fitted around the stalks of tree fruits prevent birds perching close enough to peck the fruit.

Month-by-month guide 1

JANUARY

Planting Plant new trees, bushes and vines when soil conditions are right (until March).
Routine tasks Prune newly planted cane fruits, bush fruits, vines and apples and pears (until March). Cut back summer-pruned laterals on red and white currants and gooseberry cordons (until March).

Apply sulphate of potash to strawberries, raspberries, apples and pears; nitro-chalk to apricots; balanced fertilizer to cobnuts and filberts.

Lower the tips of vine rods in the greenhouse towards the ground until the buds begin to grow. Clean the glass and top-dress the borders. To rest vines in a cold greenhouse, open the ventilators (until early March).

Move into the greenhouse plants in containers that were plunged outside after fruiting the previous year.

Check stakes and tree ties which may have become loose through wind-rock.

Cover strawberry plants with cloches or polythene tunnels at any time until mid-March for an early crop.

Check fruit in store and remove any that is diseased or rotten.
Spray guide spray peaches and nectarines against peach leaf curl and repeat 10–14 days later; spray dormant fruit trees, bushes and cane fruits with tar oil if not done in December. Begin regular checks for canker on apple and pear trees, and treat, if necessary.

MARCH

Sowing Sow alpine strawberry seeds under glass and Cape gooseberry and melon seeds for greenhouse cultivation.
Planting Plant melon and passion fruit seedlings in a heated greenhouse. Plant perpetual strawberry runners if not planted in autumn.
Routine tasks Prune newly planted pyramid plums and acid cherries; established bush and pyramid acid cherries and apricots.

Apply sulphate of ammonia (or nitro-chalk on acid soils) to black currants; sulphate of ammonia to heathland fruits, quinces and raspberries; a compound fertilizer to medlars and figs.

Mulch blackberries, raspberries, black currants, vines and newly planted apples and pears.

Begin regular feeding of grapes in the heated greenhouse.

Control weeds around trees.
Harvesting Pick strawberries in the greenhouse (March onwards).
Spray guide Spray apples against scab starting at bud burst (until late July) and against aphids, apple sucker and caterpillars; pears against scab regularly from bud burst as necessary; plums, gages and cherries against aphids and caterpillars as necessary. Spray black currants against big bud mite at late grape stage and against aphids; gooseberries against mildew regularly and against aphids if necessary; cane fruits against spur blight, cane spot at bud burst and against aphids if necessary; peaches and elderberries against aphids if necessary; grapes, citrus fruits, Cape gooseberries and passion fruit regularly against glasshouse whitefly and mealybugs if necessary; medlars and nut trees against caterpillars; greenhouse fruits against glasshouse red spider mite regularly as necessary; quinces against aphids and quince leaf blight.

MAY

Planting Harden off melon seedlings and plant out under cold glass in late May (until early June). Plant out Cape gooseberry seedlings and protect with cloches. Plant melon seedlings for greenhouse cultivation. Plant out alpine strawberry seedlings (by the end of May).
Routine tasks De-blossom newly planted two- and three-year-old trees, spring-planted runners of summer-fruiting strawberries and perpetual strawberries. Pull out unwanted rasperry canes. Thin shoots of established fan-trained peaches and nectarines and remove misplaced shoots of wall-trained plums, damsons and cherries (until early summer). Cut back the leaders of mature apples and pears grown as cordons, espaliers and dwarf pyramids and established pyramid plums. Begin thinning plums.

Apply liquid fertilizer to vines throughout the growing season. Water plants as necessary.

Control weeds around all fruits. Keep grass short around trees.

Scatter slug pellets around strawberries before strawing down. Protect strawberries from birds and frosts; ventilate on sunny days.
Harvesting Pick early strawberries and gooseberries from late May.
Spray guide Do not use pesticides during flowering. Spray apples against sawfly one week after petal-fall and against fruit tree red spider mite if necessary; raspberries and loganberries against cane spot and spur blight before flowering; all cane fruits and strawberries against grey mould when flowers open. Put down slug pellets around strawberries before strawing down and spray against mildew before flowering. Spray grapes against mildew until August; cobnuts and filberts against nut weevil.

This guide is intended as reminder of the jobs to be done each month in the fruit garden. For full details of cultivation, see under the specific fruits. The spray guides indicate when to spray – gardeners should not need to spray for every pest and disease listed, only if a particular pest or disease gets out of hand. For full information on pests and diseases, see pages 26–31, and on weed control, see pages 32–3. The timing of the tasks is based on the climate of southern Britain. Remember that local climatic conditions could mean two or three weeks later in colder northern regions.

FEBRUARY

Sowing Sow melon seeds for heated greenhouse cultivation.
Routine tasks Prune bush, standard and half-standard plums, gages and damsons and figs (until early March); young fan-trained sweet and Duke cherries, peaches and nectarines, apricots, plums and figs (until March); brutted laterals on established cobnuts and filberts; passion fruit. Cut back the tips of summer-fruiting raspberries. Cut down newly planted raspberry canes if not pruned on planting. Cut back winter-damaged tips of blackberry canes.

Apply sulphate of potash to gooseberries, red and white currants, and grapes; nitrogen as sulphate of ammonia to tree fruits; balanced fertilizer to sweet and Duke cherries, gages, plums, peaches and nectarines, blackberries, currants, gooseberries, quinces and mulberries, figs in the open.

Mulch sweet and Duke cherries and figs.

Protect blossom on fan-trained trees such as apricots, peaches and nectarines from frost with hessian or bird netting until all danger of frost has passed. Hand pollinate these fruits, if necessary.
Spray guide Treat canker on apples and pears.

APRIL

Sowing Sow melon seeds and keep in a warm place for greenhouse and cold frame cultivation.
Planting Plant citrus fruit and melon seedlings in the greenhouse. Prepare the planting site for Cape gooseberries.
Routine tasks Prune young pyramid plums and fan-trained mulberries. Pinch out selectively the laterals of vines in the greenhouse. De-blossom summer-fruiting strawberries in their first year if planted in late autumn or early spring. Apply a balanced fertilizer to citrus fruits. Begin regular liquid feeding of plants in containers (until the fruits begin to ripen).

For vines in a cold greenhouse, close the ventilators to raise the temperature.

Ventilate strawberries under cloches and tunnels on sunny days.

Control weeds in all areas.

Uncover protected plants in flower during the day to allow access for pollinating insects.
Spray guide Do not use pesticides during flowering. Spray apples and pears against aphids and caterpillars when seen, pears against pear midge if necessary; apples against capsids shortly after flowering, against suckers at green cluster stage and against mildew; peaches and nectarines against red spider mite; plums against sawfly 7–10 days after petal-fall. Give a second spray to black currants against big bud gall mite. Spray strawberries against aphids if necessary and against grey mould at flowering; raspberries against spur blight if necessary; gooseberries against sawfly caterpillars, mildew and leaf spot as necessary; medlars and nut trees against caterpillars; grapes and melons against powdery mildew as necessary; quinces against mildew (until mid-July).

JUNE

Planting Plant out melon seedlings in cold frames and Cape gooseberry seedlings outside.
Routine tasks Cut back laterals on red and white currant and gooseberry cordons and bushes (from late June to early July). Pinch out the growing points of selected shoots on established fan-trained plums and apricots (until late July). Pinch out selected growing points on cropping fan-trained figs. Cut down old canes on newly planted raspberries when new shoots appear. Select and train shoots on melons (until July). Train new shoots of blackberries and outdoor grapes.

Thin bunches of grapes in the greenhouse. Thin fruits on peaches, nectarines, apricots, plums, gooseberries and apples and pears after the June drop (until July).

Water all fruits.

Keep grass short and weeds under control.

Protect all fruit from birds.

Ventilate protected strawberries on sunny days. Remove protection when fruiting is finished. Peg down strawberry runners and remove those not wanted for propagation.
Harvesting Pick strawberries, summer-fruiting raspberries, dessert gooseberries, sweet and Duke cherries and melons in the greenhouse.
Spray guide Spray apples against codling moth caterpillars and against bitter pit in mid-June if necessary; grapes against scale insects and mildews if necessary (until August); plums against fruit tree red spider mite and plum moth if necessary; raspberries and loganberries against raspberry beetle.

Month-by-month guide 2

JULY

Planting Prepare new strawberry beds and plant out runners (until mid-September).

Routine tasks Prune cordon, espalier and dwarf pyramid apples, pears and mulberries and pyramid plums (until September). Cut back unwanted laterals on fan-trained sweet and Duke cherries. Thin out unfruitful laterals on established figs in the greenhouse. Pinch out laterals on young fan-trained apricots. Cut out old raspberry canes after fruiting, tie in new ones and remove unwanted suckers. Cut off old leaves and unwanted runners of summer-fruiting strawberries and burn them with the straw and weeds. Train in new canes of blackberries. Prune and train all grape vines.

Thin bunches of grapes in the greenhouse.

Control weeds and keep grass short around bushes and trees.

Protect fruit from birds. Support heavily laden branches of apples, plums and damsons.

Ventilate protected fruit on hot days.

Harvesting Pick strawberries, dessert gooseberries, currants, blackberries, summer-fruiting raspberries, sweet, Duke and acid cherries, apricots, melons, plums, gages, apples (dessert and cooking).

Spray guide Spray apples against codling moth caterpillars for the second time and against woolly aphids if necessary; blackberries against raspberry beetle when flowers open.

SEPTEMBER

Planting Plant runners of summer-fruiting and perpetual strawberries by mid-September if possible.

Routine tasks Cut back pinched-out laterals on fan-trained sweet and Duke cherries.

Mulch citrus trees planted in the greenhouse border.

Order new bushes and trees for winter planting.

Ventilate protected fruit on hot days.

Check and clean storage trays and boxes and the storehouse floor.

Keep grass short and control weeds.

Harvesting Pick strawberries, autumn-fruiting raspberries, blackberries, plums, damsons, peaches, nectarines, apricots, figs, apples, pears, melons, grapes, mulberries, elderberries, heathland fruits.

Spray guide Spray apples and pears against canker if necessary, after harvest, at 50% leaf-fall, and again at bud burst. Give a second spray against bacterial canker to stone fruits if necessary.

NOVEMBER

Planting Plant and prune new trees, bushes and cane fruits at any time (until March) except when the ground is frozen or waterlogged. Keep plants in a cool, frost-free place until conditions are suitable.

Routine tasks Cut back summer-pruned laterals on red and white currant and gooseberry cordons (until March). Shorten leaders on red and white currant and gooseberry bushes (until March). Prune outdoor vines and newly planted vines in the greenhouse (until December). Prune apple and pear espaliers and dwarf pyramids; fan-trained figs; elderberries and mulberries in the open (until March); quinces and medlars; established Chinese gooseberries.

Mulch trees in the greenhouse border (until February). Wash down the greenhouse interior and benching with an approved disinfectant.

Take tender plants in containers inside the greenhouse for the winter. Take hardy fruit trees in pots outside, and bury them up to their rims in an ash or sand bed.

Protect tender plants such as figs (outdoors) against frost.

Control weeds around established apples, pears, black currants, gooseberries and cane fruits.

Check the condition of supports and wires. Check that the fruit cage is closed and check its condition.

Harvesting Pick late apples, pears, quinces, medlars, plums, nuts, grapes in the greenhouse, Chinese gooseberries.

AUGUST

Routine tasks Cut back the pinched-out shoots on fan-trained plums (until mid-September). Cut out old fruiting laterals on established fan-trained acid cherries. After harvesting, cut back old fruiting laterals on peaches and nectarines in the greenhouse. Break (brut) laterals on cobnuts and filberts and leave them hanging. Thin out congested shoots on established sweet chestnuts and walnuts. Pinch out shoots on Chinese gooseberries.

Keep grass short and control weeds.

Protect ripening fruit from birds.

Begin regular checks of apples, pears, plums and quinces for brown rot and remove and burn infected fruits.

Ventilate protected fruit on hot days.

Harvesting Pick strawberries, blackberries, loganberries, autumn-fruiting raspberries, currants, heathland fruits, figs, plums, damsons, cherries, peaches, nectarines, apricots, apples, melons, mulberries, elderberries, grapes (outdoors).

Spray guide Spray stone fruits against bacterial canker in mid-August if necessary, repeating one and two months later.

OCTOBER

Sowing Sow alpine strawberries in a cold frame or cold greenhouse.
Planting Prepare the ground for all autumn planting.
Routine tasks After leaf-fall, if secondary growth occurs prune cordon apples and pears. Cut out old canes from blackberries and related hybrids after fruiting and tie in new ones.

Remove unripened figs on outdoor trees but leave embryo fruits.

Greaseband apple and cherry trees against winter moth.

Repot or pot on fruit plants grown in containers.

Tidy perpetual strawberry beds after fruiting by removing and burning old leaves and straw.

Cover perpetual strawberries with cloches or polythene tunnels.

Harvesting Pick strawberries, autumn-fruiting raspberries, blackberries, plums, apples, pears, quinces, medlars, melons, grapes, nuts, Chinese gooseberries, Cape gooseberries, passion fruit, heathland fruits. Pack apples, pears and quinces for storage.

Spray guide Spray peaches and nectarines against peach leaf curl before leaf-fall. Spray apples and pears affected by canker at 50% leaf-fall; give a final spray against bacterial canker to stone fruits.

DECEMBER

Routine tasks Prune established vines in the greenhouse.

Take strawberries in pots into the greenhouse for fruit in early spring.

Control weeds around strawberries and established apples, pears, plums and cherries.

Check fruit in store and remove any that is diseased or rotten.
Harvesting Pick late grapes in the greenhouse.
Spray guide Spray dormant bush, tree and cane fruits, outdoor vines, and dormant vines and figs in the greenhouse with tar oil against aphids, suckers and scale insects (until late January); grapes, peaches and figs in the greenhouse against mealybugs and brown scale.

Fruit in the greenhouse

There is much satisfaction and no great diffi-culty in growing out-of-season fruits if a greenhouse is available. Most tree fruits and soft fruits may be grown under glass. The warmth and protection of a greenhouse not only hastens maturity of the fruits, but also protects them from weather hazards such as gales, frosts and torrential rain, and pests such as birds. There are, however, several factors to consider before attempting to grow fruit under glass.

If a greenhouse has first to be purchased, its cost and its possible heating bills through the years must be set against the value of the fruit crops likely to be obtained. There is also the size factor. Unless a few potted trees are all that is to be grown, a greenhouse of not less than 10 ft × 8 ft is the smallest to be con-sidered. One peach, nectarine, grape or fig tree grown in the greenhouse border needs wall or roof space at least equal to this size, and more if possible. A further relevant factor is that, in general, the larger the greenhouse, the cheaper is each square yard of growing space. If fruits crop regularly and as well as they should, then in a comparatively few years the greenhouse should pay for itself.

The situation is rather different for hardy fruits such as apples, pears, cherries and plums, which are grown in pots and brought into the greenhouse to advance their time of fruiting, then taken outside for the rest of the year. Plants in containers are "plunged out-side" by burying the pot up to the rim in a bed of ash or sand or in well-drained ground, after fruiting and until early January. It is worth while growing these fruits in a greenhouse only if they are alternated with such fruits as melons. Of course, if fruit growing under glass is looked upon as a hobby, these "commer-cial" considerations do not apply.

Site
Whether or not the greenhouse is to be heated, it should be sited in a sheltered place where the low winter sun is not obstructed. Frequent strong winds can soon dissipate both artificial and sun heat and lower the tem-perature accordingly. Ideally, a lean-to greenhouse is best, built against a south- or west-facing wall. If no artificial heat is used, the lean-to is especially valuable, because the back wall absorbs the sun's heat and releases it slowly over a period. The wall is also ideal for training such fruits as peaches and figs.

Heating the greenhouse
Although heating is not necessary to advance the maturity of fruits grown under glass, it is essential for really early crops. Heating a greenhouse can be expensive and sorting the best buy from the various methods available is difficult. The main fuel types are: solid fuel such as coal, coke and wood; oil; gas; and electricity. All fuels can be burned to heat water which circulates in pipes or to heat the surrounding air by convection or using fans or ducts. Solar heating, a method that uses the sun's power to heat water or air which is stored in specially insulated containers for im-mediate or future use, has recently been de-veloped to heat greenhouses, and is used particularly in the USA. This method will probably become more popular.

Methods of heating Solid fuel systems are cheaper to run but equipment and installation charges are high. Where natural gas is avail-able, there are very cheap and efficient heat-ing units. Oil can be used in various ways, either burned to heat air directly or to work a boiler system, but the high cost of oil makes heating by this method more expensive than the previous methods. Most expensive of all is electricity, but the equipment is not unduly costly and there is much to be said for a system that provides instant, clean heat at the touch of a switch. Provided that a minimum temperature of 7°C/45°F is maintained (all that is necessary for fruit growing) and an efficient thermostat control is used, electricity need not cost as much as might be supposed. Also, when used to power a fan heater it has the added advantage of maintaining a buoyant, moving atmosphere which is bene-ficial to the plants and helps to minimize such diseases as grey mould.

Heating is not usually required until the turn of the year and can often cease in April, so fuel bills need not be high if tender plants are not grown all the year.

Maintenance and hygiene
During late spring to early autumn, the glass needs shading during warm, sunny spells.

Roller blinds are the best method, ideally coupled to an automatic opener. This method is, however, expensive to install. A favourite alternative is to apply a liquid shading compound either sprayed or painted on to the glass. It is best to select a formulation that can easily be rubbed or washed off when not required.

In the sheltered, equable conditions within a greenhouse, certain pests and diseases can flourish and become troublesome. For this reason hygiene is important. Apart from spraying or dusting infected plants with the appropriate pesticide or fungicide, the greenhouse interior should be washed down with an approved disinfectant, either when the plants are dormant or once potted plants have been taken outside. Ideally all the metal, wood and brickwork should be scrubbed annually, paying attention to crevices where female red spider mites overwinter. Forcible spraying is a less efficient alternative.

Benching should be similarly treated and all debris (including unused canes, boxes and pots) should be removed. Trees plunged outside should be sprayed with a winter wash before moving them back into the greenhouse. Permanently housed plants should be similarly treated while dormant and leafless.

Soil

Unlike plants in the open, plants in the greenhouse border are totally dependent on how good the border soil is because their roots are restricted. Ordinary top-soil from the garden is not always suitable.

A good border soil should consist of a mixture of seven parts fibrous loam (if possible made from turves stacked for six months before use), three parts peat and two parts coarse grit. Add John Innes base fertilizer at the rate of 8 oz per 2 gal bucketful of soil.

If re-soiling an existing border, it is an opportune time to check on the drainage. If the sub-soil is a layer of impermeable clay or if the ground seems waterlogged, construct a drainage system or a soakaway (see pages 18–19).

Cultivation

The following notes describe the general routine for all fruit when grown under glass.

Finer details of culture are given under the individual fruit entries. For cultivation of fruit in tubs and pots, see pages 174–7.

All the hardy fruits in this book are best planted or potted in the autumn, ideally just as the leaves fall or soon afterwards. From then on they must be kept cool. Trees under glass need plenty of fresh air, so leave the ventilators (and the door on warm days) of the greenhouse wide open unless gales or frosts are forecast.

During the dormant season from November to February, trees in the greenhouse border should be mulched with well-rotted manure or compost, or with bark after the application of a balanced fertilizer such as a brand of Growmore at 2 oz per square yard.

In early January, move in plants in containers that were plunged outside after fruiting last year and shut the ventilators to build up warmth. On mild days, the trees are sprayed over, ideally with rainwater. After a few weeks, artificial heat may be turned on if required. As the weather warms up some ventilation is needed and floors and benching should be damped down daily.

A regular watch must be kept for pests and remedial action taken as soon as possible. In particular look out for red spider mite and aphids (see pages 26–31).

When the flowers begin to open, stop the overhead spraying with water and damp down on sunny days only.

In some cases, hand pollination is needed (see pages 94–7). Once flowering has ceased and fruitlets are visible, resume regular damping and spraying. Plants in pots should be given a liquid feed at this stage, repeated at ten-day intervals.

At all times make sure that the plants do not lack water. Potted trees need watering daily, and often twice a day during hot spells. Border-grown plants need water at least once a week and two or three times a week in warm weather.

When fruits begin to ripen, cease overhead spraying but resume after picking and continue until just before leaf-fall. Potted trees should be plunged outside once all the fruit has been picked. They must be repotted annually just after leaf-fall (see pages 175–6 for details of repotting).

Soft fruits

Introduction

Soft fruit is an umbrella term for several low-growing shrubs and perennials that bear soft, juicy fruit. They are not all closely related and they have a variety of growth habits. Botanically the best-known fruits can be placed into two groups: those belonging to the rose family (Rosaceae), including the raspberry, blackberry, loganberry and allied hybrids, and the strawberry; and those classified in the gooseberry family (Grossulariaceae) including the black, red and white currant, gooseberry and Worcesterberry. Three fruits not included in these two families are grapes (Vitaceae), the melon (Cucurbitaceae) and the blueberry (Ericaceae). However, all the fruits in the soft fruit section have the common advantage of bearing fruit soon after planting – in some cases (such as the melon) within the same year. Also, soft fruits are particularly suitable for the small garden because they need far less room than do tree fruits.

Site

With good basic culture, all the soft fruits are easily grown and, once established, provide annual crops without fail. Although best grown in an open, sunny position, they do reasonably well in partial shade or in a site that gets afternoon sun only. Low-lying areas that are susceptible to late spring frosts should be avoided if possible.

If space in the garden is restricted, use walls and fences for grapes and climbing cane fruits, as well as for gooseberries and red and white currants as cordons or fans (see pages 15–17). Soft fruits such as strawberries, grapes and currants can also be grown in containers, in window boxes or in tubs on a patio, and climbing fruits can be trained over pergolas and arches (see pages 174–7).

In a small garden the fruits to be grown must be chosen carefully. If there is room, for example, for only six bushes it is tempting to grow one of each of all the main soft fruits. But it is more sensible and profitable to grow a minimum of three bushes of two favourite sorts only. In this way enough fruit can be picked for the family's needs, with some left over for jam making perhaps, or for freezing.

Personal preference will, of course, dictate the choice of fruits. If only a few sorts can be grown, black or red currants, raspberries and strawberries are a good choice because, apart from their excellent taste, all are good croppers relative to their size and those in shops are seldom as fresh as those picked straight from the garden.

With the use of cloches, cold frames or polythene tunnels the season of some soft fruits (strawberries in particular) can be extended both in the early summer and in the autumn.

Protection against birds
Another advantage of growing soft fruits is the comparative ease of providing protection against pests. Very few gardens escape bird damage to ripe fruit in summer and autumn, or to fruit buds in winter and spring. This means some sort of year-round protection is needed. A permanent fruit cage is highly recommended because it provides both efficient bird protection and allows easy access to the plants for picking, spraying, pruning and top-dressing (see page 33).

Clearing the site
Although most soft fruits grow well enough in any moderately fertile soil, it is always worth while doing some initial preparation. See pages 18–21 for details of soil preparation and drainage. A first essential is to make sure that all perennial weeds are removed. Nowadays there are selective herbicides for this purpose if necessary, although some gardeners may prefer to double dig before planting which buries the weeds. Clean, cultivated ground needs single digging before planting (see pages 18–21), and hand picking occasional weeds during this operation is all that is needed.

Planting
Strawberry plants are set out with a trowel in much the same way as any bedding plant or young perennial. Raspberry canes and blackberry layers (plants) can usually be dealt with in the same way, depending upon how much root they have. At the most a small border spade is all that is necessary.

Bush fruits generally have a more extensive root system and, because they are a fairly long-term crop, their planting ritual should be more elaborate. Plant bushes from November to March.

Dig a hole which is deeper and wider than the roots when they are spread out. The bottom of the hole should be loosened with a fork and if little or no organic matter was dug into the area initially, a spadeful or two can now be worked in. Use well-rotted manure or garden compost, or peat and bonemeal.

Set the plant in the hole and spread out the roots. Fill in the hole with the soil, occasionally giving the bush a gentle shake up and down so that the soil filters among the roots and makes close contact with them. Firm the soil gently throughout with the feet. When all the plants are in position, rake the site over so that it is level and apply a light dressing of a balanced fertilizer such as a proprietary brand of Growmore.

SUMMER-FRUITING STRAWBERRIES
Late May to mid-July.

EARLY
'Honeoye' Good flavour, crops
moderately well, large fruits, bright
red berries.

Strawberries 1

The strawberry cultivated today has resulted from the interbreeding of a number of *Fragaria* species, principally the North American *F. virginiana* as well as the South American *F. chiloensis*. This intermingling of genetic characteristics has resulted in a fruit of great variety in taste and colour, with a cropping ability and season of such versatility that it can be grown from the Tropics to the cool temperate regions of the world. It is no wonder the strawberry is the most popular soft fruit.

For the purposes of cultivation the strawberry is divided into three categories: the ordinary summer-fruiting strawberry; the perpetual or remontant strawberry that crops in irregular flushes throughout the summer until stopped by autumn frosts; and the alpine strawberry (*Fragaria vesca* subspecies *alpina*), a mountain form of wild strawberry (see page 46).

Summer-fruiting strawberries

The ordinary, or summer-fruiting strawberry, crops once only in the early summer. A few do crop again in autumn and these are called "two crop" cultivars, but they are cultivated in the same way as the others.

The expected yield per strawberry plant is about 8–10 oz.

Cultivation

Some gardeners prefer to grow strawberries as an annual crop, planting new runners each year. This method produces high quality fruits but a lower yield than that of larger two- or three-year-old plants.

Soil and situation Most soils are suitable for strawberries, but they should be well drained. On waterlogged land, if a drainage system is not practicable, grow strawberries on ridges 2–3 in high. They prefer a slightly acid (pH 6.0–6.5) light loam in a frost-free, sunny situation. They will, however, tolerate some shade and because many varieties flower over a long period, the later flowers should escape spring frosts. Strawberries are readily attacked by soil-borne pests and diseases and a system of soil rotation should be practised. Do not grow them for more than three or four years in any one site. For this reason, strawberries are best grown with the vegetables rather than with the more permanent fruit plants.

Soil preparation A strawberry bed will be down for three or four years, and the initial preparations should be thorough so that the

1 In July, dig in well-rotted manure or compost at a rate of 14 lb per square yard. Rake off any surplus manure.

2 Just before planting, lightly fork in a balanced fertilizer such as a brand of Growmore at 3 oz per square yard.

3 In July or August, plant the strawberries 18 in apart in rows 3 ft apart. Spread out the roots, keeping the crowns level with the soil surface. Firm the soil.

'Elvira' Excellent flavour, crops heavily, large, soft fruits. Good for protected cropping.

'Tamella' Moderate flavour. Fruits large, dark red, orange flesh. A very heavy cropper. Forces well, susceptible to crown rot.

'Royal Sovereign' Early to mid-season. Flavour very good. Fruits bright red, flesh pale. Susceptible to diseases and virus infection. Moderate cropper.

---

land is made fertile and free from perennial weeds. In July dig in well-rotted manure or compost at the rate of 14 lb to the square yard. Rake off any surplus because bulky organics on the surface encourage slugs, snails and millipedes. Once applied, no more organics should be needed for the life of the bed. Just before planting, lightly fork in a balanced fertilizer such as a brand of Growmore at 3 oz per square yard.

Planting and spacing The earlier the planting, the better the maiden crop in the following year. Ideally, plant in July, August or not later than mid-September. If planted in late autumn or spring, the plants are unlikely to establish well in the first year, and should be de-blossomed. This means losing the maiden crop. Plant the runners in moist soil with the crown of the strawberry just level with the soil surface; planting too deep may result in the rotting of the buds and planting too shallow may cause drying out. Plant with a trowel or hand fork, spreading out the roots well. Replace the soil and firm it. Space the plants 18 in apart in rows 3 ft apart. On a light soil they can be 15 in apart with 2½ ft between the rows. If plants are to be grown for two years only, space them only 12 in apart in the row.

Pollination The flowers are pollinated by bees and crawling insects such as pollen beetles. Imperfect pollination results in malformed fruits. All modern cultivars are self-fertile.

Watering and feeding Water regularly for the first few weeks after planting and whenever dry conditions occur during the growing season, but try to keep water away from the ripening berries because this encourages grey mould (*Botrytis cinerea*). The risk is less with trickle or drip irrigation because only the soil is wetted. Damp conditions overnight also encourage botrytis; water in the morning so that the plants are dry by nightfall. At the end of January each year apply sulphate of potash at ½ oz per square yard along each side of the row for hardiness, the development of flowers and flavour. No other feeding is necessary unless growth has been poor. In this case apply sulphate of ammonia at ½ oz per square yard in April, taking care to prevent fertilizer touching the foliage because it will scorch it.

Weed control Weeds compete for nutrients and water. Keep the rows clean by shallow hoeing and tuck any runners into the row to fill gaps. Pay particular attention to cleaning up between the rows before strawing down. Weedkillers may be used (see pages 32–3).

4 For the first few weeks after planting and during dry spells in the growing season, water regularly. Keep water away from ripening berries.

5 When the fruits begin to swell, scatter slug pellets along the rows. Cover the ground beneath the berries and between rows with barley or wheat straw.

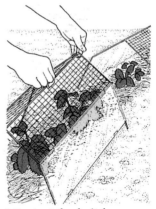

6 Protect the fruit from birds with netting stretched over cloches. Or support nets with posts at least 18 in tall. Cover posts with jars or pots first.

Strawberries 2

MID-SEASON
'Cambridge Favourite' Flavour fair.
Fruits large, salmon red, flesh pale.
Cropping heavy and reliable.
'Elsanta' Widely grown. Flavour good,
large, firm, shiny red fruits, red flesh.
Crops well but susceptible to soil borne
diseases. Resistant to mildew.

Strawing down When the fruits begin to swell and weigh down the trusses, scatter slug pellets along the rows. Then put straw down around the plants. This is to keep the fruits clean, so tuck the straw right under the berries and also cover the ground between the rows to help to keep down weeds. Do not straw down earlier than this because the straw prevents the heat from the earth reaching the flowers, which may then be damaged by frost at night. Preferably use barley straw (which is soft) or, as a second choice, wheat straw.

Protection from birds One method of protection is to use barn cloches with netting over the framework. Alternatively, make cages using ³/₄ in or 1 in plastic netting, supported by posts and wire or string. The height should be at least 18 in; about 4 ft is the ideal height for picking in comfort. Put glass jars or plastic plant pots over the posts to prevent them tearing the netting.

Harvesting

The best time to pick strawberries is in the morning when the berries are still cool. Pick them complete with stalks; try not to handle the flesh because it bruises easily.

Alternatives to strawing down

At the end of the season

Immediately after cropping cut off the old leaves (about 3 in above the crown) and unwanted runners using shears or a sickle. Tuck in runners needed to fill in any gaps in the row. In the second year a matted row can be grown by allowing runners to root in the row and reducing the space available, so that the quantity of fruit is greater but the quality suffers. The space between the rows is kept clear. Defoliation and the burning of the old straw or other debris is good horticultural practice because it is a source of pests and diseases, but it must be done as soon as cropping is over to avoid damaging fresh growth and reducing the crop the next year.

Propagation

Strawberries are easily propagated from runners which the parent plant begins to produce as the crop is coming to an end. The aim is to obtain well-rooted runners for early planting and it is achieved by pegging down the strongest runners so that they make good contact with the soil. In June or July choose healthy parent plants which have cropped well. From each select four or five strong runners. Peg them down either into moist

If straw is not available, strawberries can also be grown through black polythene. First, prepare the bed by raising a 3 in high ridge of soil. Water it well. Lay 150-gauge plastic over the ridge, tucking in the edges under the soil. Plant the strawberries

through slits in the plastic at 15–18 in intervals. Leave a 6 in run of soil between the plastic to enable rain to permeate to the roots. Alternatively, protection can be provided by placing mats around individual plants like a collar.

'Hapil' Vigorous plant. Crops well on light soils and under dry conditions. Some susceptibility to verticillium wilt. Fruits large, firm, orange red. Flavour excellent.
'Cambridge Late Pine' Flavour excellent, sweet and aromatic. Fruits dull red. Moderate cropper. Buy only Certified Stock.

LATE
'Pegasus' Flavour good, fruits large, shiny, red, attractive, flesh soft. Crops heavily. Some resistance to verticillium and red core.
'Symphony' Flavour excellent. Fruits medium to large, shiny, orange, red and firm. Crops well. Plant vigorous. Some

resistance to red core.

'Rhapsody' Flavour good. Fruits large, glossy red. Crops well. Some resistance to verticillium and red core. Vigorous.

---

open ground or into 3 in pots buried level with the soil. Pot-grown runners are best because they are easier to transplant. Fill the pots with a potting compost such as John Innes No. 3, or a peat-based compost. Peg close to the embryo plant but do not sever it from the parent at this stage. For the pegs, use 4 in pieces of thin galvanized wire bent to a U-shape. Straightened out paper clips are ideal.

In four to six weeks there should be a good root system. Sever from the parent, lift and plant out into the new bed. Keep them well watered.

Planting under mist or in a closed propagating case are other useful ways of obtaining very early runners. With these, sever the embryo plants from the parents at the first sign of roots – root initials – and peg them into 1½–2 in peat pots.

Varieties
Strawberries soon become infected with virus diseases, so it is important to plant only virus-free stock. It is best to obtain plants from a specialist propagator who guarantees healthy stock rather than accept them from a dubious source.

Clearing up the bed

In August, after cropping, cut off the old leaves and unwanted runners with shears 3 in above crowns. Rake off the leaves, old straw and other debris and burn it. Fork up the compacted earth between the rows, leaving the ground weed-free.

PROPAGATION

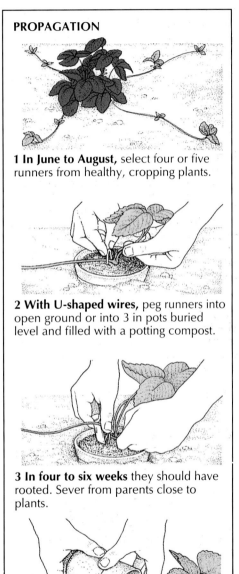

1 In June to August, select four or five runners from healthy, cropping plants.

2 With U-shaped wires, peg runners into open ground or into 3 in pots buried level and filled with a potting compost.

3 In four to six weeks they should have rooted. Sever from parents close to plants.

4 Lift out the potted runners and knock out from the pot. Plant out into the new bed and water well.

Strawberries 3

'Mara des Bois' Flavour of alpine strawberry. Medium sized, dark red berries. Crops well and is resistant to mildew.

'Bolero' Flavour excellent. Fruits firm, attractive, glossy orange red. Should

Perpetual or remontant strawberries

Perpetuals have the characteristic of producing fruit in irregular flushes throughout the summer until stopped by autumn frosts. It is useful to cover the autumn crop with cloches to extend the season, possibly into December. It is best to grow perpetuals for one year only because the size and weight of the crop deteriorate in the second year. Replant with new runners each year.

Cultivation

The basic requirements of soil, spacing, strawing down and feeding are the same as for summer-fruiting strawberries. Perpetuals crop at the hottest and driest part of the summer, so the soil should be highly fertile and moisture-retentive. Be sure to water well.

Plant in summer, autumn or spring and remove the first flush of flowers to ensure a good crop later in the season.

In the autumn, when cropping is finished, for cultivars that crop in the second year, clean up the rows, remove the old straw, surplus runners and one or two of the older leaves, and burn the debris. If the plants are grown for one year only, dig them up and burn them at this time.

Alpine strawberries

Several cultivars have been selected for garden and commercial cultivation. They make an attractive edging plant, having masses of small white flowers. They bear dark red fruits continuously or in flushes from June until November.

Cultivation

Alpine strawberries are usually grown from seed and kept for no more than two years before resowing. There are a few cultivars that produce runners, but maintaining virus-free stock is difficult.

Sowing Sow the seeds, preferably in the autumn, and overwinter the seedlings in a cold frame. Alternatively, sow in March under glass. Sow into seed boxes containing a moist seed compost such as John Innes. Maintain them at a temperature of 18°–20°C/64°–68°F. Cover the boxes with glass and shade until the seeds germinate. When two true leaves appear, prick out the seedlings 1 in apart into boxes or peat pots.

Soil preparation, planting and feeding The soil should be rich, well drained and slightly acid (pH 6.0–6.5). Just before planting apply sulphate of potash at ½ oz per square yard. Once the danger of frosts is over, but by the end of May, plant out the seedlings in the prepared, moist soil. Plant in the open or light shade. Space the seedlings 1 ft apart with 2½ ft between the rows. Water them in dry weather (about 3–4 gal per square yard every 7–10 days). For better cropping, when the flowers appear, feed every two weeks with a proprietary liquid feed for tomatoes.

Harvesting

The fruits are small but prolific and, although rather dry, have a stronger perfume than that of ordinary strawberries. Bring out this flavour by slightly crushing the fruits. Sprinkle with sugar and leave to soak overnight.

PROPAGATION

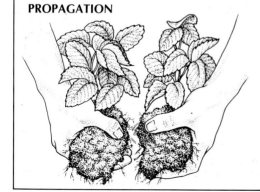

Some perpetual strawberries produce runners and are propagated in the same way as are summer-fruiting strawberries, but a few cultivars do not and these are propagated by division.

From late August to early September, dig up a mature plant and break off the new crowns or buds with as many roots as possible. Transfer them to the new strawberry bed and plant them immediately in the usual way. Do not plant the crowns too deep or they will rot.

freeze well. Crops heavily and runners satisfactorily. Some resistance to mildew and wilt.

'Calypso' Large fruits, glossy red, firm should freeze well, crops heavily. Moderately vigorous. Runners freely. Some resistance to wilt, susceptible to mildew. Flavour good.

ALPINES June to October
'Baron Solemacher' Superb flavour. Masses of tiny dark red fruits. Widely grown. Prefers slight shade.
'Alexandria' Sweet and juicy. Very bright red. Fruits long (over ½ in) and large for an alphine. Good cropper.
'Fraise des Bois' Good flavour. Fruits very small. Bright red. Prolific continuous cropper.

'Alpine Yellow' Strongly flavoured, small golden-yellow fruits. Not as heavy a cropper as the red varieties.

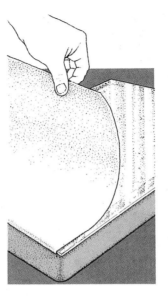

1, In autumn in a frame, or in March in the greenhouse, sow into seed boxes of moist seed compost.

2 Cover with glass and shade until germination. Maintain a temperature of 18°–20°C/64°–68°F.

3 When the seedlings have two true leaves, prick out 1 in apart into boxes or individual peat pots.

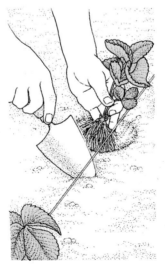

4 Just before planting, apply sulphate of potash at ½ oz per square yard to moist, well-dug soil, forking it in lightly.

5 Once the danger of frosts is over, plant out the seedlings in the prepared bed, 1 ft apart in rows 2½ ft apart.

6 In dry periods, water the plants thoroughly every 7–10 days. For better crops, feed every two weeks with liquid manure.

Strawberries 4

Protected strawberries
Early strawberries can be produced by protecting the plants in the spring with glass or plastic cloches, polythene tunnels or by growing them in cold frames. Under glass cloches, fruits can ripen three weeks earlier and with polythene 7–14 days earlier than unprotected fruits, depending on the variety and climate. Any variety can be used but, for even earlier cropping, choose early or second early varieties.

Cultivation
The cultural and feeding requirements of protected strawberries are basically the same as for unprotected plants. Use one-year-old plants rather than two-year-olds because they are smaller and need less room.

Plant runners in July to early September in the normal way, 12 in apart in rows 2½ in apart. Provide cover between January and mid-March. The earlier they are covered, the sooner they ripen; for example, if covered in February, the fruit ripens at the end of May or early June. Ventilation is not necessary in early spring but essential later on, especially at flowering time, to enable pollinating insects to visit the flowers and to prevent the build-up of extreme temperatures. Take care to avoid the twin dangers of too much ventilation, which delays ripening, and too little ventilation, which leads to fruit malformation. To ventilate, roll up the sides of polythene tunnels and remove the sides from cloches. Close the ventilation at night.

Once the crop has been gathered, take off the protection and clean up the rows, removing all runners and every other plant. The remainder are grown as summer-fruiting strawberries for the next two years.

Where there are plenty of runners, the number of plants in the row can be doubled up but after cropping, remove every second and third plant for growing on as usual.

Cloches and polythene tunnels
There are several types of glass and plastic cloches suitable for strawberries. Ideally, choose one that has a minimum height of 12 in and width of 20 in. Ventilation should be generous and easy to provide. A typical glass barn cloche is 2 ft long, 1 ft high and 26 in wide.

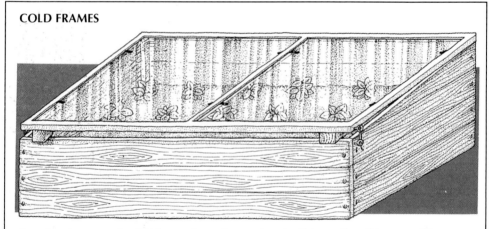

COLD FRAMES

Strawberries grown in cold frames for early cropping can be planted either in the soil in the frame, 12 in apart, or in 6 in pots in the frame. For planting in the soil, dig and manure it as for summer-fruiting strawberries. Plant the runners in July/August for fruit early in the following May. Leave the glass (or lights) off until January. The same principles of watering, feeding and ventilation as for the cloche-grown strawberries apply.

If frost is likely at flowering time, cover the frame with sacking or straw and remove it during the day.

Netting stretched over the frame keeps off birds when the glass or plastic is removed.

Polythene tunnels consist of 150-gauge clear polythene film 42–48 in wide supported by galvanized wire hoops. The film is stretched over the hoops, anchored with string tied to each hoop, and the ends of the film buried.

Pests and diseases for outdoor strawberries

Aphids are the strawberry's most common pest, resulting in twisted and yellow-green leaves and stunted growth. Spray with dimethoate, pirimicarb, heptenophos or derris when aphids are seen on the undersides of leaves. Do not spray when harvesting. Slugs, snails and beetles eat the berries. To clear them, scatter slug pellets along the rows at strawing-down time, in late May.

Grey mould (*Botrytis cinerea*) occurs as a result of a wet summer or overwatering. At flowering time (from May onwards) apply carbendazim in three sprays at 14-day intervals.

Strawberries in the greenhouse

If there is a sunny shelf in the greenhouse

STRAWBERRIES

'Cambridge Favourite'

'Royal Sovereign'

Alpine
'Baron Solemacher'

1 In July to August, plant the strawberries 12 in apart in rows 2½–3 ft apart in moist soil, spreading out the roots well.

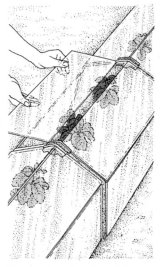

2 From January to mid-March, cover with cloches or tunnels. Ventilate on warm days, especially at blossom time. Close at night.

3 After cropping, remove the covers and dig up every other plant. The remainder are grown on in the usual way in the next two years.

Strawberries 5

strawberries can be grown in pots and, with heat, be ready to eat in March or, if the greenhouse is cold, in May.

Propagation
In late June, peg down the runners singly into 3 in pots of John Innes potting compost No. 1 buried level with the soil in the runner bed (see illustrations on page 45). Pinch out the runner just beyond the young plant.

When the new plants are well rooted, usually after four to six weeks, sever them from the parent plants and stand the pots on well-drained ground or in an open cold frame in a sunny position. Do not allow them to suffer any check due to lack of water. When the roots have filled the pots, pot on the plants into their final 6 in pots using John Innes potting compost No. 2 or a peat-based compost. Keep them well watered in hot weather and give them a liquid feed every seven days until September.

Leave the strawberries standing until the end of November, by which time they will have become dormant. Then bury the pots to their rims in peat or well-drained ground, preferably in an uncovered cold frame in a sheltered position. This prevents frost reaching the roots but in the event of very hard weather, lightly cover pots in the open with straw or bracken or close the cold frame.

Cultivation in a heated greenhouse
Bring the pots into a cool greenhouse in mid-December and maintain the temperature at just above freezing for two weeks. Space the plants out well to allow air to circulate and to prevent them becoming drawn. Then raise the temperature to 7°C/45°F but no higher because too much heat results in excessive foliage at the expense of fruitfulness. In February, when the flower trusses appear, raise the minimum to 10°C/50°F and ventilate a little if the greenhouse temperature exceeds 21°C/70°F. Maintain a moist atmosphere by damping down the paths and floor daily. Twice a week, give the plants a diluted high potash liquid feed. When the flowers

Propagation

1 In late June, peg down runners into 3 in pots as shown on page 45. In four to six weeks sever the new plants from the parents. Lift the pots and stand in a well-drained, sunny site.

2 In late July, pot on the plants into 6 in pots filled with John Innes No. 2. Keep well watered in hot weather. Feed with a liquid fertilizer every seven days until September.

3 At the end of November, when the plants are dormant, bury the pots level to their rims in peat or well-drained ground, or in an uncovered cold frame in a sheltered position.

open, increase the minimum temperature to 13°C/55°F and ventilate at 24°C/75°F. To ensure setting and good fruit shape, hand pollinate the blossoms daily with a small paint brush. During the pollination period maintain a drier atmosphere.

If the highest quality fruit rather than quantity is required, thin out the smallest flowers immediately after petal-fall, leaving eight to ten fruits to a plant.

Resume damping down floors and paths, and water the plants copiously in sunny weather. Stop feeding once the fruits begin to colour because too much feeding results in soft tasteless fruit and increases the risk of rotting. To keep the fruits clean and clear of the shelving, support the trusses with forked twigs inserted in the pots.

Cultivation in a cold greenhouse

The cultural operations are basically the same as for strawberries grown in a heated house except that the plants are brought into the greenhouse during January. When growth begins, lightly water them, increasing the amount as the plants become more leafy. When the flowers appear, twice a week apply diluted liquid feed at about a cupful per plant. During the warm days of spring and summer ventilate freely whenever the greenhouse temperature exceeds 24°C/75°F.

Suitable cultivars for both heated and unheated greenhouses include 'Honeoye', 'Tamella', 'Elvira' and 'Royal Sovereign' (see descriptions on pages 42–3).

Pest and diseases

Spray aphids with pirimicarb and introduce the predatory mite *Phytoseiulus* if glasshouse red spider mite is present. For grey mould (botrylis) apply carbendazim in three sprays at 14-day intervals starting at the flowering stage (see page 49). Grey mould should not occur if the plants are standing well spaced out on open staging.

In a heated greenhouse

4 In mid-December, bring the pots into the cool greenhouse. Raise the temperature two weeks later and again when the flowers appear in February. Apply liquid fertilizer twice a week.

5 When the flowers open, raise the minimum temperature to 13°C/55°F and ventilate at 24°C/75°F. Pollinate the flowers daily with a small brush. Do not damp down at this time.

6 When the fruit has set, resume damping down. When it begins to colour, stop feeding. Support the trusses and keep fruit clear of the shelves with forked twigs inserted in the pots.

Raspberries 1

SUMMER-FRUITING RASPBERRIES
Listed in order of ripening

EARLY
'Glen Clova' Flavour fair. Firm fruits.
Berries small to medium, dull red.
Cropping very heavy. Canes numerous
and strong. Some resistance to spur
blight. Susceptible to virus infection,

The European red raspberry (*Rubus idaeus*) can be found growing wild in cool, moist, hillside and woodland areas, from Scandinavia throughout Europe to central Asia. The stems, or canes, are biennial, in that they grow vegetatively in their first year, flower and fruit in their second year and then die back to ground level. The root system is perennial and of suckering habit, producing each growing season new replacement canes from adventitious buds on the roots and new buds from old stem bases.

Like the strawberry, the raspberry is one of the quickest fruits to crop, bearing a reasonable amount in the second year and full cropping thereafter. A good average yield is 1½–2 lb per foot run of row.

Cultivation

Most raspberries flower in late spring and the fruits ripen in early to midsummer, depending upon the cultivar and the weather: such cultivars are called "summer-fruiting" raspberries.

Some cultivars have the characteristic of flowering on the first year's growth on the topmost part in late summer and of ripening in the autumn. These are called "autumn-fruiting" raspberries and, because their cultural requirements differ in some respects, they are described separately (see page 56).

Soil and situation Raspberries grow best on a slightly acid soil of pH 6.0–6.7 that is moisture-retentive but well drained. They can be grown in dry, sandy and limy soils of low fertility, provided plenty of water is given during dry weather and bulky organic manures are liberally applied. Raspberries will not tolerate poor drainage, and even temporary waterlogging can lead to the death of the root system and subsequent death of the canes. In alkaline soils above pH 7.0, iron and manganese deficiencies may occur (see pages 18–20 for reduction of soil alkalinity and correction of iron and/or manganese deficiencies).

The site must be sheltered because strong winds damage the canes and inhibit the movement of pollinating insects. Preferably,

1 In early autumn, take out a trench in prepared ground three spades wide by one spade deep. Cover the bottom of the trench with 3–4 in layer of well-rotted manure or compost and fork in thoroughly.

2 Then, fill in the trench and fork in 3 oz per square yard of a compound fertilizer, such as a brand of Growmore.

best planted on its own.
'Glen Moy' Flavour good. Canes erect, vigorous and sufficient in number. Fruits large, firm, well flavoured. Some resistance to spur blight and aphids but susceptible to phytophthora. Unsuited to heavy wet soils. Sometimes produces autumn fruits on young canes.

'Glen Prosen' Good flavour. Canes of moderate vigour and sufficient in number. Fruits medium, firm. Crops well.
'Glen Ample' Good flavour, vigorous canes. Very heavy cropping. Large, fleshy fruits. Some disease and aphid resistance.
'Redsetter' Excellent flavour, large firm fruits well displayed. Canes of moderate vigour.

Comparatively disease free. Crops well.
'Malling Admiral' Flavour good. Berries firm, large ($1/4$–1 in), conical, dark red. Canes vigorous and numerous. Fruiting laterals long and need protection from strong winds. Cropping heavy and prolonged. Some resistance to spur blight, botrytis and virus infection.

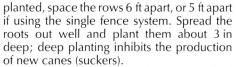

they should be planted in full sun, although they grow quite well in partial shade with a minimum of half a day's sun, provided they are not directly under trees and the soil is not too dry.

Soil preparation Prepare the ground in early autumn by forking out all weeds, particularly perennials. Then dig a trench along the intended row three spades wide by one spade deep. Cover the bottom of the trench with well-rotted manure or compost to a depth of 3–4 in and fork it into the base so that it is thoroughly mixed with the soil. With double-dug grassland there is no need for this operation because the buried turf takes the place of the organic manure. Finally, fill in the trench and fork in a compound fertilizer such as a brand of Growmore at the rate of 3 oz per square yard.

Planting and spacing If possible the rows should run north-south so that one row does not shade another too much.

Plant during the dormant season from November to March. Plant the canes 18 in apart in the rows. If more than one row is planted, space the rows 6 ft apart, or 5 ft apart if using the single fence system. Spread the roots out well and plant them about 3 in deep; deep planting inhibits the production of new canes (suckers).

After planting, cut down the canes to a bud about 9–12 in above the ground. In the following spring, when the new canes appear, cut down the old stump to ground level before it fruits. This means forgoing a crop in the first summer but it ensures good establishment and the production of strong new canes in subsequent years.

Supporting the canes
To prevent the canes bowing over when heavy with fruit and to keep the fruits clean, it is necessary to support the canes. The usual method is a post and wire fence, for which there are various alternative systems. It is easier to erect the fence before planting, although it may be left until the end of the first summer.

Single fence: vertically trained canes This is the most popular method and consists of

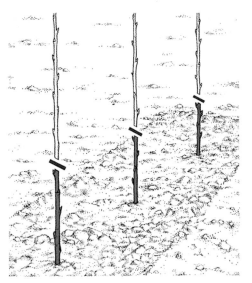

3 From November to March, plant the canes at 18 in intervals. Spread the roots out well and plant about 3 in deep. Cut down the canes to a bud about 9–12 in above the ground.

4 In late March, apply sulphate of ammonia at $1/2$ oz per square yard. Mulch with a 2 in layer of garden compost, keeping it well clear of the canes.

Raspberries 2

single wires stretched horizontally at heights of 2½, 3½ and 5½ ft. It requires the least space of the various fence systems and is ideal for the small garden. The fruiting canes are tied individually to the wires and thus are secure against winter winds. They are exposed to the sun, which enhances the quality of the fruits and reduces the incidence of fungal disease. The system has the disadvantages that the new canes are at risk of being trampled on during picking and of being damaged by strong winds in July unless temporarily supported by string tied to the lower wires.

Drive in preserved 7½ ft posts 18 in into the ground 12–15 ft apart. Use gauge 14 galvanized fencing wire.

Erect the end posts first and strut them and then drive in the intermediate posts. Finally fix the wires to the posts using straining bolts at one end and staples on the intermediates and at the opposite end.

Double fence: parallel wires The double fence is erected in a similar way to the single fence but because the top wires are not as high, the posts are only 6½ ft tall. Cross-bars 2½ ft long by 2 in across to carry the parallel wires are fixed to the end posts and to the intermediate posts. In exposed situations, double posts should be used instead of cross-bars. Parallel wires are spaced 2 ft apart at 3 ft and 5 ft from the ground. Stretch wire (or 4-ply fillis string) as cross-ties every 2 ft along the wires to prevent the canes falling down in the row.

This method has the advantage of enabling a larger number of canes to be trained in and a greater yield to be obtained from much the same area. Picking the fruits from the centre is difficult, however, and there is a higher risk of fungal diseases because of the more crowded conditions.

In an exposed garden the untied canes may be damaged on the wires, so the canes should be tied to the wires.

Scandinavian system (training in a low "V") This is a double fence system with only one set of parallel wires spaced 3 ft apart at 3 ft from the ground.

Drive two sets of posts 4½ ft long 18 in into the ground, 3 ft apart every 12–15 ft in the row.

The fruiting canes are not tied but woven around the wires to form a "V" when viewed

from the end of the row. The replacement canes are allowed to grow up the centre unsupported.

With this method the fruit is presented at a low picking height and the replacement canes are safe within the row. However, there is the risk of fungal troubles because of the crowded conditions of the canes on the wires and in the row. If more than one row is planted, space the rows 6 ft apart.

Single post system This is a method particularly suited to a very small garden. It consists of a single post to which each plant is tied. The posts are 7½ ft long by 2½ in top diameter, driven 18 in into the ground.

Initial pruning

In the first two seasons after planting, the number of canes may be few, but thereafter there should be more than enough.

In the second year thin out the weakest canes in the early summer so that the remainder grow more strongly, and pull out unwanted canes growing well away from the row. Allow about 8–10 canes to a stool.

Pruning and training established plants

As soon as fruiting is over, cut down to ground level the old canes which have fruited. Select the healthiest and strongest of the young canes, retaining about four to eight per stool.

If using the single fence system, tie the canes to the wires, 3–4 in apart. Either tie each one separately with a 6 in twist tie or secure them to the wires by continuous lacing using 4-ply fillis string. Tie the occasional knot as a precaution against the string breaking later on.

With the Scandinavian system the canes are laced around a single wire, equally on each side. Gently bend them over at the point they reach the wire and then twist the canes around the wire. No tying is necessary. Do this in late August or early September when the canes are still supple. Depending upon the length of the canes, this could mean four or six canes being twisted around each other and the supporting wires like a rope. The average number of canes from each stool should be about four to six.

For the single post system the fruiting

MID-LATE
'Tulameen' Good flavour, very large fruits, vigorous, spine-free canes. Crops well.

LATE
'Leo' Flavour good, slightly acid. Berries medium to large ($1/4$ in), bright orange-red. Cropping heavy. Canes very vigorous, stout. Slow to build up, plant two per station. Resistant to spur blight and some aphids. Susceptible to cane spot.

canes are tied to the posts and the replacement canes looped in as and when necessary.

Tipping the canes (This is not applicable to the Scandinavian system.) In late winter, about February, cut the canes to a bud 6 in above the top wire. This removes winter damage to the tips and encourages the lowest buds to break.

For very vigorous cultivars grown on the single fence system, where tipping would remove a lot of the cane, loop and tie the canes back on to the top wire and then prune about 6 in off the tips. This method gives extra length of canes, hence more crop, but the top wire must be strong.

Feeding and watering

In late January each year apply 1 oz of sulphate of potash per square yard. Every third year add 2 oz of superphosphate per square yard. In late March apply sulphate of ammonia at $1/2$ oz per square yard. The fertilizers should be applied as a top dressing covering about 18 in each side of the row.

Also, in late March, mulch with a 2 in layer of garden compost, damp peat or manure, keeping the material just clear of the canes. The mulch helps to conserve moisture in the summer and inhibits weed seeds from germinating.

Throughout the growing season keep down weeds and unwanted suckers by shallow hoeing. Be careful not to damage or disturb the roots of the raspberries. If preferred, herbicides can be used.

In dry weather water the raspberries regularly but, to minimize the risk of fungal troubles, keep the water off the canes.

Protect the fruit from birds with netting.

Propagation

Raspberries are easily propagated by forking up surplus canes with as many roots as possible at pruning time. The canes must be healthy and strong. Virus-infected plants should be dug up and burned.

Harvesting

Pick the fruits without the stalk and core, unless the raspberries are required for showing, when they are harvested with the stalk attached, using scissors.

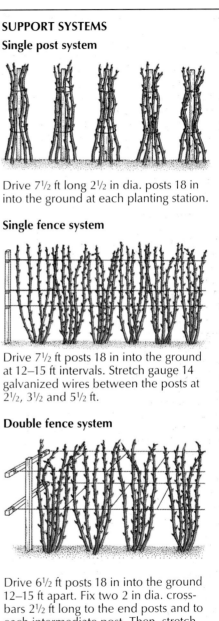

SUPPORT SYSTEMS

Single post system

Drive $7^1/2$ ft long $2^1/2$ in dia. posts 18 in into the ground at each planting station.

Single fence system

Drive $7^1/2$ ft posts 18 in into the ground at 12–15 ft intervals. Stretch gauge 14 galvanized wires between the posts at $2^1/2$, $3^1/2$ and $5^1/2$ ft.

Double fence system

Drive $6^1/2$ ft posts 18 in into the ground 12–15 ft apart. Fix two 2 in dia. crossbars $2^1/2$ ft long to the end posts and to each intermediate post. Then, stretch parallel wires 2 ft apart between the posts at 3 ft and 5 ft from the ground. Stretch wires or string as cross-ties every 2 ft along the wires.

Raspberries 3

Pests and diseases

If aphids are present, spray with dimethoate, heptenophos or pirimicarb in spring. A tar oil spray in winter gets rid of the overwintering eggs. To prevent raspberry beetle grubs feeding on the fruits in summer, spray at dusk with fenitrothion or derris when the first pink berry is seen and again 2 weeks later.

The most serious diseases of raspberries are viruses, which cause the leaves to become mottled or blotched and the canes to be stunted. Seek expert advice before destroying canes because the symptoms are similar to those caused by raspberry leaf and bud mite. New canes should be planted elsewhere.

Canes affected by cane blight in summer will wilt, snap off easily and die. Cut out and burn affected canes. Spray new canes with bordeaux mixture.

Cut out and burn canes badly affected by cane spot (see page 27).

Spur blight causes dark purple blotches around the buds and shoots wither in early spring. Cut out and burn affected canes. Spray new canes when they are a few inches high with a suitable fungicide (see page 29).

Prevent grey mould (*Botrytis cinerea*) by spraying three times with carbendazim at flowering and at two-week intervals. Remove and destroy infected fruits.

Selecting healthy plants

It is important to buy only Government-inspected stock, wherever possible, to ensure the plants are virus-free, healthy and true to name. Healthy plants should last at least ten years before starting to degenerate from virus infection. When this occurs, remove the plants and start a new row in soil that has not grown raspberries or other *Rubus* species before. If this is not possible, re-soil over an area 2 ft wide by 1 ft deep.

AUTUMN-FRUITING RASPBERRIES

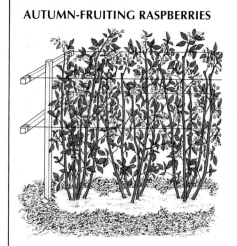

Autumn-fruiting raspberries bear their fruit on the top part of the current season's canes, extending back from the top over 12 in or more, depending upon the cultivar. The fruits ripen from the beginning of September until stopped by the autumn frosts. They do not come away from the plug or core as easily as some of the summer-fruiting cultivars, making picking more difficult. These raspberries are not usually attacked by birds, therefore netting should not be necessary. A good average yield is about ½ lb per foot run of row.

The cultural requirements (soil preparation, planting, spacing, initial pruning and feeding) are the same as for the summer-fruiting kind. Use the parallel wire method of support described on pages 54-5. The fruits are produced when the weather is becoming cooler, so they are best planted in the sunniest position possible, otherwise too few raspberries may ripen before the first frosts arrive.

Pruning established plants Each February cut down all canes in the row to ground level. In the following spring, new canes are produced which crop in the autumn. As the canes are not in the row for more than a year, it is not necessary to thin them unless they are particularly crowded. Pull out any which are growing away from the row.

AUTUMN-FRUITING RASPBERRIES

'Autumn Bliss' Ripens mid August onwards. Canes numerous of moderate height and fairly erect. Fruits large, dark, red, firm, excellent flavour. Crops well and reliable.
'Joan Squire' Similar. Follows 'Autumn Bliss'.

YELLOW AUTUMN-FRUITING RASPBERRIES
'Fallgold' Sweet, mild flavour. Berries medium to large (¼ in), golden-yellow, conical. Canes vigorous, prolific. Fruits ripen early September.

The first year

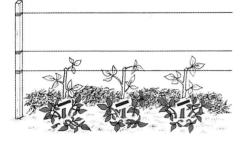

1 In spring, when the new canes appear, cut down the old stumps to ground level.

2 From June to September, as new canes develop, tie them 4 in apart on to the wires.

Second and subsequent years

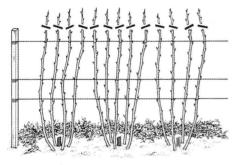

3 In February, cut the canes to a bud 6 in above the top wire. Mulch the plants.

4 In midsummer, fruit is carried on laterals from last year's canes. Thin out the weakest new growth to leave strong canes 4 in apart. Pull out new shoots growing away from the row.

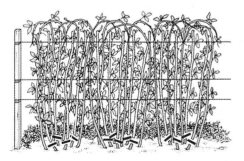

5 When fruiting is over, cut the fruited canes down to ground level. Tie in new canes 4 in apart. If growth is vigorous loop the new canes over to form a series of arches.

6 Each year in late January, apply 1 oz sulphate of potash per square yard as a top dressing 18 in each side of the row. Every third year apply 2 oz superphosphate per square yard.

Blackberries 1

The blackberry, or bramble as it is popularly called, is a rambling cane fruit found growing wild throughout the British Isles, northern Europe and in the Mediterranean region. The canes are of arching habit, thick, strong and often aggressively thorned, although there are good thornless cultivated varieties. It is usually deciduous, but not always so in mild winters.

Hybrid berries, of which there are a number of named varieties, have arisen as a result of accidental and deliberate crosses between various *Rubus* species, principally between the raspberry, blackberry and dewberry. As might be expected, they have characteristics that are intermediate between those of the parents. Most hybrid berries are not as vigorous as the blackberry and are, therefore, more suited to the small garden. There are both thorned and thornless varieties of hybrids.

A good average yield from a well-established blackberry or hybrid berry plant is 10–30 lb of fruit, depending upon the size of the plant and the cultivar.

Cultivation

Cultivated blackberries are much larger and more luscious than are wild varieties. They need little preventative spraying and can be planted in a spare corner of the garden.

Soil and situation Blackberries grow in a wide range of soils and will tolerate slightly impeded drainage. If thin dry soils cannot be avoided, improve their moisture-retentiveness and fertility with bulky organics. Hybrid berries are more demanding, and require a well-drained fertile soil, ideally a medium loam not less than 15 in deep.

Blackberries and hybrid berries flower relatively late, from the end of May onwards, and bloom over a long period, and so frost is seldom a problem. They are among the few fruits than can be successfully grown in a frost pocket, although this should be avoided if possible. They will also tolerate partial shade but fare better in full sun (particularly the hybrid berries). Because of their rambling habit, they need some support.

Planting Prepare the ground in early autumn. Fork out perennial weeds. Then, if the ground is poor, apply a 2–3 in deep layer of well-rotted manure, compost or peat over an area 2–2½ ft square at each planting site and dig it in thoroughly. Rake in 3 oz of a compound fertilizer such as a brand of Growmore over the same area.

Plant during the dormant season from November to March, preferably in the early part of the winter while the soil is still warm. Young plants, in the form of rooted tips or one-year-old bedded tips, can be obtained from a nursery. Using a hand trowel or fork, dig a hole wide and deep enough to take the roots spread out well. Plant the canes to the same depth as they were in the nursery. After planting, firm the soil and then cut down each cane to a bud at about 10 in above the ground.

Spacing Plant the canes in rows 6 ft apart. In most gardens one plant, or at the most one row, is sufficient.

Spacing between the plants depends upon the cultivar and the method of training. For the least vigorous growers, such as the thornless types and the Boysenberry and Tayberry, fan-trained plants should be spaced 8 ft apart; allow 8–12 ft between the weaving and one-way systems. For cultivars of medium vigour, such as the loganberry, 'John Innes' and 'Oregon Thornless', the relevant distances are 10 ft between fans and 10–12 ft between weaving and one-way systems. Extremely vigorous growers, such as 'Himalaya Giant' and 'Bedford Giant', should be spaced 12 ft apart when fan-trained and 12–15 ft apart for the weaving and one-way systems.

Support Support is necessary to keep the canes off the ground for easy picking and to keep the plants tidy. Out in the open, a wire fence is necessary with wires every 12 in between 3 ft and 6 ft. Erect the wires before planting the canes.

Training The fruiting canes should be trained to keep them separate from the young replacement canes to facilitate picking and to reduce the risk of the spread of fungal diseases from the old to the new.

The three methods commonly used are the fan, weaving, and rope system trained one way. The fan is best reserved for less vigorous hybrid berries. The weaving system takes full advantage of the long canes of vigorous kinds but there is much handling at

BLACKBERRIES

'Silvanberry' ['Sylvan'] Very early. Canes vigorous, thorny. Crops well. Fruits reddish black, large, good flavour. Tolerant of heavy soils.
'Waldo' Early. Long, strong, thornless canes, moderate vigour. Black glossy fruits, good aromatic flavour. Crops well.

'Adrienne' Early. Thornless, stout, vigorous. Fruits large, bright, of good flavour. Crops well.
'Fantasia' Mid to late. Very vigorous, strong canes powerfully thorned. Crops heavily. Fruits large, shiny black, good flavour.
'Oregon Thornless' A thorn-free form of the cut-leaved blackberry (*Rubus*

laciniatus). Flavour fair, mild and sweet. Fruit size small to medium. Cropping good. Growth medium to vigorous. Fruits ripen mid-August to September. Excellent for the medium-sized garden.

---

pruning time. The one-way system keeps handling to a minimum, but wastes space because young rods are trained along the wires only to one side of the plant. These fruit the following year. When new rods appear they are trained in the opposite direction.
Initial pruning In the first summer after planting, a number of young canes should spring up from the root system. Tie these securely to the lower wires in a weaving fashion. In the second summer these canes should flower and fruit. At the same time new growth springs from the base of the plant. This young growth should be secured and trained in the adopted method.

When fruiting is over, untie the old canes and cut them down to ground level. With the fan and weaving systems the young canes are then trained in to take their place. With the one-way system, the young canes are already tied in. The young growth will fruit in the next year, and so the cycle is repeated.
Subsequent pruning Pruning in the third and subsequent years consists of cutting out the rods that have fruited and replacing them with the new canes. If the replacement canes are few, the best of the old canes can be used again, but the older growth does not yield the best quality berries. Each year in February cut

back any winter-damaged tips to a healthy bud.
Feeding and watering In late February apply 2 oz of a compound fertilizer such as a brand of Growmore as a top dressing over one square yard around the base of each plant.

In late March, mulch with a 2 in layer of garden compost, peat or manure, keeping the material just clear of the canes. In dry weather water the plants but, to minimize the risk of fungal troubles, avoid the canes.

If necessary, protect the fruit from birds with netting.

Pollination
All varieties are self-compatible and only one plant is needed.

Harvesting
Blackberries are ready for picking when they are black in colour. Hybrid berries vary from claret red to black. Pick all fruit when it is ripe even if not required, because this helps the later fruit to achieve a good size.

Pests and diseases
Blackberries and hybrid berries are prone to the same pests and diseases as raspberries (see page 56).

PROPAGATION

Blackberries and hybrid berries are propagated by tip-rooting. The new canes are tip-rooted in August and September. A 6 in hole is dug with a trowel near the plant, and the tip of a young cane is bent down into it. The soil is then replaced and firmed. As new canes are produced, so more tips can be buried. In the following spring, the rooted tips are severed from the parent plant with about 10 in of stem, and then dug up and planted out in a new position. A few cultivars produce spawn (suckers), which should be lifted with as much root as possible and planted out in the new bed.

Another method is by leaf bud cuttings taken in July and August and rooted in a cold frame. This method is useful for rapid propagation when stock is limited.

Blackberries 2

HYBRID BERRIES
'John Innes' Good, sweet flavour. Large, firm, shiny black berries. Heavy cropper. Canes of medium vigour. Few spines. Ripens mid-August onwards.
Loganberry Flavour sharp and distinctive. Berries very large, up to 2 in long, burgundy red. Cropping good. Canes moderately vigorous. Fruits ripen

Cultivation

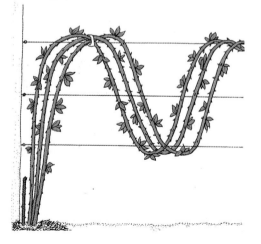

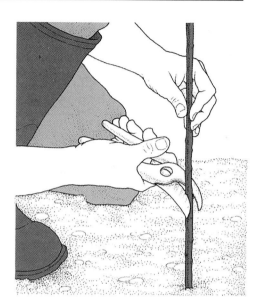

1 In early autumn, clear the ground of perennial weeds. If the ground is poor, dig in a 2–3 in layer of well-rotted manure over an area 2–2½ ft square. Fork in 2 oz of compound fertilizer over the same area.

2 From November to March, dig a hole to take the plant with the roots spread out well. Plant to the same depth as it was at the nursery. Firm the soil and cut the cane to a bud 10 in above the ground.

Weaving system

The second year

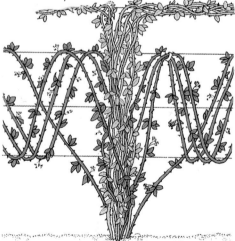

1 In summer, as the young canes appear, tie them to a strong wire support. Weave them in and out of the bottom three wires.

2 In summer, train the new canes up through the centre of the bush and along the top wire. Fruit is carried on laterals of last year's canes.

July/August. There are two good clones, LY59 (thorned) and L654 (thornless). **Thornless Boysenberry** Flavour sharp and excellent for jams and cooking. Berries large, conical, ripen to a dark purple-red. Cropping good. Weak to moderate vigour. Ripens July/August. Resists drought well, useful on light soils.

Tayberry Flavour good, mild and sweet. First berries large, smaller later in the season. Similar in shape and colour to the loganberry. Cropping good. Canes moderate in vigour, prolific, slightly thorned. Fruits ripen early July. Excellent for the small garden.

Japanese Wine Berry (*Rubus phoenicolasius*). Sweet, poor flavour. Seedy, small golden-yellow berries. Cropping light. Fruits ripen August. Canes covered with thin red bristles. Grown mainly for ornament.

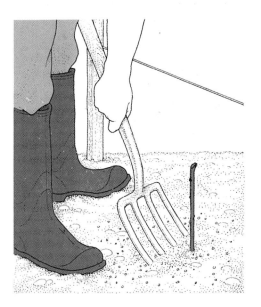

3 In late February, fork in 3 oz of a compound fertilizer such as a brand of Growmore per square yard around the base of each plant.

4 In late March, apply a 2 in layer of garden compost keeping it just clear of the canes. During dry weather, water the plants but keep the water off the canes.

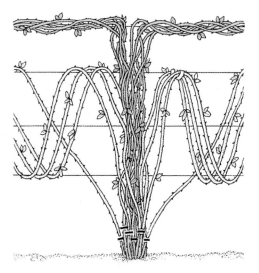

3 In October, after fruiting, cut out all fruited canes to base. If there are few new canes, retain the best of the old.

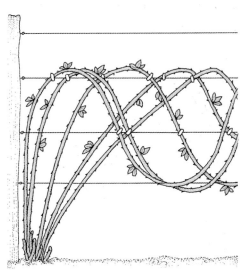

4 At the same time, untie the current season's canes and weave them round the lower three wires. In autumn, remove the weak tips from the young canes.

Black currants 1

BLACK CURRANTS
Listed in order of ripening

EARLY
'Boskoop Giant' Juicy, moderately
sweet, good flavour. A thin, rather
tender skin. Berries very large. Cropping
heavy. Bush very vigorous and slightly
spreading. Not suitable for the small

The black currant (*Ribes nigrum*) is a native of central and eastern Europe from Scandinavia to Bulgaria, also northern and central Asia to the Himalayas. It can be found growing wild, generally in damp woody places.

Selection in cultivation has given rise to stronger-growing and highly productive varieties. Black currants are grown on a stool system – that is, many shoots spring from below the ground rather than from a single stem. A well-grown black currant bush may reach 5–6 ft in height and spread and should last 15 years or more before it needs to be replaced. A good, average yield from an established black currant is about 10–12 lb.

Cultivation

It is important to buy only healthy stock because the black currant can suffer from a serious pest called gall mite (big bud mite) with its attendant reversion disease, both of which can badly debilitate the plant. For this reason many countries operate a certification scheme whereby the young stock sold by nurseries is inspected and, if healthy, a certificate to this effect is issued. In Britain only two-year-old certified black currant plants are available.

Soil and situation Black currants can be grown in a wide range of soils. Ideally it should be slightly acid (about pH 6.5), highly fertile, moisture-retentive and well drained, although black currants will tolerate slightly impeded drainage. Light soils need plenty of bulky organics. Excessively acid soils should be limed to bring the pH up to 6.5.

The site should be frost-free and sheltered from strong winds so that pollinating insects such as bees are not inhibited. Most cultivars bloom early in the spring and the flowers are extremely vulnerable to frost. In frost-prone areas, plant the late-flowering or more frost-tolerant varieties and cover the plants on frosty nights. Black currants will tolerate partial shade but prefer a sunny position.

Preparing the soil Prepare the ground in early autumn clearing away all weeds. Apply a 3 in layer of manure or compost over the whole area. If manure and compost are not available, apply a 2 in layer of peat with bonemeal at 3 oz per square yard. If the ground is fairly clean, single dig the materials in, but if rough and weedy double dig the area. Rake in a balanced fertilizer such as a brand of Growmore at the rate of 3 oz per square yard.

Planting and spacing Buy two-year-old certified bushes. Select plants with not less than three strong shoots.

Plant during the dormant season from November to March. Space bushes 5 ft apart in the row (6 ft apart for more vigorous cultivars), with 6 ft between rows.

Dig out a hole wide enough to take the roots spread out well. To encourage a strong stool system plant bushes about 2 in deeper than they were in the nursery – the soil mark on the stems gives an indication. Fill in the hole and firm.

Initial pruning After planting, cut all shoots to within 2 in of soil level. This encourages the production of strong young shoots from the base, and creates a good stool system for heavy cropping in the future, although it means forgoing a crop in the first summer. If the plants are from certified stock, the pruned shoots may be used as cuttings. They root easily so buy only half the number of bushes required and fill the vacant positions with two to three cuttings to each station.

After the hard initial pruning the young bush should produce three or four strong shoots from the base, each shoot being 18 in or more in length. If growth is poor, they should be cut down again in the winter. Assuming a strong bush has been formed, no pruning is required at the end of the first year; the young shoots are left to fruit in the following summer.

Pruning an established bush Black currants bear the best fruit on the wood produced in the previous summer, although they also crop on the older wood. Prune in early autumn or at any time in the dormant season until March.

The objective with an established bush is to stimulate a constant succession of strong young shoots to carry fruit in the next season. This is achieved by fairly hard pruning, cutting at or as near the base as possible, and by heavy feeding.

It is important to be able to distinguish the young wood from the old. This is fairly easy because the bark of the young shoots is

garden. Susceptible to leaf spot.
EARLY-MID
'Ben Connan' Large sweet berries, crops heavily. Medium vigour, compact habit. Resistant to leaf midge and some resistance to mildew and leaf spot.
MID-SEASON
'Ben Lomond' Flavour good, acid. Berries large, cropping very heavy.

Bush upright and compact, spreads a little under the weight of the crop. Flowers late and has some resistance to frost. Carries a good resistance to American gooseberry mildew.
MID TO LATE
'Ben Sarek' Large berries, good acid flavour. Small compact bush. Ideal for small garden. Some resistance to

mildew, leaf midge and frost.
'Baldwin' (Hilltop strain) The most widely grown variety. Acid flavour, rich in vitamin C. Tough skin. Berries medium and hang well without splitting over a long period. Cropping moderate to good. Bush of medium vigour, fairly compact. Suitable for the small garden.

---

much lighter in colour than that of three years old or more.

There is no need to limit the number of main branches nor to have the centre open. However, about a quarter to a third of the oldest wood should be removed annually. Cut back to a strong young shoot at or near the base or, if there is none, cut out the branch altogether.

Remove any thin mildewed shoots including those suffering from die-back in the centre. Leave a working space between one bush and the next.

Feeding and watering Black currants thrive on heavy manuring and high summer moisture. Each February apply a compound fertilizer such as a brand of Growmore over the whole plantation at 3 oz per square yard. Additionally, in March apply sulphate of ammonia at 1 oz per square yard; on acid soils apply nitro-chalk instead. Follow this with a 3 in thick mulch of manure or compost around each bush.

In dry weather apply 4½ gal of water per square yard every ten days, but keep the water off the stems as much as possible to lessen the risk of fungal trouble. This assists new growth and the developing crop.

Weed control The bushes are shallow-rooted. Do not dig around the plant but keep the weeds down by shallow hoeing or by hand weeding or by using herbicides (see pages 32–3).

Pollination
Black currants are self-compatible and are pollinated mainly by bees.

Frost and bird protection
The flowers are extremely vulnerable to spring frosts which cause the fruitlets to drop. On nights when frosts are likely, drape the bushes with hessian, fleece or a few layers of bird netting (see page 12); remove the cover in the mornings. Net the fruits against birds when the first fruits begin to colour.

Harvesting
Pick selectively when the currants ripen but before they begin to fall or shrivel. For show purposes the whole sprig should be cut off using scissors.

Pests and diseases
The most serious pests of black currants are aphids, the black currant gall mite, and glasshouse red spider mite. Use a systemic insecticide against aphids, carbendazim for gall mite, and bifenthrin, dimethoate or derris to control glasshouse red spider mite.

Of the diseases, the most troublesome are reversion disease, American gooseberry mildew, leaf spot and botrytis. Bushes affected by reversion should be dug up and burned. Mildew can be controlled by regular spraying with benomyl, which will also control leaf spot. Alternative fungicides are mancozeb or thiram. For botrytis use carbendazim or thiophanate-methyl at flowering time.

PROPAGATION

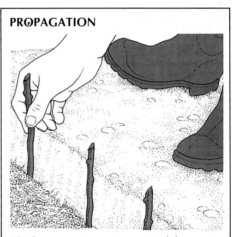

Black currants are propagated from cuttings 8–10 in long, about a pencil's width, from well-budded healthy wood of the current year's growth. Take the cuttings in October or November. Make a sloping cut just above a bud at the top and a straight cut just below a bud at the base. Insert the cuttings deeply with only two buds showing above the surface in well-drained light soil. Space the cuttings 6 in apart and firm them in the row.

At the end of the first growing season dig up and plant the rooted cuttings 12 in apart. Cut them down to within 1 in of the ground. This hard pruning should create a stooled bush.

Black currants 2

1 In autumn, clear the ground of weeds. Dig in a 3 in layer of manure or compost. Rake in a balanced fertilizer such as a brand of Growmore at 3 oz per square yard.

2 Dig a hole wide and deep enough to take the roots spread out well. Plant the bush 2 in deeper than it was at the nursery. Fill in the hole and firm the soil.

5 In February to March, apply a compound fertilizer such as a brand of Growmore at 3 oz per square yard. A month later, apply 1 oz sulphate of ammonia per square yard.

6 In July, the bush fruits best on last year's wood. New basal growths develop.

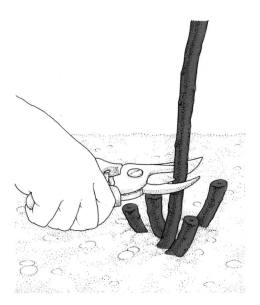

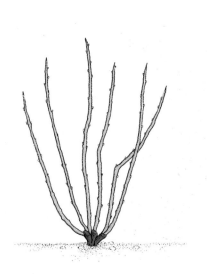

3 After planting, cut down all shoots to within 2 in of soil level.

4 In November, the severe pruning has resulted in strong new shoots appearing from the base. These will fruit the following year. No pruning is required.

The third year

In subsequent years

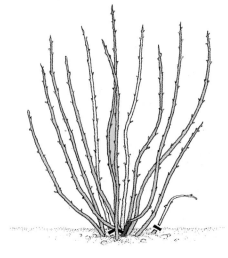

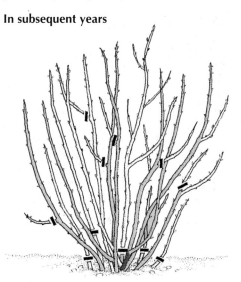

7 In November, thin out weak shoots and any branches that are too low, broken or mildewed.

8 Every winter, between November and March, remove about one-third of the bush. Cut out badly placed, damaged wood. Cut back fruited branches to a strong shoot.

Red and white currants 1

Red and white currants are basically derived from two European species, *Ribes rubrum* and *R. spicatum*. The latter species is native to northern Britain. Red currants sometimes occur as garden escapes from bird-sown seed and *R. rubrum* is also found naturalized in many areas.

Cultivation

The fruit buds are produced in clusters at the base of the one-year-old shoots and on short spurs on the older wood. Because of this fruiting habit there is a permanent framework of branches, unlike the black currant for which a succession of young wood is needed.

The red currant is usually grown as an open-centred bush on a 4–6 in stem or leg, rather like a miniature apple tree, with a height and spread of about 5–6 ft. This method of growth makes cultivation around the plant easier and keeps the fruit clear of the ground. The red currant is also grown as a single or multiple cordon, and, more rarely, as a standard or fan. A well-grown bush should yield at least 8–10 lb of fruit and a single cordon about 2–3 lb. Plants should bear well for at least ten years.

The smooth-skinned, glistening red berries are attractive and ideal for jelly, pies, juice and for wine making.

The white currant is a mutation or sport of the red currant and for cultural purposes is treated in exactly the same way. The berries, of somewhat milder flavour than the red, are also useful for jelly and for wine making.

Soil and situation Ideally, the soil should be neutral to slightly acid (about pH 6.7). It is less tolerant of poor drainage than the black currant but, provided the soil is reasonably well drained and not deficient in potash, the red currant is tolerant of a wide range of conditions.

The flowers of the red and white currants are hardier than those of the black currant, so it is a useful plant for north-facing walls and fences and for shaded areas, provided the soil is not dry and overhanging trees do not drip on the plants. It will grow in zones 7–8. A sunny position is preferable if the berries are to acquire their full flavour. The site should be sheltered but not a frost pocket.

Soil preparation Prepare the soil in the early autumn by clearing away all weeds. Apply a light dressing of well-rotted manure or compost about 1½ in thick over the whole area. If farmyard manure or compost are not available, apply a 1 in layer of damp peat. If the ground is fairly clean, single dig the dressing in; but if weedy, double dig the area. Rake in a compound fertilizer, such as a brand of Growmore, at the rate of 2 oz per square yard and sulphate of potash at ½ oz per square yard.

Selection of plants Buy plants from a reliable source because certified stock is not available. One- or two-year-old bushes are usually supplied by the nursery. Select a plant with a clear stem, or leg, of about 4–6 in with a head of about 3–6 evenly balanced sheets. The single (or multiple) cordon may be two or three years old and should consist of one (or more) straight stems with plenty of side-shoots. The standard, rarely seen nowadays, has a clear stem of about 3½ ft.

Planting and spacing Plant during the dormant season between November and March, unless the plants are container-grown, when they can be planted at any time.

Space bushes 5 ft × 5 ft (5 ft × 6 ft on fertile land) and single cordons 15 in apart, or 12 in apart on light soils. Allow 12 in between each stem of a multiple cordon; for example, double cordons should be planted 24 in apart from the main stem at ground level. Cordons should be trained up a vertical cane for straight growth and support. If planting cordons in the open, before planting erect a wire fence with horizontal wires at 2 ft and 4 ft and tie canes to the wires at each planting station.

Next, take out a hole large enough to contain the roots well spread out, and plant the bush or cordon to the same depth as it was in the nursery. Fill in and firm the soil.

Feeding and watering Each February apply a compound fertilizer, such as a brand of Growmore, over the whole plantation at 2 oz per square yard and sulphate of potash at ½ oz per square yard. On light soils also apply a mulch of rotted manure, compost or peat 2 in thick around each bush. If manure, compost or peat are not available, apply sulphate of ammonia at 1 oz per square yard. Water copiously in dry weather.

RED CURRANTS

EARLY

'Jonkheer van Tets' Good flavour. Thin but tough skin; deep red, large berries. Ripens July. A very heavy cropper. Bush moderately vigorous, fairly upright, spurring freely. Branches may need support in early years against the weight of crop. Short picking period.

'Laxton's No. 1' Good flavour, firm berries, medium to large, bright red. Ripens July. A heavy cropper. Bush vigorous, upright to slightly spreading.

MID-SEASON

'Red Lake' Good flavour, juicy, firm berries. Large bright red fruits. Ripens July to August. A heavy cropper. Easy to pick. Bush moderately vigorous, upright, spurring freely.

1 In early autumn, dig in a 1½ in layer of well-rotted manure. Then, rake in a compound fertilizer, such as a brand of Growmore, at 2 oz per square yard and sulphate of potash at ½ oz per square yard.

2 From November to March, dig a hole large enough to take the roots well spread out and plant the bush to the same depth as it was at the nursery. Delay planting if the ground is very wet or frozen.

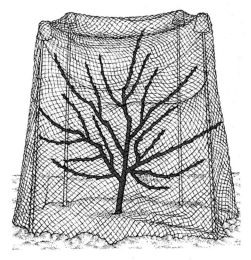

3 Each February, apply Growmore at 2 oz per square yard and sulphate of potash at ½ oz per square yard. On light soils also apply a 2 in mulch of rotted manure, compost or peat around each bush.

4 During the winter, protect the fruit buds with netting against attack by birds and frost at blossom time. Remove it during the day at flowering time.

Red and white currants 2

Pruning bush currants

The objective is to create a goblet-shaped bush with about 8–10 main branches growing upwards and outwards on a 4–6 in clear stem with an open centre. Prune in the same way as the gooseberry bush (see pages 71–3) except that the leaders are pruned to outward-facing buds, unless the branches are drooping, when they are pruned to upward-facing buds.

Pruning the single cordon: initial pruning

On planting a one-year-old rooted cutting, shorten the central leader by about one-half to an outward-facing bud. Cut back all other laterals to about 1 in at a bud, and remove any buds lower than 4 in to create a short clear stem. If planting an older pre-shaped cordon, shorten the leader by one-third and prune maiden laterals to one bud spacing 15″ apart.

In late June to early July cut back the current season's side-shoots to 4–5 leaves. Tie the leader to the cane as and when necessary throughout the growing season, but do not prune it.

The first year: Cordon

1 In winter, when planting a one-year-old shorten the central leader by about one-half to an outward-facing bud. Cut back all laterals to 1 in at a bud and remove any lower than 4 in.

Second and subsequent years A cordon is pruned in much the same way as a bush. Each summer at the end of June or early in July prune the current season's side-shoots to 4–5 leaves. Do not carry out summer pruning earlier than this or secondary growth may be stimulated. The leader is trained and tied to the cane, but not pruned in the summer until it has reached the required height, usually about 5–6 ft. From then on it is summer-pruned to 4–5 leaves.

Each winter, from November to March, cut all the previously summer-pruned laterals to about 1 in at a bud. Prune the leader to a bud leaving 6 in of new growth. Once the leader has reached the required height, it is also pruned to leave one bud of the previous summer's growth. This helps to maintain the cordon at approximately the same height for some years.

Multiple cordons, such as the double- and triple-stemmed cordon, are pruned in exactly the same way as the single, except that in the early formative years suitably low placed laterals are used to form the main stems.

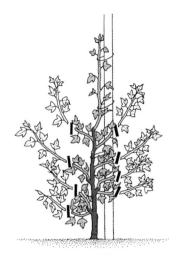

2 From late June to early July, cut back the current season's side-shoots to 4–5 leaves. Tie the leader to the cane as it extends but do not prune it.

Weed control

Red and white currants are shallow-rooted. Do not dig around the plants but keep the weeds down by shallow hoeing, hand weeding or by using herbicides.

Pollination

Red currants are self-fertile and insect pollinated, so pollination is not a problem.

Frost and bird protection

Red and white currant flowers are fairly hardy, although they will not tolerate hard frosts. Cover them with hessian, fleece or two or three layers of bird netting on frosty nights.

The berries are extremely attractive to birds in the summer, as are the fruit buds in the winter. Net the bushes in the winter and at fruit-ripening time. Remove the netting at flowering time, because netting inhibits insect pollination.

Harvesting

Red currants are ripe in July or August. Pick whole clusters to avoid injury to the fruit.

Propagation

Propagate new red currant plants in the autumn from hardwood cuttings, which should be 12 in long or more. Before planting the cuttings, remove all the buds except the top three or four. Insert into the soil with the third bud within 2 in of the soil surface and label the cuttings. After they have rooted (in about a year's time) plant out the cuttings. This method produces rooted cuttings with four good branches and a short leg.

Pests and diseases

The most serious pests are aphids (particularly the red currant blister aphid) and, to a lesser extent, sawfly caterpillars and capsid bugs. Control aphids with a systemic insecticide; control caterpillars and capsids with fenitrothion, derris or pirimiphos-methyl.

Occasionally leaf spot and coral spot can be troublesome. If leaf spot occurs, apply a suitable fungicide (see page 27). Cut back to healthy wood any branches affected by coral spot and burn the prunings.

Second and subsequent years

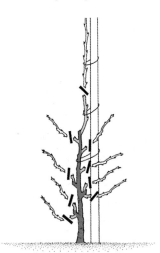

3 From November to March, prune the leader to a bud leaving 6 in of new growth. Cut all previously summer-pruned laterals to 1 in at a bud. In later years, cut the leader back to one bud.

4 From late June to early July, prune the current season's side-shoots to 4–5 leaves. Tie the leader to the cane as it extends.

Gooseberries 1

The gooseberry (*Ribes uva-crispa*) is a deciduous thorny shrub native to the cooler areas of Europe (zones 7–8).

Like the red currant, the gooseberry bears its fruit on spurs on the older wood and at the base of the previous summer's lateral growth. For this reason the gooseberry is grown with a permanent framework of branches, usually in the form of an open-centred bush on a short stem, or leg, of about 4–6 in. It is also widely grown as a cordon in single or multiple form and occasionally as a standard on a 3½ ft stem or as a fan.

The fruits may be smooth or hairy, yellow, white, green or red according to variety.

A well-grown bush should reach a height and spread of 5 ft and crop well for 12 years or more. A good average yield from a bush is 5–6 lb, and from a cordon 1–2 lb.

Cultivation

One-, two-, or three-year-old bushes can be bought from a nursery. A one-year-old bush should have about 3–5 shoots evenly placed around the stem, a two-year-old about 5–7 and a three-year-old 6–8 primary and secondary branches. Gooseberries are self-fertile and insect pollinated, so they can be planted singly if required.

Soil and situation The soil requirements of the gooseberry are similar to those of the red currant. The soil should not be allowed to become potash-deficient. It tolerates a little impeded drainage, provided it occurs below 18 in. The ideal soil, however, is a slightly acid (pH 6.7), well-drained medium loam.

The gooseberry is tolerant of cool, partial shade, but grows best in an open sunny site, which should be sheltered against strong winds, especially at flowering time in early April. Do not plant it in a frost pocket.

Soil preparation Prepare the soil in early autumn. It is essential to eliminate perennial weeds because the gooseberry is thorny and not easy to weed around. On light soils, dig in a 1½–2 in layer of well-rotted manure or compost over the whole area. On rich soils there is less need for bulky organics because too much of them encourages soft growth prone to snapping and to mildew. Rake in a compound fertilizer such as a brand of Growmore at 2 oz per square yard and sulphate of potash at ½ oz per square yard.

Planting and spacing Plant during the dormant season between November and March, preferably in autumn when the soil is warm.

Dig a hole wide and deep enough to contain the root system with the roots well spread

1 In early autumn, clear the soil of perennial weeds. Rake in a compound fertilizer such as a brand of Growmore at 2 oz per square yard and sulphate of potash at ½ oz per square yard.

2 From November to March, dig a hole wide and deep enough to take the roots spread out well. Plant the bush so that there is a clear stem of 4–6 in above ground.

EARLY
'Keepsake' Very good flavour. Fruits medium to large, green-white with a transparent, slightly hairy skin. Crops well. Ripens late but earliest for picking for cooking.

'Rokula' Dark red, good size fruits, excellent flavour medium vigour. Resistant to mildew. Crops well. Very early.

'May Duke' Good flavour when cooked. Fruits medium, oblong, dark red with smooth, downy skin. Early when picked green. Good cropper.
'Golden Drop' Rich flavour. Fruits small, round, dull green-yellow, with downy thin skin. Excellent dessert gooseberry.

---

out. Before planting, clean off any suckers at the base of the plants and any shoots too near the ground, then plant it to leave a clear stem of 4–6 in. Fill in the hole and firm the soil.

Space the bushes 5 ft apart, or on highly fertile ground 5 ft by 6 ft apart, and single cordons 1 ft apart. Allow 1 ft of space for each stem of a multiple cordon. For straight growth and support, train a cordon up a cane. If growing cordons in the open, erect a wire fence with horizontal wires at 2 ft and 4 ft and tie the canes to it.

Feeding and watering Each February apply a compound fertilizer such as a brand of Growmore over the whole plot at 2 oz per square yard and sulphate of potash at ½ oz per square yard. Mulch around the base of the plant with a 2 in layer of well-rotted manure, compost or peat on light soils, but less on medium or fertile soils. In the absence of bulky organics apply sulphate of ammonia at 1 oz per square yard.

Water copiously in dry weather but do not water irregularly or heavily at the ripening stage because this causes the fruit to split.

Formative pruning: Bush
Most cultivars have a tendency to form drooping growth and, in order to maintain an erect bush, counteract this habit by pruning the leaders to inward- or upward-facing buds or back to upright laterals. The centre of the plant is kept open to make picking and spraying easier, to ripen the wood and fruits, and to improve air circulation (which lessens the risk of mildew).

When planting a one-year-old bush, cut back each framework branch by one-half to an outward-facing bud if the shoot is upright, or to an inward-facing bud if the shoot is weeping.

The second year (or a two-year-old bush)
In November, shorten the leaders by one-half. Select well-placed shoots to form further permanent branches and cut back by one-half. Remove any suckers or low-growing shoots growing from the stem.

The third year (or a three-year-old bush)
The bush should have developed a main framework of about 6–8 branches with well-spaced leading shoots; it is at the start of its cropping life. Between November and March, shorten the leaders by one-half to a bud facing in the required growth direction. Cut out shoots crowding the centre and shorten those not required for the framework to about 2 in. Thereafter, prune the bush both in the summer and in the winter.

The second year

3 At the same time, cut back each framework branch by one-half to an inward- and upward-pointing bud. Clean off the suckers at the base and any shoots too near the ground.

4 In November, shorten the leaders by one-half to inward- and upward-facing buds. Select well-placed shoots to form further permanent branches and cut back by one-half. Remove suckers and low stems.

Gooseberries 2

MID-SEASON
'**Careless**' Good flavour. Fruits large, oval. Green skin ripening to white, smooth transparent skin. Reliable and good cropper.
'**Green Gem**' Fair flavour. Medium-sized, round. Deep green with pale green veins. Good cropper. Can be picked early for cooking.

Pruning an established bush

Each summer, in late June to early July, prune all laterals (that is, the current season's growth) to five leaves. This opens up the bush and removes any mildew and aphids at the tips of the shoots. Do not prune earlier because this might induce secondary growth. Do not prune the leaders unless mildewed.

Each winter, from November to February, cut back the leaders by one-half to a bud facing in the required direction. If the branch is weeping badly and there is a suitably placed upright lateral on it, then cut back to this.

Next deal with the laterals that were pruned the previous summer. Where fewer large dessert fruits are required, cut all of these laterals back to about two buds. Where quantity is required, pruning should be moderated accordingly. Vigorous cultivars such as 'Whinham's Industry' and 'Howard's Lancer' should be pruned less severely because this could encourage excessive growth. Cut out dead and diseased wood, and any growth crowding the centre.

As the bushes become older and branches less productive or too spreading, leave in some suitably placed strong, young shoots to replace the old which are then cut out.

The third year

5 From November to March, shorten the leaders by one-half to a bud facing in the required growth direction. Cut out shoots crowding the centre. Shorten laterals not required for the framework to about 2 in.

Pruning a single cordon Prune in the same way as the red currant cordon (see page 68).

Weed control

As with most bush fruits, the gooseberry is shallow-rooted. Keep the weeds down by shallow hoeing or with herbicides.

Protection against frost and birds

The gooseberry flowers early, during April, and spring frosts can substantially reduce the crop. On frosty nights protect the plants when they are in flower. Cover with hessian or two or three layers of bird netting, but remove it during the day to allow in light and give access for pollinating insects.

The fruit buds are attractive to bullfinches and sparrows in the winter and the ripening fruits to blackbirds and thrushes in the summer. Net the bushes in the winter and when the fruits begin to ripen.

Thinning and harvesting the fruits

For large dessert fruits start thinning the fruits in late May, removing every other one, and use them for cooking.

For small or medium dessert fruits, do not thin the fruits but leave them to ripen and develop their full flavour. Pick gooseberries

6 In May, when the fruits are large enough for cooking, thin the fruits by removing every other one. Cover the bush with bird netting to protect the fruits from birds.

'Lancashire Lad' Fair flavour. Large oblong hairy fruit. Dark red and juicy. Heavy cropper. Some resistance to mildew.

'Langley Gage' Excellent, sweet flavour. Medium, oval, smooth fruit. Pale yellow with transparent skin. Cropping variable.

'Leveller' Excellent flavour. Large oval yellow-green fruit with slightly downy skin. Very good cropper. Requires a fertile soil.

'Lord Derby' Fair flavour. Large, round dark red fruit, skin smooth with a faint down. Good cropper.

'Pax' Medium-sized berries, fair flavour. Virtually spine-free, some resistance to mildew. Crops well.

'Whinham's Industry' Sweet flavour. Fruit large, dark red and hairy. Crops heavily. Very vigorous bush.

'Whitesmith' Very good flavour. Medium to large oval fruit. Pale green with a yellow tinge. Heavy cropper.

---

for cooking when they are a good size, but still green, from late May.

Propagation
Propagate gooseberries using 12 in hardwood cuttings taken from healthy shoots in late September. First remove the weak tip and all but four buds from the upper part of the cutting. This produces a miniature, open-centred bush on a short leg. Dip the base of the cuttings in a hormone rooting powder. Insert the cuttings in the open ground with their lowest buds 2 in above the soil surface. Leave the cuttings in the nursery bed for the growing season. Lift and replant, exposing more of the stem.

Pests and diseases
The most troublesome pests are aphids, gooseberry sawfly and magpie moth caterpillars. For aphids, apply pirimicarb or a systemic insecticide, and for caterpillars apply fenitrothion, derris, permethrin or pyrethrum when flowering is over.

The most troublesome disease is American gooseberry mildew. Regular spraying with carbendazim controls it. The diseased shoots should be cut out and burnt.

WORCESTERBERRIES AND JOSTABERRIES

The Worcesterberry is a form of the North American species *Ribes divaricatum* and not a hybrid between the black currant and gooseberry as previously thought. The fruits, borne singly, are a dull black and much smaller than the gooseberry. They have an acid flavour but make good jam. The bush resembles the gooseberry in leaf and form, but is more vigorous and very thorny. It is fairly hardy and disease free. For cultural purposes treat it in the same way as the gooseberry.

The Josta is a true hybrid between the black currant and the gooseberry. It is thornless and virtually pest and disease free but extremely vigorous. The fruits are similar to the Worcesterberry. Cropping is only moderate relative to the vigour of the plant. For cultural purposes it is best treated in the same way as the gooseberry though it can be grown as a stooled bush.

The established bush

1 In late June to early July, prune all the laterals produced that season to five leaves. This opens up the bush and removes aphids at the tips of the shoots. Do not prune the leaders.

2 From November to February, cut back the leaders by one-half. Cut back laterals pruned in the previous summer to about two buds. Cut out diseased and dead wood and growth that crowds the centre.

Grapes 1

GRAPES (OUTDOORS)
Listed in order of ripening.

WHITE
EARLY
'Siegerrebe' Very good flavour with trace of muscat for dessert and wine. Berries golden-brown, medium in well-shaped bunches. Ripens late August to

Grapes (outdoors)

The art of growing grapes, or viticulture, has a long and illustrious history. The vine grows wild in the temperate regions of western Asia, southern Europe and parts of North Africa and it is thought to have originated in Asia Minor.

The vine is a perennial deciduous climber which clings to supports by tendrils. The leaves are heart-shaped and 4–8 in in size.

In the 1860s the vine pest *Phylloxera vastatrix* decimated the vineyards of Europe. The European vine (*Vitis vinifera*) was salvaged by grafting scions on to rootstocks of the more vigorous and *Phylloxera*-resistant American vine. Hybrids have also been raised by cross-pollination with the American vines *V. labrusca*, *V. rupestris* and *V. riparia*. These crop heavily and are *Phylloxera*- and mildew-resistant but many consider that they produce poorer quality wine.

Cultivation

Grape vines are sun-loving plants hardy in zones 9 and 10 and in warm, sheltered areas in zone 8. The black cultivars require greater warmth and a longer ripening season than the white cultivars, so most vines grown in the open in cooler areas are white, although there are a few hardy black grape cultivars.

Soil and situation The grape vine is fairly tolerant of a wide range of soils (although they must be deep and well drained) and it requires a soil pH of 6.5–7.0. Chalky soils are less suitable because of the risk of chlorosis.

The choice of site is important because it must be both sheltered and in full sun at an elevation of not more than 300 ft in southern Britain. Further south in warmer areas the vine is grown at higher altitudes. In the open, a south-facing or south-west-facing slope with the row running from north to south is ideal but not essential. In cooler areas, vines can be grown against a south-facing wall or fence. Avoid planting vines in a frost pocket.

Soil preparation If there is any possibility that the soil may become waterlogged, a drainage system must be installed (see pages 18–19).

Two or three weeks before planting, prepare the soil by double digging to break up any hard layers and to clear away perennial weeds. If the soil is very acid, dig in lime at the rate of 7 oz per square yard. If the soil is poor, dig in well-rotted manure or compost at the rate of one barrowload per 20 square feet. Rake in a balanced fertilizer such as Growmore at the rate of 3 oz per square yard.

All vines require a system of supporting horizontal wires. For vines against a wall, space wall wires 10–12 in apart (see pages 14–17). For vines in the open, drive 6½ ft wooden posts 2 ft into the ground spaced 8–10 ft apart. Reinforce the end posts with struts. Use gauge 12 and 14 galvanized wire secured to the end posts with straining bolts and stapled to the intermediate posts. Attach a single gauge 12 wire 15 in from the ground and two gauge 14 wires every 12 in above. Zig-zag the double wires so that they cross at each post. Insert a cane at each planting station except where it coincides with a post.

Planting Plant a one-year-old grape vine between October and March. Overwinter a weak vine of less than ¼ in diameter in a cold frame and plant it out when the danger of frost is over. Dig a hole wide and deep enough to take the roots fully extended. Against walls or solid fences plant vines 4 ft

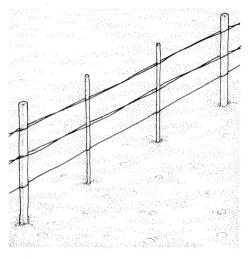

1 Before planting, drive 6½ ft posts 2 ft into the ground, 8–10 ft apart. Stretch one gauge 12 wire 15 in from the ground. Stretch two gauge 14 wires every 12 in above, zig-zagged from post to post. Insert a cane for each plant.

early September. Heavy cropper. Moderately vigorous. Does not grow well on alkaline soils.
'Précoce de Malingre' Good flavour for dessert and wine. Berries large in medium bunches but sets erratically. Ripens late September. Light cropper. Poor to moderate vigour.

'Madeleine Angevine 7972' Fair flavour for dessert and wine. Berries medium in moderately-sized bunches. Ripens late September to early October. Heavy cropper. Vigorous and fairly hardy. Prone to mildew.

MID-SEASON
'Muller Thurgau' Delicate flavour,

excellent for wine. Berries small to medium. Ripens mid-October. Heavy cropper. Vigorous. Needs good weather for pollination.
'Seyval' Reasonably good flavour for wine. Berries medium in moderately-sized bunches. Ripens mid- to end October. Hybrid. Some resistance to mildew. Heavy cropper. Moderately vigorous.

---

apart and 9 in from the wall. In the open plant vines 4–5 ft apart in rows 5–6 ft apart. Place the vine in the hole and spread out the roots. Return the soil and firm it down well. Ensure that the union of a grafted plant is above soil level. Tie the vine to the supporting cane or post. Water it if it is dry and apply a mulch of well-rotted manure or compost.

Pruning and training
Vines grown against walls and fences are usually pruned by the rod and spur system used for greenhouse vines (see pages 78–81).
The Guyot system Vines grown in the open are usually trained in the Guyot system, which can be single or double in form. With the single Guyot there is one fruit-carrying arm, with the double Guyot there are two; the double is the most popular method and is described below.

Each year, allow three new main stems, or rods, to develop. Retain two rods for fruiting and cut back the remaining stem to produce replacement rods for the following year. The fruiting arms are trained close to the ground to take advantage of its radiated warmth.

IMPROVING THE CROP
If all the bunches of fruit that set are allowed to mature, the quality of the crop suffers and the vine may crop poorly or not at all for several years after. Reduce the number of bunches as soon as it is possible to tell which look shapely, well set and of good size. With the rod and spur system, if two bunches are growing on one spur, remove the poorer. Allow two or three bunches on a three-year-old vine, four or five bunches on a four-year-old vine and full cropping thereafter.

It is not necessary to thin berries on the bunch if the grapes are grown for wine, but do thin dessert grapes (see page 80).

In early September, gradually remove the lower leaves to expose the bunches to sunlight and improve the air circulation. Do not remove all the leaves at once because this may lead to sun scorch.

Check the grapes two or three times a week and cut away any diseased or damaged berries.

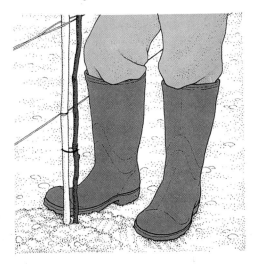

2 From October to March, in prepared ground plant the vine to the same depth as it was at the nursery. Firm the soil and water (if dry). Tie the vine to the supporting cane. Cut the rod down to two good buds from the union or from ground level.

3 From February to March, apply a general fertilizer, such as a brand of Growmore, at 2 oz per square yard and sulphate of potash at ½ oz per square yard. Mulch each plant with well-rotted compost to a depth of 2–3 in. Repeat annually.

Grapes 2

LATE
'Chasselas d'Or' ('Royal Muscadine')
Excellent flavour for dessert and wine.
Berries medium and round in long
bunches. Ripens late October. Suitable
only for growing against a wall.

The first year At planting, cut the rod down to about 6 in from ground level if the vine is on its own roots or, if it is a grafted plant, 6 in above the graft union, leaving at least two good buds. From April to September following planting, train one shoot up the cane or post and pinch out all others to one leaf. In November that year cut the rod down to within 15 in of ground level, leaving three good buds.

The second year During the summer, train in three shoots vertically. Pinch back any laterals to one leaf as they develop. In November the vine should be pruned as for an established vine (below).

Pruning an established vine Each November, (except the first) cut back the arms that bore fruit the previous summer to the replacement shoots. Tie down on to the lowest wire one replacement shoot to the left and one to the right. Cut down the remaining shoot to three or four buds to provide replacement shoots for the following year. Cut back the immature wood on the replacement shoots, leaving about 2–2½ ft of strong growth either side.

Third and subsequent years From April to August, tuck in the vertical fruit-carrying laterals between the double wires. Cut them back to two or three leaves above the top wires, as necessary, and remove any sub-laterals. Train the three replacement shoots from the centre for the following year up the cane or post. Pinch back any sub-laterals on the replacement shoots to one leaf and remove any blossom. Remove any surplus shoots coming off the main stem.

Feeding and watering In February, apply a balanced fertilizer, such as Growmore, at a rate of 2 oz per square yard and sulphate of potash at a rate of ½ oz per square yard.

In spring, mulch each vine with well-rotted compost to a depth of 2–3 in.

The grape vine is prone to magnesium deficiency (see page 28). Spray with a mixture of ½ lb magnesium sulphate (coarse Epsom salts) in 2½ gal water and a few drops of mild liquid detergent. Repeat this two weeks later.

Throughout the growing season, feed dessert grapes with a general liquid fertilizer once a week until the berries begin to ripen.

Wall-grown vines need regular watering because the soil near walls dries out rapidly.

Harvesting
Even when the grapes are fully coloured they are not ripe because they need a finishing period for sugars to form. This varies from 4–5 weeks for mid-season varieties to 8–10 weeks for late varieties.

Handling the grapes destroys the bloom, so with dessert grapes cut the branch carrying the bunch 2 in either side of the point where it hangs using secateurs.

Pests and diseases
Outdoor vines are less prone to pests than those grown in a greenhouse although typical greenhouse pests and diseases may occur outside as well, especially on vines grown against a wall (see page 81). Net the vine to keep birds away from the ripening fruits.

Powdery mildew can be very troublesome on outdoor vines and a regular fungicidal programme against this disease should be adopted as soon as it occurs (see page 28). Spray against grey mould (see page 27) at blossoming and repeat every two weeks until three weeks before harvesting. Dig up and burn vines infected with honey fungus and change the soil.

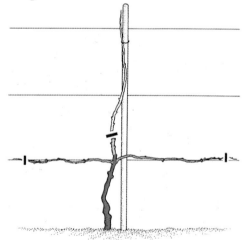

7 In November, tie down one replacement shoot to the left and one to the right on to the lowest wire. Cut them back leaving about 2–2½ ft of strong growth. Cut down the remaining shoot to three good buds.

BLACK

MID-SEASON

'Cascade' ('Seibel 13.053') Fair flavour. Berries small in tight, small bunches. Ripens early October. Resistant to mildew. Very vigorous. Fairly hardy.

'Boskoop Glory' A sweet grape of excellent dessert flavour for an outdoor grape. Bunches and berries of medium size. Moderate vigour. Crops well. Ripens late September–early October.

LATE

'Brant' Sweet flavour. Berries and bunches small. Ripens mid-October. Heavy cropper. Vigorous and relatively mildew-resistant. Good wall cover.

Strawberry Grape Musky flavour for dessert. Berries large, bunches small. Ripens late October. Moderate cropper. Fairly vigorous. Best grown against a warm wall.

The first year

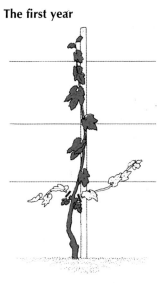

The second year

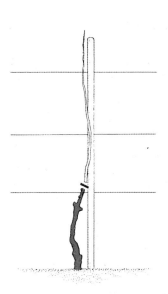

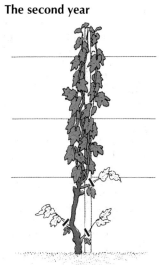

4 From April to September, allow one shoot to develop and train it vertically up the cane. Pinch back to one leaf any other shoots.

5 In November, cut the rod down to within 15 in of ground level, leaving three good buds.

6 From April to August, train the three shoots vertically. Pinch back any laterals to one leaf as they develop.

Third and subsequent years

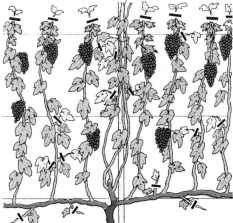

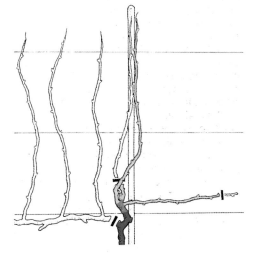

8 From April to August, train three shoots vertically from the centre. Pinch back any laterals produced on them to 1 in as they develop. Tuck in the vertical fruit-carrying laterals through the double wires. Cut them back to three leaves above the top wires.

9 In November, cut out the two arms that bore fruit in summer to the replacements. Tie down one replacement shoot to the left and one to the right. Cut back each to leave 2–2½ ft of strong shoot. Cut down the remaining shoot to three good buds.

Grapes 3

GRAPES IN THE GREENHOUSE
Sweetwater varieties are quick maturing and ripening. Thin-skinned, they are sweet and juicy. They deteriorate rapidly if left hanging for long after ripening. Ideal for the unheated greenhouse.
EARLY
'Buckland Sweetwater' Fairly good, sweet flavour. Fruits round, pale green

Grapes in the greenhouse

A much wider range of dessert grapes can be grown in the greenhouse than outside in a cool climate zone and, if the greenhouse is heated, this range can be extended.

Cultivation.

A grape vine can be planted in an inside border or outside with the main stem, or rod, led into the greenhouse through a hole cut low down in the wall. It can also be container-grown (see pages 174–7).

The advantages of planting in an outside border are that less frequent watering is required because of natural rainfall and that there is less risk of faulty watering. The advantage of an inside border is that the soil is warmer in early spring, especially if the vine is started early with artificial heat.

Soil and situation For an inside border, particularly if the roots are restricted, an open porous soil is required. Make up a mixture of seven parts loam, three parts peat and two parts coarse grit. Add 12 oz of John Innes base fertilizer or equivalent per 2 gal bucketful of soil, and 2¾ oz of ground chalk per 2 gal bucketful. The soil in an outside border should be deep and well drained with a pH of 6.5–7.0 (see page 74).

The vine is usually planted at the side, 9 in away from the wall and the rod trained up towards the ridge, parallel with the glass. In a small greenhouse it is best planted at the gable end farthest away from the door and then trained along the length of the house under the ridge. Or, plant the vine at one side, near the corner and run the rod horizontally along the side wall, with the fruit-carrying laterals trained vertically from it.

Planting Good drainage is essential. If in doubt, lay land drains or a soakaway (see pages 18–19).

Construct a system of supporting wires to run horizontally along the sides of the house. Use gauge 12 or 14 galvanized wire at 9 in intervals and finish 18 in below the ridge with a minimum distance of 15 in from the glass to prevent scorching and distortion.

Usually grape vines are supplied in containers, so vines can be planted in the greenhouse at any time of year. Planting between November and December is best so that the initial pruning can be done immediately.

Dig a hole large enough to take the roots fully extended. Plant the vine, spreading out the roots. (If the plant is pot-grown, simply tease out the perimeter roots with the fingers.) Replace the soil and firm it. Water well.

The first year

 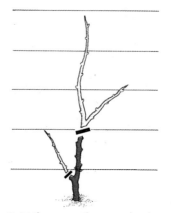 

1 From November to December, prepare the border soil and erect a support system. Plant the vine, spreading out the roots.

2 At the same time, cut back the main stem by two-thirds of the previous summer's growth. Cut remaining laterals to one bud.

3 In summer, allow the main stem to reach 10 ft. Cut back laterals to five leaves. Pinch out sub-laterals to one leaf. Tie loosely to the wires.

ripening to amber, in short, broad bunches. Sets freely. Heavy cropper. Not vigorous.
EARLY TO MID-SEASON
'Foster's Seedlings' Good flavour. Fruits oval, green-yellow ripening to amber, very juicy. Large bunches. Sets freely. Heavy cropper. Fairly vigorous.

LATE
Black Hamburgh (Schiava Grossa) Most reliable sweetwater grape, of excellent flavour. Sets and ripens well under cold glass. Bunches and berries of good size. Crops well and must be thinned. Muscat cultivars have the finest flavour. They hang well if a little warmth is provided. They are not free-setting and

need warmth and hand pollination. In cooler areas this means artificial heat.
EARLY
'Frontignan' Good flavour for dessert. Fruits small, black and white varieties.
'Madresfield Court' Very good flavour. Fruits large, oval, black with tough skin in long, large bunches. Tends to split. Good cropper. Moderately vigorous.

Pruning and training

Vines in a greenhouse are usually pruned by the rod and spur system (below). The replacement system, which is similar to the single Guyot system used for grapes grown outdoors (see pages 75–6), can also be used but it is more difficult.

If the vine is planted in November or December, cut back the main stem by two-thirds of the previous summer's growth. Cut any remaining laterals to one bud. If the vine is planted during the growing season, leave the initial pruning until leaf-fall to avoid the risk of the wound bleeding.

The first year After the initial pruning allow the main stem to grow unchecked to about 10 ft and produce lateral shoots. In summer, cut back the laterals at five or six leaves and pinch out any sub-laterals to one leaf. Tie the main stem and laterals loosely to the wires, leaving room for expansion. In November or December, immediately after leaf-fall, cut back the vine by two-thirds, and the laterals on the main stem to one good bud.

The second year From March to April, the topmost bud forms the new extension leader, which should be grown on unchecked. In the summer, if growth is vigorous, allow two laterals to bear fruit. Pinch out these laterals

at two leaves beyond the flower bunch. Stop unfruited laterals when they have five leaves. In December, shorten the leader by about one-half. Cut back laterals to 1 in, leaving two good buds.

Third and subsequent years The vine is now established and routine cultivation can begin. In a cold house open the ventilators so that the vine rests from January to March. In April close down the ventilators to increase the temperature, which encourages the buds to break. At the beginning of the year leave the rod hanging with the top almost touching the ground to prevent the sap from rising to the apical buds and stimulating only those to grow. When the buds on all the spurs have started to grow tie the rod back into position.

In May, increase the temperature slowly, ventilating at first if the temperature exceeds 18°C/64°F, and letting it increase to 21°C/70°F by the end of May.

If artificial heat is used growth can be started in February, maintaining a minimum temperature of 8°C/46°F, gradually increasing to 20°C/68°F minimum by the end of May.

Keep the atmosphere humid by damping down the borders on fine days. Until flowering begins, spray the rods each morning from above with a fine spray but not in bright sun.

The second year

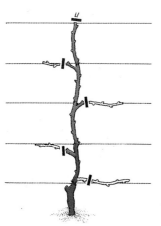
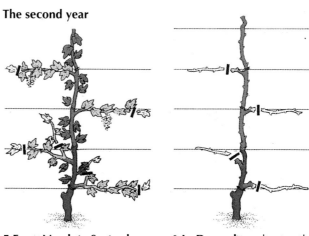

4 In November/December, immediately after leaf-fall, cut back the vine by two-thirds, and the laterals on the main stem to one good bud.

5 From March to September, the new leader extends. If allowing two laterals to bear fruit, pinch out these to two leaves beyond the flowers.

6 In December, shorten the leader by about one-half. Cut back laterals to about 1 in, leaving two buds.

Grapes 4

The side-shoots develop quickly and by May in a cold house (and earlier in a heated house) it is possible to select those which are to be retained. The flower trusses begin to appear when there is 18–24 in of growth. Allow two leaves to form beyond the flower bunch and then pinch out the growing tip. Keep the strongest side-shoots with the best flower bunches, one shoot only to a spur and rub out all others. Secure each chosen fruiting lateral to a wire, gradually bringing it down to the horizontal (or up to the vertical if growing a horizontal rod).

From about mid-May, it may be necessary to put shading on the roof.

Throughout the summer pinch back any sub-laterals to one leaf and barren laterals to five leaves. Towards the end of the summer allow one or two laterals at the top of the rod to grow freely to take up any excess sap and prevent the fruits from splitting.

Pollination

Once the flowers are open, hand pollination is necessary. Some cultivars set fruit readily and for these it is sufficient to give the rods a sharp tap at about midday each day until flowering is over. With less free-setting cultivars, such as the muscats, stroke the flowers gently with cupped hands. The pollen collects on the palm and fingers and is passed on to the stigmas. Ideally cross-pollination is best (see pages 94–7).

Thinning

From June onwards the berries swell quickly and thinning must be completed over a period of 7–10 days while the stalks on the grapes are easily accessible. Thin with a pair of long-bladed scissors. Leave plenty of grapes at the shoulders of the bunch and remove most of the interior berries first and then the smallest. Aim for a spacing of about a pencil thickness between one berry and the next. Touch dessert grapes as little as possible so that the bloom is not disturbed.

When the grapes start to ripen, check the bunches two or three times a week for diseased or split grapes. Cut them away with grape scissors.

Watering and feeding In February or March when growth starts, soak the bed with water. A second watering one week later may be necessary if the roots are dry. After watering, mulch with well-rotted manure or compost. In hot weather, every 7–10 days apply enough water to vines in an inside border to penetrate the soil deeply. Water vines planted

Third and subsequent years

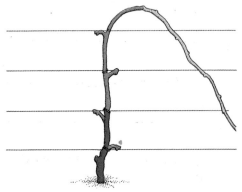

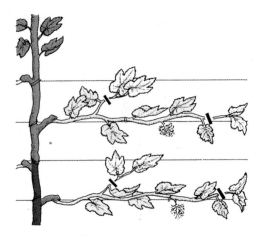

7 In January, undo all the ties except one about one-third of the way up the rod. Let the rod almost touch the ground. When the buds on the spurs begin to grow, tie the rod back into position.

8 When the flower trusses appear, pinch out the growing tips two leaves beyond them. Tie in each fruiting lateral to a wire, gradually bringing it to the horizontal. Pinch back sub-laterals to one leaf.

ripening to amber with white bloom, in long bunches. Fairly vigorous.
'Muscat Hamburgh' Excellent flavour for dessert and wine. Fruits oval, dark red-purple with blue bloom. Medium bunches. Heavy cropper. Fairly vigorous.

Vinous cultivars are late ripening and must hang for a long time in a warm

greenhouse to develop their full flavour.
'Alicante' Good flavour. Fruits oval, jet-black with thin blue bloom, in unshapely bunches. Heavy cropper. Free-setting. Vigorous.
'Gros Colmar' Fair flavour. Fruits large, round, black with thick skins in well-shaped bunches. Heavy cropper. Very vigorous.

'Lady Downe's Seedling' Very good flavour. Fruits round, black in tapering bunches. Not free-setting. Fairly vigorous.
'Syrian' Fair flavour. Fruits oval, white in large bunches. Very vigorous. Very late ripening.
'Trebbiano' Good flavour. Fruits oval, white in very large bunches. Heavy cropper. Vigorous. Very late ripening.

---

in an outside border if the weather is dry. Gradually reduce watering as the grapes ripen and be careful not to subject a vine near the harvesting stage to a sudden influx of water because this may cause the berries to split.

When the grapes start to change colour the risk of splitting increases. Black and tawny cultivars are particularly suceptible. Do not damp down the greenhouse late in the day because a humid atmosphere also encourages splitting. Open a leeside vent 1–2 in at night. Avoid rapid rises in temperature because this causes condensation.

Apply a high potash feed suitable for tomatoes every 14 days when growth begins, increasing to every seven days when the vine is in flower but stop when the fruit starts to colour. If growth is poor, give a high nitrogen or general purpose feed in summer.

After picking the fruits, from September onwards, cut back the laterals by about one-half. During the summer, when the rod reaches the full extent allowed by the height of the greenhouse, stop it by pinching out the growing point. In December, prune it back to 1 in of new growth, keeping the top about 15 in from the ridge and cut back to one bud all the laterals produced the previous summer.

Harvesting
Late varieties need to hang on the vine for a long time in a warm greenhouse to develop their full flavour. Heat the greenhouse in late autumn and early winter for cultivars such as 'Syrian' which do not ripen fully until December. For harvesting details see the relevant section on page 76.

Pests and diseases
Some pests and diseases are more likely to affect grapes grown inside the greenhouse than those which are grown outside. Nevertheless, pests and diseases typical to outdoor vines may affect greenhouse vines (see page 76).

To protect against scale insects and mealy-bugs, in winter scrape off with a knife and burn old bark fibres on rods and spurs. Do not cut away any green tissue. If necessary spray with an insecticidal soap in late May and again in June. Spray with bifenthrin against glasshouse red spider mite as soon as seen. Spray against glasshouse whitefly with a pesticide containing pyrethrum, or permethrin at four-day intervals as required. Alternatively, use biological control against these pests, see page 30.

9 In summer, when the rod reaches the top of the house, pinch out the growing point. Thin the bunches with long-bladed scissors.

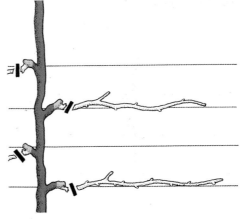

10 In December, prune back the pinched-out growing point to 1 in of new growth. Cut back to one bud all the laterals produced the previous summer.

Heathland fruits 1

Bilberries or whortleberries
The bilberry (*Vaccinium myrtillus*) is a low, suckering shrub with green stems 1–2 ft tall, and small, narrow leaves. The urn-shaped flowers are whitish-green to pink. The globular fruits are ⅓ in wide and purple-black, with a waxy-white patina and they ripen from late summer to autumn. Native to Europe and northern Asia, it is rarely cultivated.

Low bush blueberries
In the USA the bilberry and its close ally *Vaccinium angustifolium* are known as low bush blueberries. *V. angustifolium* is also known as low sweet blueberry and *V. myrtilloides* as velvet-leaf blueberry. Both are native to eastern USA and Canada and are seldom cultivated in the accepted sense, but where in the wild they are the dominant plant (blueberry barrens), they are often managed commercially by burning over every two to three years in winter. This eliminates weed scrub and encourages vigorous young growth from the base. They are not cultivated because they provide far less fruit than the taller high bush cultivars. They are, however, easy to cultivate, requiring almost the same conditions as the high bush blueberries. They differ in that they tolerate drier soils and need full sun for good crops.

They are best planted 12–15 in apart each way in beds 3 ft wide with access paths in between. Feeding is the same as for high bush blueberries.

Pruning as such is not necessary, but in the second or third year cut back hard half the plants to promote young, vigorous stems. One or two years later the other half is cut back. Thereafter the plants are treated regularly in this way.

Harvesting and storing is as for high bush blueberries (see page 84). Pests and diseases are not a problem.

High bush blueberries
There are two species of high bush blueberry, *Vaccinium corymbosum* and *V. ashei,* the former species being the most important. Both form bushes to 6 ft or more in height with narrow oval leaves about 2 in long and white, sometimes pink-tinted flowers in dense clusters. The fruits are up to ½ in wide.

Cultivation
The blueberry is a decorative shrub and it can be grown as an ornamental with rhododen-

High bush blueberries

1 Before planting, dig out a 1 ft square hole at each planting station. Fill it with an equal mixture of peat, or leaf-mould, and soil.

2 In autumn or spring, plant the bushes 5 ft apart in rows 6 ft apart. With a trowel make a hole large enough to take the root ball. Set the plant in it. Firm the soil.

BLUEBERRIES

The following cultivars are derived from *Vaccinium corymbosum*. They will set fruit with their own pollen but for maximum crops at least two cultivars should be planted together.

'Berkeley' Very large, light blue berries of good flavour. Medium vigour.

'Bluecrop' Fast-growing cultivar with big clusters of large, light blue berries. A consistently heavy cropper of good quality. Bush upright, then spreading. Vigorous.

'Earliblue' Similar to 'Bluecrop' but the berries ripen earlier.

'Jersey' A vigorous cultivar of erect habit bearing large handsome foliage. The large, light blue berries are sweet and of good flavour. Excellent as a dual purpose bush for the shrub border.

'Rancocas' This cultivar produces a good crop of quality, small fruits over a long harvesting period. Good shapely habit.

---

drons and other acid soil shrubs. It can also be grown in large pots or tubs filled with an acid rhododendron compost.

Soil and situation Blueberries require moist but well-drained acid soil with a pH of 4.0–5.5. If the pH is much above the upper limit, chlorosis occurs and the plants may die. Suitably acid sandy or clay soils should be liberally enriched with moss peat or acid leaf-mould at not less than one large bucketful per square yard.

As with most members of the heather and rhododendron family (Ericaceae), blueberries rely upon an association with a fungus for their existence. The fungus thrives where organic matter is abundant, so it is important to apply plenty of peat or acid leaf-mould to the soil. If the soil is thin and sandy, apply the organic material to the whole site. For most soils, it is usually sufficient to dig out 1 ft square holes at each planting station and fill these with an equal mixture of peat and soil, or leaf-mould and soil. Include some coarse sand if the surrounding land is heavy. Hoof and horn or dried blood at 2 oz per hole may also be added if the land is poor. Alternatively, apply sulphate of ammonia to the soil surface at ½ oz per hole after planting.

The site may be in sun or slight shade and should be sheltered from strong winds. Blueberries are hardy throughout the British Isles and *V. corymbosum* will grow in zone 4 but does not thrive if the temperature falls regularly below −28°C/−18°F. A frost-free growing season of at least five months is needed and ideally a warm summer with plenty of rain.

Planting Two- to three-year-old plants are usually available in containers. In autumn or spring, set out the plants 5 ft apart in rows 6 ft apart. If the plants are pot-grown, gently knock them out of their containers and carefully spread out the perimeter roots without breaking up the root ball. Fill the planting holes with an equal mixture of peat and compost and firm fairly lightly. Then, using a trowel, make a small hole large enough to take the root ball, set the plant in the middle and firm the soil. Larger plants are planted as described in the Introduction to Soft Fruits (page 41).

Pruning Regular pruning is not essential. If young plants fail to branch naturally, in spring cut back the longest stems by about one-third. After the third year, bushes that are becoming dense should be thinned, removing

The established bush

3 In spring each year, apply a dressing of sulphate of ammonia at 1 oz per square yard. At the same time, mulch with peat, leaf-mould, sawdust, or pulverized bark.

4 From November to February, cut back some of the fruited branches that have become twiggy to a vigorous shoot. Cut close to base any damaged or dead branches.

Heathland fruits 2

the oldest, barest stems to ground level or to where a low strong side-shoot emerges.

Feeding and watering In spring, apply a dressing of hoof and horn or dried blood at 2 oz per square yard or sulphate of ammonia at 1 oz per square yard. On poorer soils, every other year in winter apply a general fertilizer, such as a brand of Growmore, at 2–3 oz per square yard. To maintain the humus content, mulch annually in spring with peat, leaf-mould or pine needles to a depth of 1–2 in. Other important sources of humus are composted sawdust and pulverized bark.

Blueberries need plenty of moisture in the summer. In dry weather, water them copiously, preferably (although not necessarily) with collected rainwater.

Harvesting and storing

The berries should be picked when they are blue-black with a white waxy bloom and start to soften. They should be eaten fresh within a few days, but if spread thinly on trays and kept in a cool cellar or refrigerator they will last for at least a couple of weeks.

Pests and diseases

In Britain there are no pests and diseases of importance. In the USA a rust disease can be troublesome. It cannot be cured so infected plants should be scrapped and disease-resistant varieties planted.

Once the berries have formed, protection from birds is essential (see page 33).

Cranberries

The common or small cranberry (*Vaccinium oxycoccus* or *Oxycoccus palustris*) has long wiry stems with tiny, narrow, pointed leaves. The small, pink flowers are carried in clusters. The fruits are about 1/3 in wide, red or pink, sometimes with brown-red spots. Cranberries sold in Britain come from the USA and are the fruits of *Vaccinium macrocarpum* (*Oxycoccus macrocarpus*). This is a slightly more robust species than the common cranberry, with blunt-tipped leaves and much larger fruits.

Cultivation

Like the low bush blueberry, the cranberry is not grown as a regular fruit crop in Britain. In the USA the crop is of very limited import-

ance and has acquired a highly specialized form of agriculture including the construction of artificial bogs which can be flooded and drained. It requires moister conditions than the blueberry to thrive and, ideally, a soil of greater acidity. Despite this, both cranberry species are easy to grow if the right rooting medium can be provided.

Soil and situation Cranberries need a constantly moist soil of high organic content with a pH of 3.2–4.5 A naturally moist, acid soil is ideal, but if not naturally peaty, fork generous amounts of moss peat into the top 6–9 in. Or, prepare trenches as described in the box opposite. Cranberries should be cultivated in a sunny site.

Planting Plant one- or two-year-old divisions, rooted cuttings or seedlings 12 in apart each way in autumn or spring, or during mild spells in winter. Any long trailing stems should be partly buried, or held down by sand or small pegs, to prevent them from being blown about. Rooting usually occurs along the pegged-down stems.

Pruning and feeding No pruning is required, but any semi-erect wispy stems can be sheared off annually in early spring. Feeding is not usually necessary, but if growth is poor, apply hoof and horn at 4 oz per square yard or sulphate of ammonia at 1/2 oz per square yard. Plants in peat-filled trenches benefit from a light dressing of general fertilizer every other year. An old matted bed can be rejuvenated by almost covering it with a layer of fine peat and sand.

Harvesting and storing

See high bush blueberries (this page).

Pests and diseases

These are negligible in Britain, but in the USA various grubs attack the fruits. A permethrin spray when the flower buds are swelling and again as the flowers fade provides control.

Cultivars

One or two are available in Britain and a few are obtainable in the USA. Among vigorous and free-fruiting cultivars of *Vaccinium macrocarpum* are 'Early Black', 'Hawes', 'Searless Jumbo' and 'McFarlin'. 'Stevens' is a particularly good new cultivar.

PREPARING THE CRANBERRY BED

Where the soil is acid but not naturally moist, dig shallow trenches about 3 ft wide by 9 in deep and line them with heavy-duty polythene. Return the soil with peat to the waterproofed trench and lightly firm. Spread and rake in hoof and horn at 4 oz per square yard or sulphate of ammonia at ½ oz per square yard.

This trench method can be used on alkaline soils, filling in this case with pure moss peat or a mixture with up to half by bulk of coarse washed sand. The same fertilizers should be used.

Before planting, unless the ground is already wet, soak the bed thoroughly, using rainwater if possible.

Cranberries

1 In autumn or spring, plant the divisions, cuttings or seedlings 12 in apart in the prepared ground. Bury any trailing stems.

2 In early spring, shear off any semi-erect wispy stems. If growth is poor, apply ½ oz sulphate of ammonia per square yard.

Melons 1

Melons in cold frames

The sweet melon (*Cucumis melo*) is a tropical climbing annual, native to central Africa.

Three types of sweet melon are commonly grown: they are cantaloupe, musk and winter. Cantaloupes have grey-green or ochre-coloured, thick, rough skins which are not netted but deeply grooved. They are most suitable for cold frame, cloche or tunnel cultivation. Musk melons are small with fine netting on smooth skins and a musky flavour. Winter melons are large, smooth-skinned fruits, often yellow with little or no musk odour. Musk and winter melons are best grown in a greenhouse.

Cultivation

The melon can only be grown successfully in cool temperate regions of zone 8 when protected by glass or polythene. In warmer zones (9 and 10) it can be grown outside without protection.

Soil The melon requires a fertile, not too rich, well-drained soil with a pH of 6.7–7.0.

Sowing the seed Sow the seed from mid- to late April in 3 in pots of seed compost in a heated greenhouse at a minimum of 18°–21°C/64°–70°F or on a sunny windowsill in a warm room. Sow two seeds ½ in deep in each pot and remove the weaker seedling if both germinate. Cover the pots with glass or clear plastic.

After germination, remove the glass or plastic and grow on the seedlings at a minimum of 13°–16°C/55°–60°F. Gradually harden them off and plant out in late May or early June. If the roots fill the pot before it is time to plant them out, pot on into a 5 in container of John Innes No. 1 compost.

Planting Three to four weeks before planting, clear the site of perennial weeds. Single dig it and, if the soil is poor, dig in a 2 in layer of well-rotted manure.

Two weeks before planting, in late May or early June, dig out holes one spit deep and 1 ft across. Dig in a spadeful of well-rotted manure at each planting site and mound up the soil. Water well if the soil is dry and place

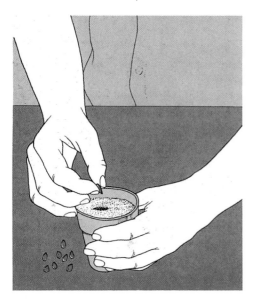

1 From mid- to late April, sow two seeds ½ in deep in 3 in pots. Maintain at 18°–21°C/64°–7.0°F. Harden off gradually. Thin to one seedling.

2 A week before planting, dig out holes one spit deep and 1 ft across. Incorporate manure and mound up the soil. Cover the mounds with the cloches or tunnels to warm the soil.

MELONS IN COLD FRAMES
EARLY
'Charantais' Excellent flavour. Fruits small, round, slightly ribbed, grey-green skin, flesh orange-scarlet.
'Ogen' Good flavour. Fruits small, round, orange-yellow ribbed with green, flesh pale green, firm and thick. Early. Very suitable for colder areas.

'Sweetheart' Excellent flavour. Fruits medium, with firm, salmon pink flesh. An F₁ hybrid of the Charantais type. Suitable for colder areas.

MID-SEASON
'Tiger' Good flavour. Fruits medium, flattish, orange and green mottled and netted skin, flesh orange.

the glass or polythene in position a week before planting to warm the soil.

With a trowel, scoop out a hole wide and deep enough to take the root ball. When the seedlings have three or four leaves, plant them leaving 1 in of the soil ball above ground level as a precaution against soft rot. Do not firm the soil but gently water in each plant, keeping the water off the stem.

Plant at 3–4 ft intervals down the centre of a run of cloches or a polythene tunnel, or plant a single seedling in the centre of each cold frame.

After planting, close the cloches, tunnels or frames for 7–10 days. Provide temporary shading if there is hot sun until the melons are established.

Stopping and training Pinch out the growing point at the fifth leaf to encourage the production of side-shoots. Two or three weeks later, when these side-shoots appear, select the four strongest and remove all the others. In a cold frame, train the four shoots in an X-shape, one to each corner. Under cloches or tunnels, train one pair of shoots each way.

Ventilation Once the plants are established, gradually increase the ventilation and remove the shading. When the flowers appear, ventilate freely to maintain a drier atmosphere, which helps pollination. In warm weather, during flowering, remove the covering entirely to allow access to pollinating insects. Replace the protection at night. To aid pollination occasionally pollinate by hand (see pages 89 and 94–7).

Increase the ventilation when the fruits are swelling. In hot weather, from late July to early September, shade the glass or polythene to avoid sun scald. When the melons start to ripen, ventilate freely.

Thinning When the fruits reach the size of large gooseberries select the four most evenly shaped fruits, one on each shoot, and remove all other flowers and fruits. Stop the sub-laterals to two or three leaves beyond the selected fruits. Pinch out the growing point of each main shoot and remove any new growths as they appear.

3 In late May, make a hole wide and deep enough for the root ball. Plant the seedlings 3–4 ft apart with the soil ball 1 in above ground. Water in, avoiding the stem.

4 In mid-June, select the four strongest shoots, remove all the others. Train one pair of shoots each way. In warm weather and at pollination ventilate fully.

Melons 2

Place a tile or flat piece of wood under each melon to keep it clear of the soil and to prevent rotting.

Feeding and watering After selecting the fruits, water regularly and generously to swell the fruits rapidly, but do not wet the stem. Avoid irregular flushes of water that will cause the fruits to split or drop.

When the fruits are about the size of walnuts, feed every 7-10 days with a liquid feed suitable for tomatoes. As soon as the fruits start to ripen, stop feeding and gradually reduce watering.

Harvesting

The fruits are mature when they have the characteristic melon scent and when circular cracking appears near the stalk. They yield slightly to finger pressure at the end away from the stalk. When lifted, they should part easily from the stalk.

Pests and diseases

See Melons in the greenhouse, page 90.

SUPPORT THE FRUIT

Support each fruit with a net sling tied to the roof rafters or wires once the melons are the size of tennis balls.

5 Thin the fruits when they are gooseberry-size. Select the four best fruits and remove the rest. Stop the sub-laterals at two or three leaves beyond the retained fruits. Pinch out the growing points.

6 In mid- to late July, water regularly. Feed the fruits every 7-10 days with diluted liquid feed. Protect each fruit from the soil with a tie.

'Burpees Hybrid' (Cantaloupe) Good flavour. Fruits large, slightly oval, ochre-coloured. Flesh orange, coarse-textured. Also suitable for cold frames and cloches.

'Hero of Lockinge' (Musk) Good flavour. Fruits large; oval, golden. Flesh white, fine-textured. Good for forcing.
'No name' (Cantaloupe) Excellent flavour. Fruits medium, oval, green and yellow. Flesh amber-yellow, fine-textured. Also suitable for cold frames and cloches.

'Ringleader' (Musk) Very good flavour. Fruits large, oval, orange-yellow. Flesh green, fine-textured. Forces well.
'Superlative' (Musk) Very good flavour. Fruits large, almost round, green. Flesh scarlet, fine-textured. Also suitable for cold frames and cloches.

Melons in the greenhouse

The melon is a relatively small climbing plant and can be grown in most modern greenhouses, provided the length from the base of the side wall to the eaves and up to the ridge is not less than 6 ft. Most cultivars of melon can be grown in a heated house but, in a cold house, the choice is limited to the Cantaloupes and the more cold-tolerant Casaba cultivars.

Cultivation

The melon is usually grown as a single cordon. Occasionally it is grown as a double cordon. It is planted at the side of the house and trained up to the ridge for maximum light and heat.

Soil For soil preparation see Melons in cold frames, page 86.

In the greenhouse, the right drainage and soil conditions are provided by growing the melons on a continuous ridge of compost along each side of the house. Single plants may be grown on mounds of compost or in 9 in pots of John Innes potting compost No. 2 standing on the greenhouse staging.

Sowing the seed Melons take three to five months from seed-sowing to harvesting, depending on the temperature, light and variety. Seed sown in February should yield in June and seed sown in March should yield in July, but the greenhouse must be heated at least until April. A minumum of 18°C/64°F is necessary for germination. May is the earliest time for sowing seeds without heat and these plants should yield in early to mid-September. To give plants intended for the cold house an early start, sow the seed at the end of April in a slightly heated greenhouse, on a sunny windowsill or in a propagating case. The fruits should ripen in late August.

For details of sowing the seed, see Melons in cold frames, page 86.

When the seedlings appear, about one week after sowing, remove the glass or plastic sheet and maintain a minimum night temperature of 16°C/60°F. During the day the temperature may rise sharply and ventilation should be given at 27°C/80°F. Give the seedlings maximum light. Once they have made three or four true leaves, they are ready for planting.

Planting A week before planting, prepare the soil to allow time for it to settle and warm up. Fork over the existing border soil. Prepare a light loam for the ridges by thoroughly breaking up well-rotted turves. Add 2 oz of a compound fertilizer, such as a brand of Growmore, and 2 oz steamed bonemeal per 2 gal bucketful of soil. Alternatively, mix one part well-rotted manure with five parts loam.

With the prepared soil, make the ridges 12 in high by 24 in wide. Firm the ridges without compacting them and water well.

Construct a system of horizontal, supporting wires each side of the house. Fix gauge 16 galvanized wires at 12 in intervals, 15 in from the glass. Tie in two canes per plant to the undersides of the wires, one from the soil to the eaves and the other from the eaves to the ridge. If permanent wires are not possible, attach 6 in square mesh plastic netting, stretched taut, to the gable ends.

Plant the seedlings (see Melons in cold frames, page 86). Space them 15 in apart for single cordons and 24 in apart for double cordons.

Melons may also be grown in commercially prepared polythene bags containing peat or a bark-based compost, or on specially prepared bales of wheat straw.

Stopping and training Train the cordons up the canes, parallel with the glass, and tie the stems with raffia at regular intervals. If the melons are grown in bags or on straw bales, tie them loosely to allow for subsidence or the plant may be uprooted.

Pinch out the growing point at 5-6 ft to encourage the production of laterals. As these appear, tie them to the horizontal wires or plastic netting. Stop each lateral by pinching back at five leaves to encourage the formation of the side-shoots which bear the flowers. Pinch back these side-shoots to two leaves beyond the flower. Remove any flowers produced on the stem.

Pollination Male and female flowers are borne separately on the same plant. Pollinate by hand (see page 95) when there are at least four female flowers open, each on a different side-shoot. The female flowers can be recognized by the embryo fruit which appears as a swelling behind them. One male flower will pollinate four female flowers.

Melons 3

Thinning If the plant sets more than four fruits, when they reach the size of walnuts thin them down to four good fruitlets of about the same size by pinching off the others.

Feeding See Melons in cold frames, page 88. Regular watering and feeding are especially important with pot-grown melons.

Ventilation Create a humid atmosphere by damping down the path and gently misting the leaves. Do not damp down but allow the atmosphere to dry out during pollination and when the fruits start to ripen.

In early spring, maintain a minimum nighttime temperature of 21°C/70°F and a minimum daytime temperature of 24°C/75°F. Later, increase these to 24°C/75°F at night and 30°C/86°F in the day. Ventilate during the day when the temperature exceeds this, but close the vents at night except in really hot weather. From late July to early September, lightly shade the glass on the south side with greenhouse shading wash or lime wash to avoid scald. As the fruits begin to ripen, open the ventilators fully to dry the atmosphere but keep the soil moist.

Supporting the fruits Once the melons have reached the size of tennis balls, provide support for each fruit with a net sling tied to the roof rafters or wires, otherwise the fruits are likely to break off under their own weight. These slings can be either special melon nets or squares of 2 in netting.

Harvesting

Harvest in the same way as melons grown in cold frames (see page 88).

Pests and diseases

In the greenhouse protect against glasshouse red spider mite by keeping the atmosphere humid. If infestation occurs, introduce the predatory mite *Phytoseiulus persimilis*. For whitefly, use the parasite *Encarsia formosa*. Dust at regular intervals with sulphur against powdery mildew.

Destroy any plants with verticillium wilt and sterilize the soil. Prevent soft rot (collar rot) by keeping the stem dry. If signs of the disease are present, remove decayed tissue (see pages 26–31).

1 One week before planting make up a compost of loam with 2 oz of steamed bonemeal and 2 oz compound fertilizer to a 2 gal bucketful of soil on top of the border soil, making a ridge 12 in high by 24 in wide.

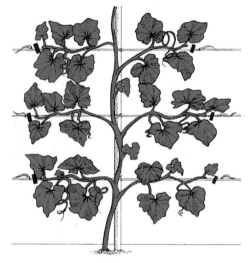

4 Tie the cordon stems to canes. Pinch out the growing point at 6 ft. Tie in laterals to the horizontal wires. Stop each lateral at five leaves.

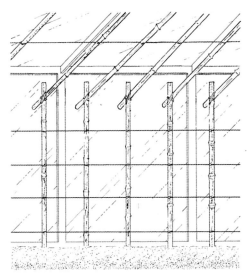

2 Before planting stretch wires across the sides of the house at 12 in intervals and 15 in away from the glass. Tie in two canes per plant, one from the soil to the eaves, the other from the eaves to the ridge.

3 From February onwards, plant seedlings raised in a heated greenhouse 15 in apart with the top of the root ball 1 in above the surface. Do not firm. Maintain at 16°C/60°F. Damp down the paths.

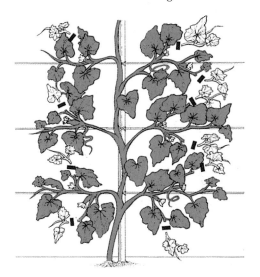

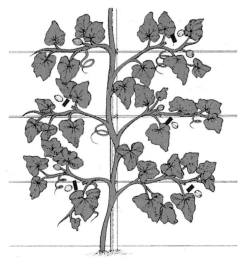

5 Pinch back resulting side-shoots to two leaves beyond the flower. During pollination and as the fruits begin to ripen, open the ventilation fully. Maintain a drier atmosphere.

6 When the melons are the size of walnuts, thin the fruits to four of the same size to each plant by pinching off the others. Water generously and give a liquid feed every 7-10 days.

Tree fruits

Introduction
Tree fruits (also somtimes referred to as top fruits) form a group comprising all the larger growing fruits which, in the natural state at least, attain tree form. The exceptions to this are the fig, elderberry, mulberry, quince and medlar, which may have several main stems and be more shrub-like in appearance; they are, however, still classified as tree fruits.

Botanically, the most familiar tree fruits are members of the rose family (Rosaceae), including the apple, pear, plum, cherry, peach, apricot, quince and medlar; the mulberrry and fig are outsiders belonging to the mainly tropical family Moraceae. Also included in the tree fruit section are the most popular nuts: walnuts, sweet chestnuts, cobnuts and filberts.

Tree fruits are not difficult to grow provided the soil is well drained but moisture-retentive and of a moderate to good depth (see pages 18-21). The site must be sunny and not prone to severe late spring frosts (see pages 10-13).

Unlike growing soft fruits, cultivating tree fruits in the garden is a long-term project. Full fruiting capacity is reached by the tree only after several years, but with care it will then continue for a lifetime. However, the fruit grower is compensated by the fact that the fruiting season for tree fruits is much longer than that of soft fruits. Furthermore, if fruits such as peaches or figs are grown in a greenhouse the season can be prolonged.

Rootstocks
Apples, pears, peaches, cherries, apricots and plums can all eventually make sizeable trees if grown on their own roots; some even become too large for most gardens. For this reason they are grafted on to rootstocks which control their eventual size. Usually apples are grafted on to a range of apple rootstocks to produce dwarf or less vigorous trees which are ideal for the small garden (see pages 100-1). Pears are traditionally grafted on to quince rootstocks and this lessens their vigour and ultimate size. A dwarfing rootstock for cherries has proved harder to find but a less vigorous one has now been produced, although it is not as dwarfing as some of the apple stocks.

Pruning and training
For all tree fruits, initial training and subsequent pruning is necessary to keep them in good shape and productive throughout their lives. Methods of training, particularly pruning, can seem daunting to an amateur but this need not be so if the instructions with each fruit entry in this book are followed closely. There is also a companion volume on pruning in this series.

Pruning terms The terms used frequently in fruit tree pruning are defined as follows. Maiden describes a one-year-old, for example, a maiden tree. A scion is a variety grafted on to a rootstock of another tree; the union is where the two join. A branch is a limb that arises from the trunk. Primary branches are the first formed, and secondary branches arise from the primary ones. A leader is a main central stem of a tree or a shoot selected to extend a main branch; a lateral is a sideshoot. Spurs are short laterals that bear flower buds and which can occur naturally or be induced by selective pruning of the laterals. Flower buds, or blossom buds, are unopened flowers, often referred to as fruit buds. Wood buds open to give rise to a shoot, as opposed to a flower. Suckers are shoots that grow from below the ground or below the union.

Choice of site

The site should be chosen with care and the soil cleared of perennial weeds, either with a selective herbicide (see pages 32-3) or by hand weeding during digging. If some weeds still persist, herbicide treatment can be given again after the tree is planted, but take care to choose one which will not damage the tree.

Protection against birds

In areas where bird damage is expected (and few rural or suburban districts are exempt), protection is necessary. For small tree forms, such as dwarf bush trees, cordons or espaliers, this can be provided by a fruit cage, ideally one with tubular steel or metal alloy poles and netting, although 7 ft headroom is a minimum (see page 33). It is generally impracticable to protect larger tree fruits against bird damage.

Wall- and fence-trained trees

If there is no room in the open garden for free-standing tree fruits, good use can be made of walls and fences if restricted tree forms such as fans, cordons or espaliers are grown. North-facing walls can be used in this way for Morello cherries. Some plums and gages are even more successful on walls than in the open, ripening well in the sheltered and warmer environment. Figs are invariably best grown on a warm wall (see page 15-16).

Pollination

Unlike most soft fruits, which will produce an adequate crop even if only one plant is grown, many tree fruits are totally or partially self-compatible. This means that some cultivars cannot produce a good crop of fruit if their flowers are fertilized with their own pollen. In such instances, at least two different compatible cultivars must be grown close enough for bees to be able to carry pollen from one to the other. Sweet cherries provide the best example of self-sterility, but practically all the tree fruits set heavier crops if two or three cultivars are planted together. They must, of course, flower at the same time and produce plenty of good pollen. Before buying any fruit tree, consult the pollination tables on pages 94-7.

Storage

If it is decided to plant enough apples and pears to provide fruit for the late autumn to winter period, storage facilities are necessary. This can be provided by a cool but frost-free cellar or shed (see page 179). Late apples and pears finish ripening many weeks after they have been picked, and so they should not be stored with mid-season varieties until this ripening has taken place because the gases given off by the earlier varieties shorten the storage life of the later ones. Deep-freezing is suitable for these two fruits only if they are to be used in cooking when thawed.

Fruit under glass

Figs, peaches and nectarines all produce their most luscious fruits under glass in cool areas. Artificial heat is not required although ripening can be hastened by its use early in the season. Wall or roof space not less than 10 ft long is needed for a well-developed peach or a fig rooted in the floor of the house. Alternatively, much smaller trees can be grown in large pots and housed in all but the smallest greenhouse. Space outside should be set aside where hardy potted trees can be plunged up to their pot rims to keep the roots protected during the winter after the fruit has been picked (see pages 38-9).

Pollination 1

Pollination is the transfer of pollen from the anthers or male parts of the flower to the stigmas or female parts of the flower. This results in fertilization and the eventual production of fruit. It is usually carried out by bees or other insects or by the wind. Occasionally, it is necessary to pollinate by hand (see opposite).

The flowers of most garden fruits contain both anthers and stigmas. Some fruits, such as melons and cobnuts, bear separate male and female flowers on the same plant.

Some fruit trees, such as peaches, nectarines, apricots and certain plums and gages, are self-compatible – that is, they can be fertilized by their own pollen. Others, such as nearly all sweet cherries, elderberries and many varieties of apples and pears, are self-incompatible; they must be grown with another cultivar of the same fruit that flowers at the same time so that the two cultivars can fertilize each other.

Pollination groups
Different cultivars of plums, gages and damsons, apples, pears and cherries are divided into pollination groups according to when their flowers are open and ripe for pollination. Those cultivars that appear in the same pollination group will cross-pollinate because their flowers are open at the same time. Those in adjacent groups are also acceptable because in most years their seasons of flowering overlap. The most common and popular cultivars are listed in the pollination groups below. The pollination groups are listed in order of the flowering season; Pollination Group 1 is the earliest.

STRUCTURE OF BLOSSOM (APPLE)

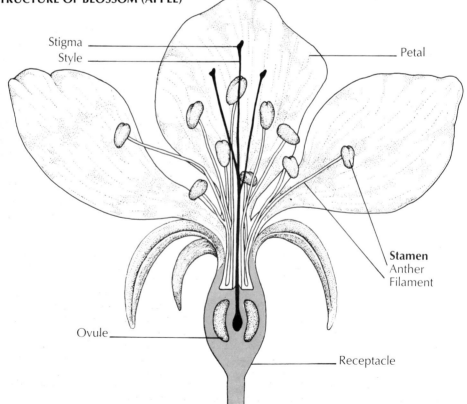

Stigma
Style
Petal
Stamen
Anther
Filament
Ovule
Receptacle

Incompatibility groups

Not all cultivars of the same fruit can cross-pollinate, even when they appear in the same pollination group. This is called cross-incompatibility. These cultivars are divided into incompatibility groups and will not set fruit with their own pollen or that of any cultivar which appears in the same incompatibility group. They will cross-pollinate with cultivars in another group or in adjacent groups (provided they flower at the same time).

Ineffective pollinators

Some cultivars of apples and pears, although not strictly cross-incompatible, are ineffective pollinators. This can occur for a number of reasons.

Most cultivars are diploid, that is, they have the normal number of chromosomes. A few are triploid, that is they have 1½ times the normal number. Triploids, shown in the pollination groups as (T), are poor pollinators and should be grown with two diploid cultivars to pollinate each other and the triploid.

Some cultivars of pears are known to be ineffective pollinators and are indicated (IP) in the pollination groups. Also some cultivars of both apples and pears flower only every two years (biennially) or irregularly, designated (B) in the pollination groups. These cannot, therefore, be relied upon to pollinate other cultivars.

Many triploids, ineffective pollinators and irregular-flowering cultivars are good cultivars in their own right and popular with gardeners. If planting these cultivars, remember to plant other cultivars near them to provide the necessary pollen.

HAND POLLINATION

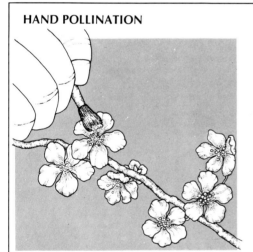 

Some fruits require hand pollination, such as those inaccessible to pollinating insects because they are grown under glass, or those whose flowers open early in the year when few insects are about.

Test to see if the pollen is being shed by drawing the finger-tip over the anthers, which should deposit yellow grains on the finger. Pollinate at midday when conditions for fertilization are best and when the weather has been warm and dry for two or three days. Very gently transfer the pollen from the anthers to the stigmas by using a soft camel-hair brush or a piece of cotton wool on a matchstick.

When male and female flowers are borne separately, as on the melon, another method may be used. Test the male flowers with the finger-tip to ensure that pollen is being shed. Strip the petals off the male flower and press its centre against the centre of each female flower.

Carry out hand pollination every day until flowering is over.

Pollination 2

Apples

No apple tree is completely self-compatible, so more than one cultivar should be grown.

Pollination Group 1 Gravenstein (T); Lord Suffield; Red Astrachan; Stark Earliest.

Pollination Group 2 Alkmene; Baker's Delicious; Beauty of Bath; Bismarck (B); Christmas Pearmain (B); Devonshire Quarrenden (B); Egremont Russet; George Cave; George Neal; Golden Spire; Idared; Irish Peach; Keswick Codlin (B); Laxton's Early Crimson; Lord Lambourne; Margil; McIntosh Red; Melba (B); Merton Charm; Norfolk Beauty; Rev W. Wilks (B); Ribston Pippin (T); St Edmund's Pippin; Warner's King (T).

Pollination Group 3 Allington Pippin (B); Arthur Turner; Belle de Boskoop (T); Blenheim Orange (TB); Bountiful; Bramley's Seedling (T); Brownlees' Russet; Charles Ross; Chivers Delight; Cox's Orange Pippin; Crispin (T); D'Arcy Spice; Discovery; Duchess Favourite; Emneth Early; Emperor Alexander; Epicure (B); Fortune (B); Granny Smith; Greensleeves; Grenadier; Holstein (T); James Grieve; John Standish; Jonagold; Jonathan; Katja; Kent; Kidd's Orange Red; Lord Grosvenor; Lord Hindlip; Mère de Menage; Merton Knave; Merton Worcester; Miller's Seedling (B); Ontario; Peasgood's Nonsuch; Queen; Rival (B); Rosemary Russet; Spartan; Stirling Castle; Sturmer Pippin; Sunset; Tom Putt; Tydeman's Early Worcester; Wagener (B); Winter Gem; Worcester Pearman.

Pollination Group 4 Annie Elizabeth; Ashmead's Kernel; Autumn Pearmain; Claygate Pearmain; Cornish Gillyflower; Cox's Pomona; Delicious; Duke of Devonshire; Dumelow's Seedling; Ellison's Orange; Encore; Gala; Gladstone (B); Golden Delicious; Golden Noble; Hawthornden; Herring's Pippin; Howgate Wonder; Ingrid Marie; King's Acre Pippin; Lady Sudeley; Lane's Prince Albert; Lord Derby; Monarch (B); Orleans Reinette; Pixie; Superb (Laxton's) (B); Tydeman's Late Orange; Woolbrook Russet.

Pollination Group 5 Gascoyne's Scarlet (T); King of the Pippins (B); Merton Beauty; Mother; Newton Wonder; Northern Spy (B); Royal Jubilee; William Crump; Winston.

Pollination Group 6 Bess Pool; Court Pendu Plat; Edward VII; Laxton's Royalty; Suntan (T).

Pollination Group 7 Crawley Beauty.

There are no incompatibility groups but 'Cox's Orange Pippin' and 'Kidd's Orange Red' are cross-incompatible, as are 'Cox's Orange Pippin' and 'Holstein'.

Pears

Although the cultivar 'Conference' is sometimes described as self-compatible, no pear cultivar is fully self-compatible.

Pollination Group 1 Brockworth Park; Maréchal de la Cour (T); Précoce de Trévoux.

Pollination Group 2 Bellisime d'Hiver; Beurré Alexandre Lucas (T); Beurré Clairgeau; Beurré d'Amanlis (T); Beurré d'Anjou; Beurré Diel (T); Beurré Six; Doyenné d'Eté; Duchesse d'Angoulême; Emile d'Heyst; Louise Bonne of Jersey; Marguerite Marillat (IP); Packham's Triumph; Passe Crassane; Princess; Seckle.

Pollination Group 3 Beurré Dumont; Beurré Hardy; Beurré Superfin; Conference; Doyenné Boussoch (T); Dr Jules Guyot; Durondeau; Fertility; Fondante d'Automne; Hessle; Jargonelle (T); Joséphine de Malines; Laxton's Progress; Merton Pride (T); Roosevelt; Souvenir du Congrés; Thompson's; Williams' Bon Chrétien.

Pollination Group 4 Bristol Cross (IP); Beurré Bedford (IP); Calebasse Bosc; Catillac (T); Clapp's Favourite; Doyenné du Comice; Glou Morceau; Gorham; Improved Fertility; Laxton's Foremost; Marie Louise; Napoleon; Nouveau Poiteau; Onward; Pitmaston Duchess (T); Santa Claus; Winter Nelis; Zépherin Grégoire.

There are two incompatibility groups.

Incompatibility Group 1 Fondante d'Automne; Laxton's Progress; Louise Bonne of Jersey; Précoce de Trévoux; Seckle; Williams' Bon Chrétien.

Incompatibility Group 2 Buerré d'Amanlis; Conference but one way only – 'Beurré d'Amanlis' will pollinate 'Conference'.

Plums, damsons and gages

Some cultivars are self-compatible and are shown (SC). All cherry plums are self-compatible.

Pollination Group 1 Angelina Burdett; Blue Rock; Heron; Jefferson; Mallard; Monarch (SC); Utility.

Pollination Group 2 Ariel; Brahy's Greengage (SC); Coe's Crimson Drop; Coe's Golden

Drop; Curlew; Denniston's Superb (SC); Guthrie's Late (SC); President; Warwickshire Drooper (SC).
Pollination Group 3 Allgrove's Superb; Bryanston Gage; Bountiful (SC); Czar (SC); Early Laxton; Early Rivers; Edwards (SC); Golden Transparent (SC); Goldfinch; Late Orange; Laxton's Cropper (SC); Laxton's Gage (SC); Merryweather Damson (SC); Merton Gem; Opal (SC); Pershore (SC); Purple Pershore (SC); Reine-Claude Violette; Severn Cross (SC); Thames Cross; Victoria (SC); Washington.
Pollination Group 4 Blaisdon Red (SC); Bradley's King Damson (SC); Cambridge Gage; Count Althann's Gage; Early Transparent Gage (SC); Farleighh Damson; Giant Prune (SC); Kirke's; Ontario (SC); Oullin's Golden Gage (SC); Wyedale.
Pollination Group 5 Belle de Louvain (SC); Blue Tit (SC); Late Transparent; Marjorie's Seedling (SC); Old Greengage; Pond's Seedling; Red Magnum Bonum; Shropshire Damson (SC).

There are three Incompatibility groups.
Incompatibility Group 1 Allgrove's Superb; Coe's Golden Drop; Coe's Violet Gage; Crimson Drop; Jefferson.
Incompatibility Group 2 Cambridge Gage; Late Orange; Old Greengage; President.
Incompatibility Group 3 Blue Rock; Early Rivers.

There are exceptions to these incompatibility groups. In Incompatibility Group 2, 'Late Orange' and 'President' will set full crops when pollinated by 'Cambridge Gage' or 'Old Greengage', but 'Cambridge Gage' and 'Old Greengage' will set poor crops when pollinated by 'Late Orange' or 'President'. In Incompatibility Group 3, 'Early Rivers' will set a full crop when pollinated by 'Blue Rock', but 'Blue Rock' will set a poor crop when pollinated by 'Early Rivers'.

Sweet cherries
With the exception of the self fertile cultivars all sweet cherries are self incompatible and considerable cross incompatibility between cultivars also exists. It is essential to check the compatability of chosen cultivars before purchase.

Below is a selection of sweet cherry cultivars arranged in compatibility groups in order of flowering, with the earliest first. Provided at least two cultivars within any one group are chosen, the pollination requirements will be met. For example, 'Early Rivers' will pollinate 'Noir de Guben' and vice versa, but 'Merton Favourite' will not pollinate or be pollinated by 'Van'.
Pollination Group 1 Early Rivers; Noir de Guben.
Pollination Group 2 Merton Favourite; Merton Glory.
Pollination Group 3 Merton Bigarreau; Roundel.
Pollination Group 4 Governor Wood; Napoleon Bigarreau; Van.
Pollination Group 5 Bigarreau Gaucher; Bradbourne Black.
Pollination Group 6 Self fertile: Lapins (Cherokee) Sunburst; Stella; Sweetheart; Celeste; Cristalina. Will pollinate self-incompatible cultivars in Group 4.

Acid and Duke cherries
These are much more straightforward than sweet cherries because some acid and Duke cherries are self-compatible and no cross-incompatibility is known. Sweet cherries are not suitable pollinators for acid and Duke cherries but both acid and Duke cherries can pollinate sweet cherries, although most of them flower too late.

'Ronald's Late Duke', 'Wye Morello', 'Montmorency Morello' and 'Flemish Red' are self-compatible. 'May Duke', 'Royal Duke' and 'Archduke' are partly self-compatible, that is, they set a moderate crop with their own pollen but do better with cross-pollination. 'Reine Hortense', 'Belle de Chatenay', 'Olivet' and 'Coe's Carnation' are self-incompatible.

Other fruits
Most other fruits are self-compatible. Nevertheless, cropping is usually improved when cross-pollination is available.

Two exceptions are blueberries and elderberries, most of which are partly self-incompatible. Two cultivars should be planted.

Apricots, peaches, nectarines and melons usually require hand pollination (see page 95). Pollination of cobnuts and filberts can be assisted by pruning during the flowering season, when the shaking of the branches helps to disperse the pollen. Tapping or shaking the vine rods during the flowering season helps to pollinate grapes.

Planting fruit trees

Good establishment, healthy growth and eventual successful cropping of a fruit tree depend a great deal on how well it is planted.

Preparation

Before planting prepare the ground in early autumn as described on pages 18-21. Then, for each tree, prepare an area 3 ft square by single digging clean ground and double digging weedy land. Prepare the ground overall for closely planted trees such as those on dwarfing rootstocks. Apply lime if the pH is less than 5.8 (see page 18).

Just before planting, fork in a balanced fertilizer, such as Growmore, at a rate of 3 oz per square yard with bonemeal at 2 oz per square yard.

Time to plant

Plant in the dormant season, from November to March (the earlier the better while the soil is still warm). Container-grown trees can be planted at any time. Do not plant when the soil is frozen hard or very wet.

If the tree arrives from the nursery when the soil conditions are not right, heel it in in a sheltered part of the garden. If the ground is too cold and hard to heel in, keep the tree in an unheated, frost-free place such as a garden shed. Unpack the upper parts of the tree but keep the roots in damp straw wrapped in hessian until planting.

Staking

Mark out the planting position and drive in a stake to a depth of 18 in on heavy soils and 24 in on light. Standard trees require 7½-8 ft posts, half-standards 6-6½ ft and bush 3½-4 ft. Central-leader trees need a stake as long as the height of the tree plus the depth into the soil. A large-headed standard, such as a sweet cherry, is best supported by two stakes 18 in apart with a crossbar (to which the tree is tied) nailed just below the stake tops. The top of the stake should be 2-3 in clear of the tree's head to avoid chafing the lowest branches. Stakes come in a variety of materials (see page 23).

Trees on very dwarfing rootstocks, for example apples on M9, are best staked permanently. But for trees on more vigorous stocks, the stake can usually be removed after four or five years, depending on the vigour. Before removing the stake, check by rocking the tree that its anchorage is sound.

Planting

If the roots are a little dry, soak them for an hour before planting. Keep them covered.

On the day of planting, dig out a hole deep and wide enough to take the roots fully spread out. Mound the soil in the centre. Keep the fertile top-soil separate from the lower layers. Fork the bottom and prick the sides of the hole to allow the roots to develop outwards. Dig in into the base rotted-down turf or a bucketful of well-rotted manure, compost or peat. Trim off with secateurs any broken or long tap roots. If planting a container-grown tree, gently tease out the soil and roots around the edge of the root ball.

Place the tree on the mound with the stem 2-3 in away from the stake. Ensure that the lowest branches clear the top of the stake. Plant the tree to the same depth as it was in the nursery, indicated by the soil mark. Keep the union between scion and rootstock at least 4 in above the soil surface to prevent the scion from rooting.

Fill in the holes; this is easier if one person holds the tree while another fills it in. Sprinkle a little of the fertile top-soil over the roots first then return the remaining soil a spadeful at a time. Occasionally shake the tree gently so that the soil falls among the roots. Finally, firm the soil and level off the surface.

Next, mulch the tree with well-rotted manure, compost or peat over an area 18 in in radius to a depth of 2-3 in, keeping the material 1-2 in clear of the trunk to prevent fungal diseases from infecting the base.

Tie the tree to the stake. A one-year-old can be secured with plastic chainlock strapping using a figure-of-eight tie, but older trees need a more substantial tie with a cushion between stake and tree to prevent chafing. There are numerous proprietary makes, or one can be made (see page 23).

Bushes require one tie placed 1 in from the top of the stake. Half-standards and standards require two ties, one at the top and one halfway down. Nail the ties to the post to prevent them slipping down.

Where rabbits or other animals are troublesome protect the trunks with wire netting.

Each year in April, July and October check the tree ties and if necessary loosen them to avoid constriction. Re-tie home-made ties.

Planting against a wall

The soil at the foot of a wall can become very dry and poor, especially if it is protected from rain-bearing winds or is sheltered by overhanging eaves.

Where the soil is poor and the drainage is bad, construct a soakaway or a single line of tiles 3 ft deep to take the water away (see page 18-19). Re-soil over an area at least 6 ft × 3 ft wide × 2 ft deep with a fibrous, medium chalky loam, if possible made from turves stacked for six months before use. Add rubble to the loam in the ratio ten soil to one rubble. Two weeks before planting thoroughly mix in John Innes base fertilizer at the rate of 8 oz per 2 gal bucketful of soil.

The tree should be planted about 9 in from the wall base. During the growing season, water it when the soil is dry, applying 4 gal at a time around the base of the tree.

HEELING IN

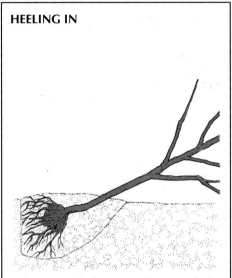

Take out a shallow trench. Unpack the tree and lay it in the trench at an angle. Cover the roots with moist, friable soil.

1 If the roots are dry, soak them for an hour before planting. Trim off broken or long tap roots with secateurs.

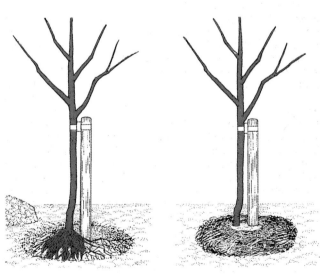

2 Drive in stake. Dig a hole deep and wide enough to take the roots fully spread out. Mound the soil slightly in the centre.

3 Set the plant on the mound 2-3 in away from the stake with the union at least 4 in above the soil surface. Replace the soil, firming gently. Mulch well.

Apples and pears 1

DESSERT APPLES
Listed in order of ripening. (NB The "season" is the eating not ripening period.)
★ Recommended for flavour.

'Gladstone' Pleasantly flavoured. Flesh soft, green-white. Small to medium size, colour green-yellow, almost

Introduction and rootstocks

The domestic apple (*Malus domestica*) is of complex hybrid origin but it has evolved, under human influence, from various species, all of them belonging to the series Pumilae. It has been estimated that up to 1980 there were at least 6,000 named cultivars of apples in the world.

Like the apple, the pear (*Pyrus communis*) has long been cultivated. It is a native of northern Europe, and can also be found growing wild in parts of Britain.

Site

Ideally, the site should be frost-free, in full sun, and sheltered from strong winds. Pears flower in late April to early May and apples in the first half of May, when they are at risk from spring frosts. The gardener in a frost-prone site should consider growing trees on dwarfing stocks or using the restricted forms whose small size makes it practicable to protect them by covering the trees on frosty nights. With apples, the alternative is to plant cultivars that flower late, but this is not applicable to pears because even the later cultivars flower in the danger period.

Ample sunshine is important, particularly for pears, if the fruits are to develop their full colour and flavour. Apples will tolerate some shade, provided they receive at least half a day's sun in the growing season. Where there is a choice, allocate the sunniest position for pears and dessert apples, and the less sunny positions for culinary apples, for which colour and flavour are not so critical.

Shelter is essential because both kinds of fruit are insect pollinated and strong winds inhibit the insects' flight, which results in poor pollination. Wind-breaks, either living or artificial, should be provided on exposed sites or, again, choose apples and pears on dwarfing stocks or in restricted forms because they are easier to shelter than are taller trees (see pages 10–13).

Soil

The ideal soil for both apples and pears is a medium well-drained loam, not less than 24 in deep and slightly acid (pH 6.7). They are, however, tolerant of a wide range of soils. Pears and dessert apples require good drainage, whereas culinary cultivars can be grown in heavy soil and marginally poorer drainage, but the soil must never be waterlogged.

Light sandy soils are acceptable provided bulky organics are incorporated and heavy mulching and watering is practised. Thin soils over chalk are unsuitable because lime-induced chlorosis and lack of water and nutrients generally occur. Deep soils over chalk can support apples and pears quite satisfactorily.

Soil preparation

In early autumn, prepare the soil by clearing away perennial weeds over an area 3 ft square. Fork in a compound fertilizer such as a brand of Growmore at 3 oz per square yard.

Planting and staking

In the dormant season, from November to March, plant the tree to the same depth as it was at the nursery, spreading the roots out well (see pages 98–9).

Bush trees, half-standards, standards and spindlebushes require stakes and tree ties. The restricted forms are supported by wall or fence wiring.

Selecting the rootstock

Apples and pears are not grown on their own roots for a number of reasons. Some will not root easily, some are prone to root troubles, and some make large unproductive trees. To overcome these problems, apple and pear cultivars are grafted by the nursery on to various rootstocks.

The rootstock is the most important influence on the eventual size of the tree. An apple grafted on to a dwarfing stock, for example, will stay small, whereas on a vigorous stock it will eventually become large. It can also affect how long it is before the tree will fruit and its cropping capacity, so it is important to know the rootstock on which the tree is grafted or, when ordering a new tree, to indicate to the nursery what size of tree is required so that the appropriate rootstock is selected.

The stocks most widely used are listed below in order of vigour. The size of the tree quoted under the rootstock is an estimate only and will vary according to conditions.

covered with a dark red flush and a few broken stripes, light to moderate, spreading. Season late July to mid-August. Tendency to biennial bearing. Hardy.
'George Cave' Refreshing flavour, crisp texture. Medium-size fruits. Colour light red flush and stripes over green background. A regular and heavy

cropper. Medium vigour, upright and then spreading habit. Season mid-August. Flowers early. Like many early apples tends to drop prematurely. Fairly hardy.
★ **'Discovery'** Good flavour, sweet and crisp, much loved by birds and wasps. Small to medium. Green-yellow, almost entirely covered bright red.

Cropping regular and good, but can be slow into bearing if not on a dwarfing stock. Growth moderate. Upright and then spreading habit. Season end August to mid-September. Blossom fairly frost-tolerant.
★ **'Merton Knave'** Sweet, richly flavoured, crisp texture. Fruits small to medium. Flushed red overall.

ROOTSTOCKS
Apples
M27: Extremely dwarfing Requires a fertile soil. Will not thrive in poor soils or with competition from grass and weeds. Excellent for the vigorous cultivars such as the triploids. Makes a bush tree about 5–6 ft in height and spread. It is unsuitable for weak cultivars. Trees on M27 need staking throughout their lives.

M9: Very dwarfing One of the most dwarfing stocks, M9 is widely used, making a bush tree about 6–10 ft in height and spread. It soon bears fruit, usually from the third year onwards, sometimes even in the second year. It requires good soil conditions and will not tolerate neglect, or competition from grass and weeds. The root system is brittle and as a bush tree it requires staking throughout its life. An excellent stock for the small garden. Used for dwarf bush, spindlebush, dwarf pyramid and cordon.

M26: Dwarfing M26 makes a dwarf bush tree 8–12 ft in height and spread. It tolerates average soil conditions. It soon bears fruit, usually within three or four years of planting. As a bush tree, it requires staking for the first four or five years, longer on exposed sites. Used for bush, dwarf pyramid, spindlebush, cordon and occasionally espalier and fan. It is a suitable stock for the small garden.

MM106: Semi-dwarfing MM106 makes a bush tree 12–18 ft in height and spread. It is tolerant of a wide range of soils. Trees on this stock soon bear fruit – usually within three or four years – and can produce heavily in later years. As a bush tree it requires staking for the first four or five years. Used for bush tree, spindlebush, cordon, espalier and fan.

MM111 and M2: Vigorous Bush trees on these stocks make trees 18–22 ft in height and spread, but their growth varies according to soil and cultivar. They make large trees on good loamy soils, but only medium-sized trees on poorer sandy soils. Used by nurseries for bush, half-standard and standard trees, espaliers and occasionally cordons and fans. They are slow to

fruit in comparison with the more dwarfing stocks, sometimes taking seven to eight years. They are too vigorous for most gardens except where the soil is poor.

Pears
Pears are usually grafted on to quince rootstocks, which make them small to medium-sized trees. Some pears have a weak and spreading habit, and others are vigorous and upright, therefore the sizes given below are only an approximation.

There are three rootstocks: Quince C, Quince A and Pear. Both Quince C and A are suitable for the garden.

Quince C: Moderately vigorous Quince C makes a bush pear tree about 8–18 ft tall. It bears fruit in four to seven years. It is suitable for highly fertile soils and vigorous cultivars, but not where conditions are poor. Used for bush, cordon, dwarf pyramid and espalier.

Old stocks of Quince C may be infected with a virus, so where possible obtain stock certified as virus-free. If in doubt, use Quince A because there is not much difference in vigour between the two.

Quince A: Medium vigour Slightly more vigorous than Quince C, it is the stock upon which most pears are grafted. It bears fruit in four to eight years. Bush pears on Quince A make trees between 10–20 ft in height and spread. It is used for all forms of pear tree except standards.

Certain pear cultivars are not compatible with quince and these have to be double worked by nurseries. This means a piece of pear graftwood compatible with both the quince rootstock and the pear variety, such as 'Beurré Hardy', is used as an intermediate between the two. Varieties requiring double working include 'Bristol Cross', 'Dr Jules Guyot', 'Doyenné d'Eté' and 'William's Bon Chrétien'. If this is not done, the pear could eventually separate at the graft union.

Pear stock: Very vigorous Pears grafted on to pear rootstock make very large standard trees, too big for most gardens.

Apples and pears 2

Cropping regular. Moderate growth. Upright and then spreading habit. Season late August to September. Blossom fairly frost-tolerant.
'Worcester Pearmain' Flavour sweet and perfumed when fully ripe. Texture a little chewy. Fruits small to medium, round, conical. Cropping regular. Growth moderately vigorous. Upright and then

Selecting the tree form

Just as important as the correct choice of rootstock is the choice of tree form.

There are two basic types of trees, those that are planted in open ground and pruned in the winter, and those that are grown in restricted form, usually against a wall or fence, and pruned mainly in summer.

Where a gardener has plenty of land and a heavy yield is the main criterion, the unrestricted winter-pruned trees planted in the open are the best choice. Where the gardener has little room, or prefers the neat look of well-trained summer-pruned trees, or wants to fill a blank space on a wall or fence with fruit trees, then the restricted forms should be chosen.

Trees in the open

The tree forms commonly grown in the open are the dwarf bush, bush, the half-standard and the standard. These are all open-centred trees and they differ in appearance only in the length of stem or trunk before the first permanent branch and in the size of the head, or framework.

There is also the central-leader tree, sometimes called the spindlebush, which is widely grown in commercial orchards.

Dwarf bush tree The dwarf bush tree has an open centre and is goblet-shaped with a short stem of about 18–24 in. It is used only for apples because there is as yet no truly dwarfing stock for pears. Dwarf bush apples are grafted on to M9 and, because of their small size, are suitable for any garden. The soil must be very fertile, however, and the trees have to be fed and watered regularly or they will be stunted. Gardeners with less fertile soils should choose trees on the more vigorous stock M26.

Dwarf bush trees are easy to prune, spray and pick, and they soon bear fruit, but obviously their cropping capacity is not as great as that of larger trees. It is best not to plant dwarf bush apples in a lawn because they cannot compete with grass but if this is unavoidable, maintain a grass-free area for at least 2 ft around the base and water the tree regularly.

Bush tree The bush tree has a clear stem or trunk of about 20–30 in before the first primary branch is reached. Usually, the bush apple is grafted on to M26, MM106, MM111 or M2, and the bush pear on Quince C or Quince A.

Apples on the rootstocks M26 and MM106 develop into moderately-sized trees which bear fruit in about the third or fourth year. Trees on M26 are suitable for the small to medium garden and on MM106 for the medium to large garden. Bush trees on MM111 and M2 eventually become medium-sized to large trees and are best reserved for the larger orchard if this is the size of tree required. They are slow to bear fruit, taking five to eight years depending upon the variety and the growing conditions.

Bush apples and pears are suitable for the medium to large garden and can be planted in a lawn provided the grass does not inhibit the young tree's growth. They are not suitable as shade trees because the head is too low.

Half-standard and standard The half-standard has a clear stem of 4–4½ ft and the standard 6–7 ft. Both are grafted on to vigorous stocks and eventually make very large trees. For this reason they require more pruning and larger equipment than do smaller trees – for example, a long ladder for picking and a fairly powerful sprayer for pest and disease control. Vigorous trees are slow to bear fruit but, because of their large size, they eventually yield heavy crops.

Central-leader tree (spindlebush) The central-leader tree, or spindlebush, is cone-shaped. It consists of a central stem on which are carried horizontal branches starting at 2 ft from the ground.

The tree is supported by an 8–9 ft pole and the horizontal branches are achieved by tying them down in the early formative years. During the training it does not look attractive in the garden, but because this kind of tree shape allows plenty of sunlight to reach all parts, it can yield heavy crops.

Apples are grafted on to M9, M26 or MM106 and pears on to Quince A and sometimes on to Quince C.

Restricted tree forms

The restricted tree forms are used where trees have to be contained in some way, for example against a wall or fence. They are

spreading habit. *Season* September to October. Fairly resistant to mildew, susceptible to scab and canker. Blossom fairly frost-tolerant.
'Katy' ('Katja') Sub-acid, juicy, fair flavour, flesh crisp. Fruits medium, round, conical with a red flush on yellow-green background. Cropping very heavy and regular, requires thinning. Medium vigour. Upright and then

spreading habit. *Season* early September to October. Fairly hardy, suitable for the north.
'James Grieve' Excellent flavour, very juicy, flesh yellow, tender, somewhat soft. Fruits medium to large, flushed pale yellow, striped and blotched crimson. Occasionally russet. Cropping regular and good. Medium vigour.

Rather upright habit. *Season* September to October. Early fruits can be picked green for cooking. Subject to scab and canker. Blossom has some degree of frost-tolerance.
★ **'Fortune'** Flavour sweet, aromatic, flesh firm at first, but later soft. Fruits medium, round to slightly conical, golden-yellow, flushed and striped

---

TREES IN THE OPEN: SPACING AND YIELDS

Dwarf bush tree
Spacing Plant the trees 8–10 ft apart.
Yield A good average yield from an established tree is about 40–60 lb.

Bush tree
Spacing Plant bush apples on M26 rootstock 10–15 ft apart; those on MM106 12–18 ft apart; and bushes on MM111 or M2, 18–25 ft apart. Plant bush pears on Quince C rootstock 10–14 ft apart and those on Quince A 12–15 ft apart. Choose the smaller spacing on light sandy soils or with the weak cultivars, and the wider spacing on good fertile land or with vigorous cultivars.
Yield A good average yield from a well-grown bush apple on the less vigorous rootstocks is 60–120 lb and from a pear 40–100 lb.

Spindlebush
Spacing Plant apples on M9 rootstock, or in poor soils on M26, with 6–7 ft between the trees and 12 ft between the rows. If on M26 or MM106 rootstocks on good soils, leave 8 ft between trees and 14 ft between rows. Space pear trees 8 ft apart in the row with 12 ft between rows.
Yield A good average yield ranges from 30–160 lb depending upon the rootstock, cultivar and the growing conditions.

---

ideal for the small garden or where space is limited. However, because they are restricted, the yield in comparison with trees in the open is relatively small.

The main restricted tree forms for apples and pears are the cordon, the espalier and the dwarf pyramid. The fan is occasionally used.

The cordon is intended for a low fence. If closely planted, many cultivars can be grown in a relatively small space and the gardener can more easily meet the cross pollination requirements (see pages 110–13).

The espalier may be planted against a low or high fence, depending upon the number of

arms it is intended to have. Its long horizontal arms require more room than the cordon. It is a handsome form (see pages 114–17).

The fan requires a high wall, the height depending on the kind of fruit grown (see pages 14–17). Unlike the cordon or espalier it cannot be planted against a low fence unless the gardener is prepared to increase the height with trellis work. The fan is used mainly for stone fruits such as peaches, cherries and plums, and for this reason it is described only on those pages.

The dwarf pyramid The dwarf pyramid is a small tree, pyramidal or Christmas tree-like in shape and kept this way by summer pruning. If, like the cordon, it is closely spaced, many trees can be planted in a relatively small area. Close attention to summer pruning is necessary, however, to maintain space between the framework branches and adjoining trees, otherwise a row of dwarf pyramids can soon degenerate into an unproductive hedge.

Although a restricted form, the dwarf pyramid is intended for planting in the open, not against a wall or fence (see pages 118–21).

Cultivars
The choice of cultivars depends upon the personal preferences of the gardener. Nevertheless, when making the final selection, ensure that the cultivars will pollinate each other (see pages 94–7).

Many triploid cultivars (see pages 94–7) are very vigorous and are not suitable for growing in restricted form unless grafted on to the dwarfing rootstocks M9 for apples and Quince C for pears.

Those cultivars specially recommended for flavour are marked with an asterisk in the descriptions (above). The season refers to the period when the fruit is mature and fit to eat or cook. The picking date and maturity are not necessarily the same; a late apple, for example, is picked in October but might not be ready to eat until December. The season can be considerably affected by locality, climate, cultural treatment and, for stored fruit, the storage conditions. The seasons given are applicable to warmer areas, for example southern Britain, and in the northern areas they will be one or two weeks later.

Apples and pears 3

bright red on the sunny side. Cropping heavy, but sometimes biennial. Moderately vigorous, spreading habit. Season September to October. Fairly resistant to scab. Blossom fairly frost-tolerant.
'Greensleeves' Pleasant, moderately acid flavour, crisp and juicy. Fruits medium, conical, green-yellow with a trace of russet around the stalk.

Trees in the open
The dwarf bush, bush, half-standard and standard are commonly grown in the open.

Selecting the tree
A nursery can supply one-year-old, two-year-old or three-year-old trees. Trees older than this are not recommended because they may not establish well.

A one-year-old, or maiden, tree consists of a straight stem with or without laterals. A maiden with laterals, called a feathered maiden, is a better choice because if the laterals are suitably placed they can be used as primary branches, and a year is saved in the formative pruning stage. The maiden is the least expensive type, but it requires initial shaping and takes longer to bear fruit.

Trees of two and three years old will have already been partly shaped by the nursery and, being older, bear fruit sooner.

Soil preparation and planting
Prepare the soil in early autumn (see page 98). Plant the tree in the dormant period from November to March, driving in a stake first.

Pruning
Prune in the winter, from November to February, but not when the air temperature is below freezing.

The first winter The work of forming the head begins with the maiden tree.

Unfeathered At planting, shorten the maiden tree to 24 in for a dwarf bush or to 30 in if a bush tree is to be formed. Cut back to just above a bud, making a sloping cut away from the bud and ensuring there are three or four good buds beneath it. This cut stimulates the formation of primary branches the next year.

Feathered Cut back the main stem to a lateral at about 24 in for a dwarf bush or 30 in for a bush, ensuring there are two or three suitably placed laterals just beneath it. Remove all others flush with the main stem. Shorten the selected laterals by about two-thirds to an outward-facing bud.

The second winter (or the two-year-old tree) In the dormant season, select three or four strong leaders to form the primary branches, taking care to select those that are evenly spaced and have formed wide angles with the main stem. The wide angles ensure a stronger

Pruning a feathered maiden

1 In November to March, prepare the soil and drive in a stake. Plant a maiden tree to the same depth as it was at the nursery. Tie to the stake. Cut the main stem back to a bud or lateral at about 24 in for a dwarf bush, 30 in for a bush.

The second year

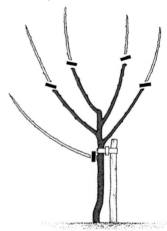

2 In November to March, select four of the primary branches that have formed wide angles to the stem. Cut back vigorous ones by one-half and less vigorous ones by two-thirds. Prune to outward-facing buds. Remove unwanted branches.

---

joint; a narrow-angled branch may break off under the weight of the crop later on. Notice the effect of apical dominance, that is, the topmost shoot is the most upright and it is often unsuitable because it is too central and forms a narrow angle with the stem. If this is so, cut it out, heading back to the next branch. Next, shorten the selected primary branches by one-half and shorten the less vigorous ones by two-thirds. Cut each to an outward-facing bud. The remaining shoots are removed altogether.

During the summer, the branch growth following the hard pruning should be strong, with secondary branches forming.

In the third winter (or the three-year-old tree) Select about four more widely spaced branches. The framework now consists of about eight branches. Shorten these by one-half or, if weak, by two-thirds, cutting back to outward-facing buds. Prune back to about four buds those laterals not required for secondary branches and those competing with the leaders. If the tree is growing vigorously, some laterals on the outer part of the tree can be left unpruned to form flower buds. Shoots crowding the crotch of the tree should be removed. The centre should be open, but not completely barren of growth. Growth from the main stem lower than the primary branches should be cut off to maintain the clean leg. Protect the cuts.

The fourth winter The tree is entering the cropping phase of its life, but a little more formative pruning is still necessary, as described for the third winter. Weak cultivars may need further formative pruning for the next two or three winters.

Winter pruning the cropping tree By the fourth or fifth year the tree should start bearing fruit. From then the pruning guidelines are flexible, exactly how much is pruned depends on the condition of the tree.

Before pruning an older tree, remember that the harder the tree is pruned, the more growth is obtained, but in consequence the less fruit is produced. Thus, a heavily pruned tree will be vigorous but unfruitful, whereas a lightly pruned tree may crop heavily, but the fruit will be small and the framework weak and badly shaped. It is a question of balance between growth and fruitfulness.

The third year

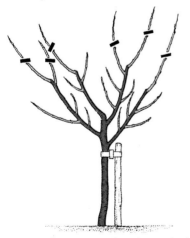

3 In November to March, select a further four well-placed new growths to form permanent branches. Cut back vigorous ones by two-thirds. Prune to outward-facing buds.

Fourth and subsequent years

4 In November to March, the branch framework has now been formed and leader pruning can cease, unless growth is weak. Leave laterals on the outer parts of the tree unpruned. Cut back laterals on the inside to about 4 in.

Apples and pears 4

'**Lord Lambourne**' Moderately sweet and aromatic, flesh fine, crisp, cream-coloured. Fruits medium, skin green-yellow with red flush and darker stripes. Compact tree. Crops heavily and regularly. Season October to November. Some scab-resistance.
'**Alkmene**' Excellent Cox-like flavour, crisp and juicy. Fruits medium size, golden yellow, flushed red. Moderate vigour,

Pruning the cropping tree

Before pruning apple or pear trees that are past the formative stage, it is important to distinguish between the spur-bearing and the tip-bearing cultivars. A spur-bearing cultivar produces fruit buds on the two-year-old as well as on the older wood, where they are carried on short stubby shoots called spurs. Where these shoots become very branched, typically on old wood, they are called spur systems. The spur-bearer is the most common type of apple and pear tree.

A tip-bearing cultivar produces fruit buds at the tips of slender shoots made in the previous summer. A few spurs are also produced on the older wood, but considerably fewer than on a spur-bearing. The tip-bearer has a more gaunt appearance in comparison. There are also partial tip-bearers, which produce spurs on the older wood as well as fruit buds at their tips. For pruning purposes they are treated a spur-bearers.

Examples of spur-bearing cultivars are the apples 'James Grieve', 'Cox's Orange Pippin' and 'Sunset', and the pears 'Conference', 'Doyenné du Comice' and 'William's Bon Chrétien'. Among the tip-bearers are the apples 'Irish Peach' and 'Worcester Pearmain' and the pear 'Joséphine de Malines'. Examples of partial tip-bearers are the apples 'Bramley's Seedling' and 'Discovery'.

There are three basic pruning techniques: spur pruning, renewal pruning, and regulatory pruning.

Spur pruning As mentioned above, spur-bearing cultivars form spurs naturally, but they can also be induced to form spurs. Each winter cut back a proportion of maiden laterals to four or five buds. Choose those that have insufficient room to extend as secondary branches.

In the following summer, a lateral so pruned produces one or two shoots from the uppermost buds, but usually the lower buds develop into flower buds by the end of the growing season.

In the second winter, cut back the laterals to the topmost flower bud, thus removing the previous summer's growth. However, where there is room and no risk of the spur overlapping an adjoining branch, extend the spur system by cutting back to three or four wood buds on the previous summer's growth.

After some years, a spur system may become crowded and complicated and, as a result, the fruits are too numerous and therefore small. Then spur thinning is undertaken by reducing the length of the spur systems, cutting away the weakest buds and those on the undersides of the branches.

Renewal pruning of spur-bearers This also depends upon the tendency of many apple and pear cultivars to produce flower buds on unpruned two-year-old laterals. It is best reserved for the strong laterals on the outer part of the tree, where there is room for such growth.

In the winter, select a proportion of strong, well-placed laterals on the outer part of the tree and leave them unpruned. Prune the others as described in spur pruning. During the following growing season, the terminal bud on each unpruned lateral extends to produce a further maiden shoot, while most of the remaining buds develop into flower buds.

In the second winter, cut back the laterals to the topmost flower bud. In the following summer the cut-back laterals produce fruit.

In the third winter, half the laterals that have fruited can be retained as an elongated spur system. The others are cut back to leave a 1 in stub. This severe shortening stimulates the production of a new lateral from the stub, and so the cycle is repeated.

To sum up, at any one time the tree carries a number of one-year-old laterals unpruned, two-year-old laterals pruned back to a flower bud, and three-year-old laterals which are stubbed back to 1 in after fruiting — or left if there is room.

Regulatory pruning This applies to the tree as a whole rather than to specific parts of it as in spur or renewal pruning. Basically it entails keeping the centre open by removing crowding and crossing branches and cutting out dead, diseased and broken wood. There is no need to prune the leaders after the early formative years except with poorly growing cultivars, which require the stimulus of hard pruning.

The framework branches, laterals and spurs also should not be crowded. As a rough guide, in an old tree no main branch upright, then spreading. Cropping regular and good. Season October to December. ★ 'Ribston Pippin' Rich, sweet flavour, flesh yellow, firm, somewhat dry, crisp and aromatic. Fruits medium, round, conical, irregular. Colour yellow with dull brown-red flush, a few stripes and russet. A regular, heavy cropper. Growth moderate. Triploid. Season November to January. A parent of 'Cox's

Orange Pippin'. Blossom fairly frost-tolerant. ★ 'Egremont Russet' Good, nutty russet flavour, flesh green-yellow, firm. Fruits medium, yellow almost covered with russet. Crops well. Moderate vigour, upright. Season October to December. Blossom fairly frost-tolerant. ★ 'Sunset' Excellent aromatic flavour, flesh creamy yellow, crisp and juicy. Fruits small to medium, round and flattened, regular.

Colour golden-yellow with red flush and russet in the eye. Cropping regular and very heavy, requires thinning. Season November to December. A small tree, which succeeds in many areas where 'Cox's Orange Pippin' grows with difficulty. ★ 'Cox's Orange Pippin' Generally considered to be the finest flavoured desert apple. Flesh tender, yellow, juicy,

---

should directly over-shade another by less than 18 in, nor should branches be closer than 18 in when side by side. Laterals should be spaced about 18 in apart and spurs not less than 9 in along the framework of branches.

If in later years, as a result of light pruning, the tree over-crops (with consequent small fruit) and growth is weak, adopt a policy of harder pruning to reduce the number of flower buds and to stimulate new growth. Simplify some of the over-long spur systems, and where they are crowded cut out some of them altogether. Increase the amount of renewal pruning.

Pruning of tip-bearers In the winter, prune lightly on the regulatory system (see above). Leave any maiden shoots less than 9 in long unpruned because they have fruit buds at their tips. Prune longer laterals back to four buds. This induces short shoots in the following summer with fruit buds at their tips – spur pruning in effect.

Always prune the leaders of tip-bearing cultivars because this induces more laterals to bear fruit in the following year.

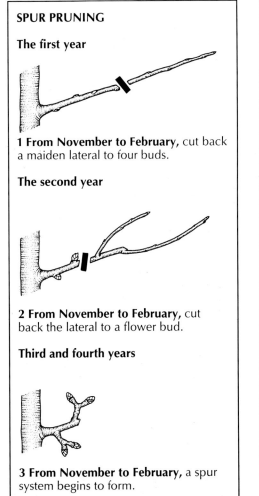

SPUR PRUNING

The first year

1 From November to February, cut back a maiden lateral to four buds.

The second year

2 From November to February, cut back the lateral to a flower bud.

Third and fourth years

3 From November to February, a spur system begins to form.

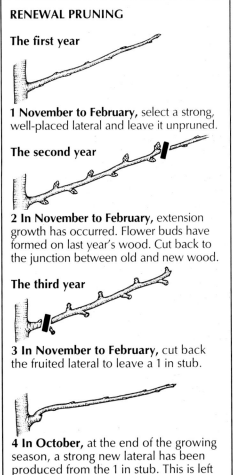

RENEWAL PRUNING

The first year

1 November to February, select a strong, well-placed lateral and leave it unpruned.

The second year

2 In November to February, extension growth has occurred. Flower buds have formed on last year's wood. Cut back to the junction between old and new wood.

The third year

3 In November to February, cut back the fruited lateral to leave a 1 in stub.

4 In October, at the end of the growing season, a strong new lateral has been produced from the 1 in stub. This is left unpruned, to repeat the cycle.

Apples and pears 5

aromatic. Fruits medium, conical, regular. Colour golden-yellow with brown-red flush and streaks with patches of russet. Trees medium-size, fairly upright, with slender branches which are usually numerous. Season October to December. The blossom is not hardy and the tree develops canker in cold and wet soils. Also very susceptible to scab and mildew. Difficult.

The central-leader tree (spindlebush)

The success of this form depends upon producing wide-angled branches off the central leader. Therefore buy a feathered maiden, because the laterals on such a tree are naturally formed at the correct angle.

Soil preparation and planting

Prepare the soil in the early autumn (see page 98). A spindlebush requires a long stake to support the central leader. The stake should be 8–8½ ft long by 1½–2 in top diameter (see page 23).

Drive the stake in first, 18 in deep on a heavy soil and 2 ft deep on a light soil. Plant the tree and tie it to the stake.

Pruning and tying down in the first year (or the one-year-old tree)

During the dormant season from November to February, select three or four laterals to form the first tier of branches starting at not less than 24 in from the ground. Choose strong, well-placed laterals coming off the main stem at a wide angle. Prune these back by one-half to an outward-facing bud. Remove the rest of the laterals entirely. Cut back the central leader to the third bud above the topmost selected lateral.

By August the original laterals will have extended and possibly new laterals will have been produced. A new central leader will have grown on. Tie the leader to the stake using a figure-of-eight tie with soft thick string such as 4-ply fillis. Choose three or four good laterals that form a wide angle with the main stem and gently tie the extension growth of each down to 30 degrees above the horizontal with soft thick string secured to 9 in long wire pegs pushed into the ground. Remove any upright laterals and those directly beneath the central leader.

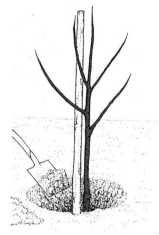

1 In November to March, prepare the ground and drive in a stake. Plant the feathered maiden tree to the same depth as it was at the nursery. Tie it to the stake.

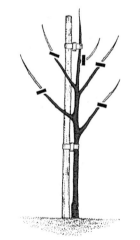

2 At the same time, select three or four laterals to form the first tier of branches at about 24 in from the ground. Prune them back by one-half to an outward-facing bud. Remove remaining laterals entirely.

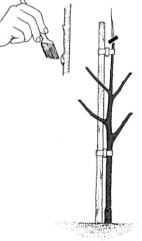

3 Then, cut back the central leader to the third bud above the topmost selected lateral. Protect the pruning cuts with a wound paint.

'Kidd's Orange Red' Flavour very good, sweet, rich and aromatic, crisp and juicy. Fruits medium-sized, can be small unless thinned, orange red with russetty patches. Moderate vigour, upright then spreading. Cropping good. Season November to January. 'Captain Kidd' is a more highly coloured sport.

★ **'Orlean's Reinette'** High quality, sweet rich flavour, crisp, very juicy. Fruits medium to fairly large, somewhat flattened, quite regular. Colour golden-yellow with slight red flush and cinnamon russet. Cropping moderate. Growth strong, upright and spreading. Season December to February.

Pruning in the second winter

Cut back the central leader by about one-third of the previous summer's growth to a bud on the opposite side to that of the previous year. The technique of cutting to an opposite bud is called "zig-zagging" and helps to maintain the more or less straight growth essential in the central leader. Remove any upright laterals and those competing with the leader. Prune each remaining lateral by one-quarter to a downward-facing bud. Check the string ties to ensure there is no constriction and remove any where the branch has set at about 30 degrees.

In August, again tie down suitable new laterals to form branches.

Pruning the cropping tree

In the third and subsequent years a similar procedure is followed. The central leader is pruned by one-quarter (if weak by one-third) to induce the lower buds to produce new laterals. The more vigorous the leader is, the lighter it is pruned. Branches are allowed to grow from the central stem at regular intervals, choosing those with a wide angle. Narrow-angled laterals are removed. The higher placed branches must be kept shorter than those beneath to allow sunlight to reach the lower parts. After the laterals at the very top have fruited, they must be pruned on the renewal system (see page 106). Tying down is discontinued once the branches have set at the required angle. The need for tying down decreases once the tree is cropping because the crop pulls the branches down.

Each winter cut back the extension growth of the central stem to a weaker side branch once it has reached a height of 7–8 ft. Tie up the side branch to the stake and treat it as the new leader.

The second year

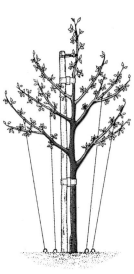

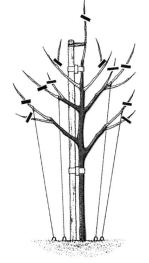

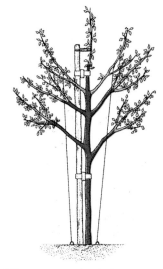

4 By August, the original laterals will have extended and a new central leader will have grown on. Tie the leader to the stake. Tie down the extension growth to 30 degrees above the horizontal using soft string.

5 In winter, cut back the central leader by one-third of the previous year's growth to an opposite-facing bud. Remove any upright laterals. Prune remaining laterals by one-quarter to a bud.

6 Every year, check the string ties. Remove the ties where the branch has set at 30 degrees. In August, tie down new laterals. Cut back the leader to a weaker lateral. Tie it up as the new leader.

Apples and pears 6

'Golden Delicious' The most universally planted cultivar. Pleasant flavour but in Britain unlikely to produce the quality comparable with imported fruit. Flesh yellow-white, crisp. Fruit small to medium, round, oblong, slightly ribbed. Skin green-yellow to golden-yellow. Cropping usually regular, occasional biennial. Growth moderately vigorous.

Restricted tree forms: The cordon

A cordon consists of a single straight stem furnished with side-shoots or fruit spurs which are kept short by summer pruning and sometimes by winter pruning. It may be planted and trained vertically or obliquely, usually the latter because it requires less height and its growth is more easily controlled. There are also multiple cordons, with two or more stems.

The cordon is a form that, perhaps more than any other, is suited to the small garden. It is closely planted, so many cultivars can be grown in a relatively small space and the gardener can more easily meet the cross-pollination requirements of apples and pears. Cordons can be grown against walls and fences or out in the open on a wire fence.

Choice of rootstock

For apple cordons, the rootstock M9 is the most suitable where space is very limited and the cordons are to be kept down to a height of 5–6 ft. The soil must be fertile, however. If in doubt about the soil, obtain trees on a slightly more vigorous stock. M26 (dwarfing) and MM106 (semi-dwarfing) are widely used and are satisfactory for most situations. MM106 is especially useful for cultivars that do not spur easily. the rootstocks M2 and MM111 (vigorous) are recommended where the soil conditions are very poor.

For pears, the cordons must be grafted on to Quince A or C rootstocks.

Selecting the tree

Cordons of one, two or three years old can be planted. If selecting a maiden tree, preferably choose one with plenty of laterals because these are the foundation of the fruit spurs to come. Two- or three-year-old cordons will be quicker to bear fruit, but they must be well furnished with spurs and laterals.

Spacing

Space the cordons 2½ ft apart on medium to good soils or 3 ft apart on poor, shallow or sandy soils with the rows 6 ft apart.

It is best, although not essential, that the rows run north-south.

Support system

Cordons may be planted against a wall or fence or out in the open on a wire fence. On walls and wooden fences erect horizontal wires every 2 ft as described on pages 15–17. Out in the open drive in wooden posts every 12 ft to hold the wires. The posts may be 2½ in × 2½ in oak or 3½ in top diameter in other woods. Set the posts 2 ft deep or 3 ft in sandy soils. The end posts should be strutted. Alternative materials include iron, steel or concrete posts. Erect the wires at 2 ft, 4 ft and 6 ft and use gauge 10 wire for the upper wire and gauge 12 for the other two. Securely tie 8 ft bamboo canes to the wires at an angle of 45 degrees, with the tops pointing towards the north if the rows run north-south, or to the east if they run east-west. Space the canes at 2½–3 ft intervals to correspond with the planting stations.

Planting and training oblique cordons

Prepare the soil in the early autumn (see page 98). Plant in the dormant season, November to March, unless using container-

The first year

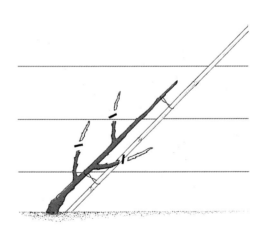

1 From November to March, plant the maiden tree with the scion uppermost, against a cane secured to wire supports at about 45 degrees. Do not prune the leader. Cut back any feathers to four buds.

Season November to February.
★ **'Ashmead's Kernel'** Sweet aromatic flavour, firm, crisp, yellow flesh. Fruits medium, round with somewhat flattened sides. Skin green-yellow with a brown flush and covered with russet. A tendency to light cropping. Trees of moderate vigour. Season December to March. A fruit for the connoisseur.

'Winter Gem' Flavour good, rich, juicy, firm. Fruits medium-size, flushed pinkish red over yellow. Moderate vigour, spreading. Crops well. Season November to March.

★ **'Tydeman's Late Orange'** Good flavour, flesh creamy, firm, crisp, but not juicy. Fruits small to medium, round, conical. Skin golden-yellow with orange-red flush and russet patches. Tends to crop biennially. Growth vigorous. Season January to March. Blossom fairly frost-tolerant.

grown plants. Against walls and solid fences, the cordon should be planted 6–9 in away from the structure to allow room for the growth of the trunk. Set the cordon at an angle of 45 degrees with the union above ground and the scion uppermost, and then securely tie the cordons to the cane using thick soft string or plastic chainlock strapping in a figure of eight. If the one-year-old tree has laterals, shorten those over 6 in long to four buds. Thereafter, prune each summer. Do not prune the leader.

It is not wise to allow a cordon to crop in the first year after planting, so in the spring remove any flowers, taking care not to cut the growing shoot just behind the blossom.

Summer pruning: Modified Lorette System
Summer pruning is necessary to confine the growth to the limited space available. It also induces the production of fruit spurs close to the main stem. The Modified Lorette System is the simplest method.

Summer prune in about mid-July for pears and in the third week of July for apples in southern England. Prune seven to ten days later farther north. Cut back to three leaves all mature shoots of the current season's growth that are growing directly from the main stem. Cut back those mature sub-laterals arising from existing side-shoots or spurs to one leaf beyond the basal cluster or rosette of leaves. Mature shoots have a stiff woody base, dark leaves and are 9 in or more long. Leave immature shoots until mid-September. Do not prune shoots that are shorter than 9 in because they usually have fruit buds at their tips.

Pruning the cropping tree
Each May, once the cordon has passed the top wire and reached the required height (usually 7 ft), cut back the extension growth to its origin. Each July subsequently, cut the leader to 1 in. From mid-July onwards the remaining shoots on the cordon are pruned on the Modified Lorette System (see above).

If, later on, there are secondary growths from shoots pruned in July, cut them back to mature wood just before leaf-fall. In areas

Second and subsequent years

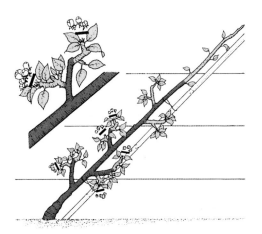

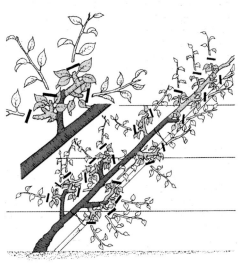

2 In spring, after a further year's growth, spurs will have formed on the cut-back feathers. Remove any flowers as they appear, leaving intact the growing shoot behind the blossom.

3 In late July, cut back laterals longer than 9 in arising directly from the main stem to three good leaves from the base, ignoring the basal cluster. Cut back sub-laterals from existing spur systems to one leaf beyond the basal cluster.

Apples and pears 7

where secondary growth is prolific after pruning, for example in high rainfall regions, delay pruning until later in the summer. If much secondary growth still occurs, then stop summer pruning altogether and prune in the winter instead, pruning to one bud from existing spurs and three buds on laterals arising directly from the main stem.

Winter pruning
Normally neither the leader nor the side-shoots are pruned in the winter except when a tree makes too much secondary growth, or makes poor growth, or to renovate it.

When a young cordon does not produce sufficient side-shoots, resulting in bare areas of stem, laterals may be induced by pruning the leader (previous summer's growth) by up to one-third of its length. Treat newly planted tip-bearers in the same way.

Neglected cordons can be brought back into shape by winter pruning. Thereafter prune them in the summer. Overlong or complicated spur systems should be reduced to two or three fruit buds.

Secondary growths

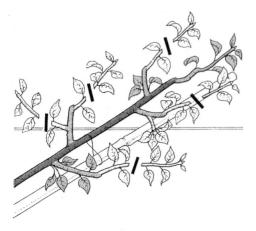

Just before leaf-fall, if further growth has developed from pruned shoots, cut it back to mature wood. In high rainfall areas, where much secondary growth occurs, stop summer pruning and prune from November to March instead.

LOWERING THE CORDON

When the cordons reach the top wire they may be lowered to obtain a longer stem. Lowering also helps to check the vigour of an over-vigorous cordon. Lower carefully five degrees at a time and not lower than 35 degrees, so that there is no risk of breaking the stem. Lowering the angle slows down the movement of sap and limits extension growth while encouraging fruit bud production.

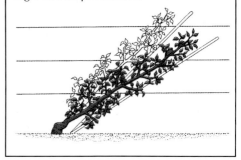

The fruiting cordon

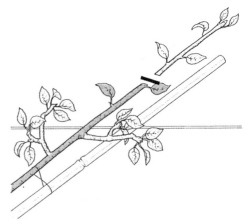

1 In May, when the leader has passed the top wire and reached the required height of about 7 ft, cut back the extension growth to its origin.

★ **'Suntan'** 'Cox'-type flavour, but more aromatic and acid. Fruits large, flat to conical, skin golden-yellow, flushed heavily with brown-red and faint stripes with some russet. Good cropper. Growth vigorous, upright and then spreading. Season December to March. Triploid. Flowers very late, escapes frost.

★ **'Sturmer Pippin'** Good flavour, flesh yellow-green, crisp and firm. Fruits medium, round to conical. Skin green-yellow, brown flushed. Regular cropper, growth compact. Season January to April. Best left on the tree as late as possible before picking. Requires a light soil and warm situation to develop its full flavour.

'Idared' Fair flavour, can also be cooked. Flesh white, somewhat juicy. Fruits large, flattish and ribbed. Colour yellow with red flush on the sunny side. Cropping regular. Growth moderately vigorous, rather spreading. Season November to May. Stores well.

MULTIPLE CORDONS

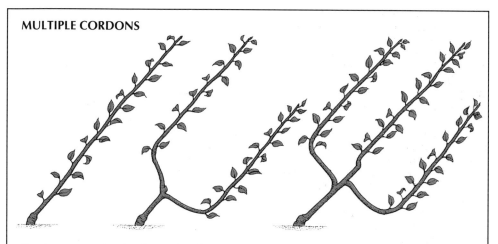

Cordons may also be formed with two, three or more arms, trained either vertically or at an angle. The training of a multiple cordon is initially similar to the formation of the first horizontal arms of an espalier. Thereafter each stem of the multiple cordon is treated as a single cordon. Vertically trained cordons are generally more vigorous and often less fruitful than those trained at an angle of about 45 degrees. The angle can be reduced further (see Lowering the cordon).

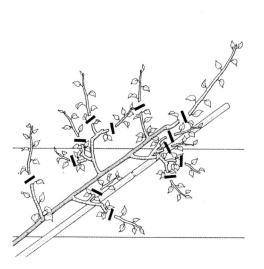

2 Each July, cut back the leader to 1 in. Cut back to three leaves all mature laterals longer than 9 in growing directly away from the main stem and those from existing side-shoots and spurs to one leaf beyond the basal cluster.

OVERCROWDED SPUR SYSTEMS

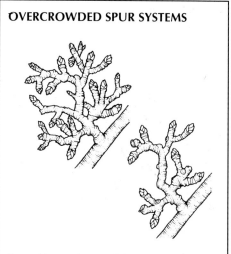

From November to February, as the tree matures thin out in the winter by reducing over-long, overlapping or complicated spur systems to two or three fruit buds. Remove buds that are weak on the underside and shaded parts of the branches.

Apples and pears 8

CULINARY APPLES
Listed in order of ripening.

'Emneth Early' ('Early Victoria') Flesh green-white, rather soft. Cooks to a froth. Fruits medium, skin yellow-green. Crops heavily, needs hard thinning. Growth compact, upright, moderate. Season July to August.

Restricted tree forms: The espalier

An espalier consists of a central stem from which horizontal fruiting arms (tiers) grow at about 15–18 in intervals. The tree is trained in one plane and makes a handsome boundary marker or can be used to cover walls or fences.

Choice of rootstock and spacing

If a small espalier apple is required, for example, against a low fence, the tree should be on the M9 rootstock. This means obtaining a maiden tree and shaping it, because pre-formed espaliers on this stock are not usually available. For more than one espalier, plant 10 ft apart.

For most gardens, espaliers on M26, spaced 10–12 ft apart, or MM106, spaced 12–15 ft apart, are suitable. Where more vigorous trees are required, to clothe a large wall for example, they should be on the vigorous stocks M2 or MM111 spaced 15–18 ft apart. Pears should be on Quince A or C rootstock.

Selecting the tree

The number of horizontal amrs or tiers required depends on the height of the wall or fence. Most nurseries supply two-tier and three-tier espaliers and further arms can be trained in if required. A formed espalier is much more expensive but crops sooner.

Support system

On walls and fences erect the horizontal wires to coincide with the espalier arms (as described on pages 14–17); usually each tier is 15–18 in apart. Out in the open, drive in posts to hold the wires every 12–18 ft, depending upon the spacing of the espaliers. The end posts should be strutted. Plant the espaliers centrally between the posts. Use gauge 10 galvanized wires and strain tight with straining bolts on the end posts.

Soil preparation and planting

In early autumn, prepare the soil (see page 100). Plant in the dormant season from November to March. To allow room for the trunk to grow when sited against a wall or fence, the espalier should be planted 6 in away.

Formative pruning

Formed espaliers may be obtained or the

The first year

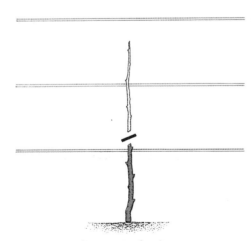

1 From November to March, plant an unfeathered maiden tree. Cut back the stem to within 15 in of ground level just below the wire. Select three good upper buds, the lower two buds pointing in opposite directions.

2 From June to September, train the shoot from the top bud vertically up a cane. Train the shoots from the two lower buds at an angle of 45 degrees to the main stem. Tie them to canes fixed on the wire support.

'Grenadier' Flesh white, crisp, acid. Cooks to a froth. Fruits large, round, conical, a little uneven. Skin pale green, fading to light yellow, smooth. Crops well. Growth moderate. Season August to September. Resistant to apple scab. A good pollinator for 'Bramley's Seedling'.
★ **'Rev. W. Wilks'** Flesh tender, white, sub-acid. Cooks to a golden froth.

Fruits large, flat, conical, slightly irregular. Colour pale creamy-white with light red flush and stripes. Cropping good, but inclined to be biennial. Growth compact and dwarfish. Season September to November. A good apple for the small garden.
★ **'Golden Noble'** Flesh tender, yellow, acid. Cooks to a froth. Fruits medium,

round, slightly flattened, regular. Skin clear yellow with light russet. Good, regular croper. Growth vigorous. Season September to January. Susceptible to scab and canker. Suitable for the north. One of the best cooking apples.

gardener may prefer to start off with a maiden tree and carry out the formative pruning as described below.

The first year Plant an unfeathered maiden tree in the dormant season between November and March. Cut back the stem to within 15 in of ground level, making sure that room for a short leg is left, together with three good topmost buds. The two lower ones should point in opposite directions.

In spring carefully direct the shoot from the top bud vertically up a cane and the others to the right and the left. It is difficult to obtain horizontal shoots in the first year without a check to growth and it is best to train the two shoots initially at angles of about 45 degrees to the main stem. This can be achieved by tying them to canes secured to the wire framework.

During summer the angle can be varied so that a weaker shoot is encouraged to catch up by raising it a little towards the vertical.

In November, at the end of the first growing season, lower the two side branches to the horizontal and tie them to the wire supports. Prune back the central leader to within 18 in

of the junction, with the lower arms to coincide with the next wire. The intention is to promote a further three growths – one to continue the central axis and the other two to form a second tier of side branches. Shorten surplus laterals from the main stem to three buds. Prune the two horizontal leaders to downward-pointing buds, removing about one-third of each shoot. If growth has been particularly satisfactory, perhaps because of a good growing season, the leaders can be left unpruned.

Second and subsequent years The next years are a repetition of the first, with subsequent tiers of branches being trained in. In November lower the side branches to the horizontal and secure them to the wire supports. Cut back the central leader to within 18 in of the last tier of arms at the next wire. Cut back unwanted laterals from the main stem to three buds. The horizontal leaders should be cut back by one-third, cutting to downward-pointing buds, if growth has been poor.

Cut back competing growths from the main stem to three leaves during the summer.

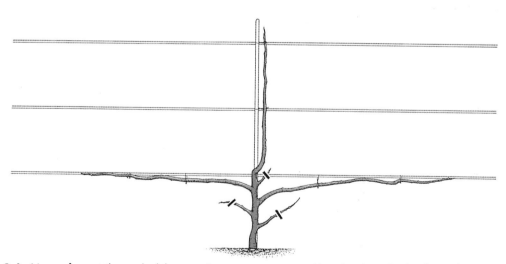

3 In November, at the end of the growing season, lower the two side branches to the horizontal and tie them carefully to the wire supports with soft string. Cut back surplus laterals on the main stem to three buds.

Apples and pears 9

'Bountiful' Good flavour, sweet yet acid, needs little sugar in cooking. Fruits medium to large. Moderate vigour, compact tree. Crops heavily. Season September to January.
'Warner's King' Flesh tender, white, acid. Very large, skin pale green to pale yellow. A good cropper. Growth vigorous. Season October to November. Susceptible to scab and canker. Triploid.

There is a tendency for vertical shoots to grow from the horizontal arms. These laterals are pruned in summer, cutting each back to three leaves above the basal cluster. Do not tie the extension growth of the horizontal arms until the end of the summer because early tying checks growth. In November train and prune both the horizontal and vertical leaders in the same way as before. This regime of winter and summer pruning should continue until the desired number of tiers has been built in.

The number of tiers finally achieved depends on soil, site and inherent vigour, but four or five is usual. Eventually both the central axis and the horizontal arms fill their

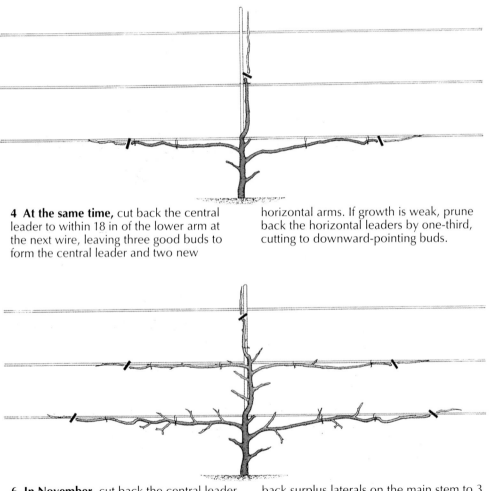

4 At the same time, cut back the central leader to within 18 in of the lower arm at the next wire, leaving three good buds to form the central leader and two new horizontal arms. If growth is weak, prune back the horizontal leaders by one-third, cutting to downward-pointing buds.

6 In November, cut back the central leader to within 18 in of the lower arm, leaving three good buds to form the new central leaders and two new horizontal arms. Cut back surplus laterals on the main stem to 3 buds. Tie down the extension growth of each arm to the horizontal. If growth is poor, prune back the leaders by one-third.

'Howgate Wonder' Fair flavour, sub-acid, flesh fairly crisp, creamy. Fruits large to very large. Skin golden-yellow with pale red flush and streaks. Cropping prodigious. Growth vigorous. Season November to February. Often produces a late flush of blossom and so suitable for frosty areas and the north.

★ 'Blenheim Orange' Culinary or dessert. Fine sub-acid flavour, flesh crisp, yellow. Fruits medium to fairly large, flattened, round and regular. Skin yellow, flushed and striped dull red and fine russet. Cropping sometimes biennial. Growth very vigorous and must be on dwarfing stock to crop early and keep the tree small. Season November to January. Triploid. Suitable for the north. The finest dual-purpose apple.

'Lane's Prince Albert' Flesh tender, green-white acid, cooks well. Fruits large, round, conical. Skin pea-green with distinct red stripes, smooth and shiny. A most reliable cropper. Habit small, spreading tree. Season January to March. Suitable for the north.

---

allotted space. From then onwards cut back the new terminal shoots to their origin each May and summer prune subsequent growth.

The fruiting stage
Each summer The fruits are carried on spur systems on the horizontal arms. The spurs are formed by the summer pruning of laterals on

the Modified Lorette System in exactly the same way as for cordons. Regard each arm as a horizontal cordon (see pages 110–13).

Winter After a few years of fruiting, the spur systems may become complicated and should be simplified by removing clusters of weak buds and by cutting back some of the spurs to two or three fruit buds.

Second and subsequent years

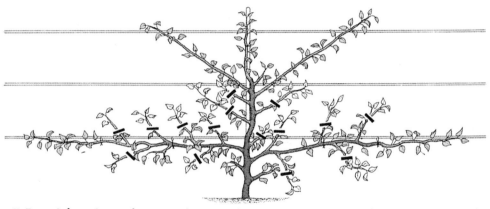

5 From July to September, train the second tier of branches in the same way as in the previous years (see caption 2, page 114). Cut back competing growths from the main stem to three leaves. Cut back laterals from the horizontal arms to three leaves above the basal cluster.

Mature tree

7 In May, when the final number of tiers is produced and the tree has filled its allotted space, cut back the new terminal growths of the vertical and horizontal arms to their origins. From now on prune them each summer as if they were cordons.

Apples and pears 10

The dwarf pyramid

The dwarf pyramid was evolved by commercial fruit growers as an easier method of producing apples and pears intensively. The pear, in particular, when grown on Quince rootstock, responds well to this method of training and in recent years the technique has been extended to plums. With apples and pears the aim is to produce a central-leader tree some 7 ft high with a total branch spread of about 4 ft through the tree, tapering to the top to form a pyramid.

It is essential to keep such a closely planted and compact tree under control. This control is exerted by a combination of summer pruning, early cropping, the complete removal of any vigorous upright shoots, and the choice of a rootstock capable of sustaining the required balance between steady cropping and the renewal of bearing wood.

Choice of rootstock

M9 and M26 rootstocks are suitable for apples in most gardens and either Quince A or the re-cloned Quince C (when it becomes generally available) can be used for pears.

The first year

1 From November to March, at planting, cut back the maiden to a bud within 20 in of ground level.

2 From July to August, four or five strong shoots will have been produced. No pruning is necessary.

★ 'Bramley's Seeding' Flesh firm, pale yellow, acid, excellent cooker. Fruits large, flat round. Colour green-yellow, red flush with broad broken stripes. Cropping regular, sometimes biennial. Habit extremely vigorous. Season November to March. Triploid. Blossom very hardy, suitable for the north. The most famous of all cooking apples, but unsuited to small gardens unless on very dwarfing rootstocks.

'Edward VII' Flesh extremely firm but yellow, acid, juicy. Cooks dark red and transparent. Fruits oblong, regular, skin pale yellow with faint brown-red flush. Cropping moderate. Growth vigorous. Season December to April. Flowers late. Suitable for frost pockets.

'Annie Elizabeth' Flesh crisp, white, acid. An excellent cooker. Fruits medium to large, oblong, conical, irregular. Skin pale yellow, flushed and striped brilliant red. Cropping regular. Growth vigorous, upright. Season December to June. Fruits tend to drop, primarily because of short stalk. Very good cropper. Very suitable for the north.

Planting and staking

In early autumn, prepare the soil (see page 100). Plant in the dormant season from November to March. Individual stakes are not necessary unless planting only one or two trees. With a row of trees, support them by erecting two posts at the ends of the row, and stretch two horizontal wires between them, one at 18 in and the other at 36 in. Tie the trees to these, using string or strapping.

Spacing

Space apples on M9 rootstocks at 4–5 ft apart, and apples on M26 rootstocks and pears 5–6 ft apart. Allow the wider spacing on fertile soils. The rows should be 7 ft apart.

Pruning and training

The first year A start is made with a maiden tree, which is cut back to about 20 in on planting during the dormant season from November to March. Prune to a bud on the opposite side to the graft. The result of this initial pruning is the production of four or five strong shoots. The uppermost shoot grows vertically.

The second year

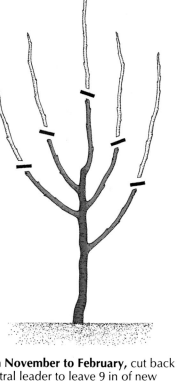

3 From November to February, cut back the central leader to leave 9 in of new growth. Cut to a bud that points in the opposite direction to the last pruning. Cut back side branches to downward-pointing buds to leave 8 in of the maiden extension.

4 From July to August, cut back laterals not required for the framework to three leaves or 3–4 in and sub-laterals to one leaf beyond the basal cluster. Leave leaders unpruned.

Apples and pears 11

DESSERT PEARS
Listed in order of ripening

★ **'William's Bon Chrétien'** Very juicy and sweet with a strong musky flavour, flesh white and transparent. Fruits fairly large, oval, uneven. Skin smooth, golden-yellow with russet dots and faint red stripes. A regular cropper.

The second year In the following winter prune the central leader to leave about 9 in new growth, taking care to cut to a bud that points in the opposite direction to the last pruning. This is aimed at keeping the successive stages of the central stem as straight as possible, in a series of zig-zags. It would be easier not to prune the leader at all because the stem would be straighter if left untouched, but such pruning is necessary to stimulate the annual production of side branches during the formative stages. These side branches, perhaps four in number and evenly spaced around the tree, are pruned back to within 8 in of the maiden extension, cutting each to a downward-pointing bud to maintain the horizontal direction.

During the following summer begin summer pruning, starting in mid-July for pears and about the end of July for apples. Cut back laterals (the current season's growth) longer than 9 in arising directly from the side branches to three leaves, and laterals from existing spurs to one leaf beyond the basal cluster. Leave immature shoots until September and then prune them in the same way.

Third and subsequent years

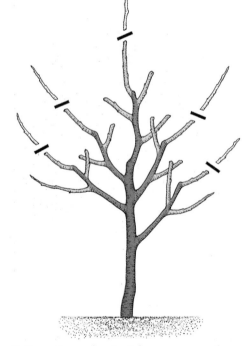

5 From November to February, prune the central leader to leave about 9 in of new growth, cutting to a bud on the opposite side to the previous pruning.

6 From July to August, throughout summer cut back laterals to three leaves or 3–4 in and sub-laterals to one leaf beyond the basal cluster. Prune the leaders of the side branches to six leaves.

Do not prune the leaders in summer.

Third and subsequent years Prune the central leader in winter. Aim to leave about 9 in of new growth, cutting to a bud that is pointing in the opposite direction from the bud to which the stem was pruned in the previous winter. This stimulates the production of new side branches. Cut back any secondary growth that may have occurred as a result of summer pruning to a mature bud.

Every summer, prune the current season's growth on the side branches using the Modified Lorette System (see page 111), treating each side branch as if it were a cordon. Prune the branch leaders to six leaves.

When the tree reaches 7 ft, further extension growth should be stopped by cutting back the leader to its origin each May. Prune any other shoots that need restriction, such as vigorous upright shoots at the top or branch leaders growing into adjacent trees.

In the winter it is occasionally necessary to shorten branches to a downward-pointing shoot in an attempt to maintain the essential horizontal position of the fruiting arms. Trim overcrowded spurs at the same time.

7 From November to February, prune the central leader to leave 9 in of new growth. Remove entirely any over-vigorous shoots. Shorten the branches to downward-pointing buds as necessary to maintain the horizontal position of the fruiting arms.

THE MATURE TREE

When the tree has reached the required height of about 7 ft, cut back the leader to its origin each May. Thin fruiting spurs as necessary. Maintain the central stem and retain the pyramid shape by close pruning and removal of vigorous shoots.

121

Apples and pears 12

★ **'Beurré Superfin'** Sweet and perfumed flavour, flesh white, melting, juicy. Fruits medium, conical. Skin golden-yellow, patched with fine brown russet. Cropping and growth habit moderate. Season October. Pick early and eat while still firm.
'Louise Bonne of Jersey' Sweet flavour, flesh white, melting. Fruits medium, long.

Cultivation

Feeding and mulching Apply fertilizers as a top dressing over the rooting area, which is roughly equivalent to the spread of the tree and slightly beyond. Inorganic fertilizers can scorch grass, therefore brush well in and water the grass if the weather is dry. If the soil tends to be acid, with a pH lower than 6.7, sulphate of ammonia should not be applied because it makes the soil more acid. Instead use nitro-chalk, which does not affect the pH.

In early March, mulch newly planted and young trees with well-rotted manure, compost or peat to a depth of 2 in over a radius of about 18 in, but keep the mulch just clear of the stem.

Dessert apples In late January apply sulphate of potash at ³/₄ oz per square yard. Every three years, in late January apply superphosphate at 2 oz per square yard. In late February apply sulphate of ammonia or nitro-chalk at 1 oz per square yard.

Dessert apples in grass See Culinary apples.

Culinary apples The same rate and timings given for dessert apples apply except that extra nitrogen is necessary, so double the application of sulphate of ammonia or nitro-chalk. This also applies to dessert apples grown in grass which need extra nitrogen to compensate for the nitrogen taken up by the grass.

During heavy rainfall in spring and summer, and in high rainfall areas, certain apple cultivars ('Cox's Orange Pippin' in particular) suffer from magnesium deficiency (see page 28). At the first signs, apply three foliar sprays at 14 day intervals, using 8 oz magnesium sulphate in 2½ gal water, plus a spreader (¼ fl oz washing-up liquid). To avoid a recurrence, apply the magnesium sulphate as a top dressing, in April, at 1 oz per square yard over the rooting area.

Pears, dessert and culinary Pears benefit from additional nitrogen. Apply all the fertilizers at the same rates and timings as given for culinary apples.

Watering To ensure good establishment and strong growth, young trees (especially newly planted ones) need to be watered in the growing season whenever the soil is dry. As a guide, apply 4 gal per square yard every ten days throughout the dry period.

Cropping trees also respond to irrigation by producing much heavier crops of larger and better quality fruit. Lack of water may induce a biennial bearing pattern (see page 126). The total amount of water needed is 4 in (18 gal per square yard) in July, 3 in (13½ gal per square yard) in August and 2 in (9 gal per square yard) in September.

Obviously, in the cool wet regions these totals will be met by natural rainfall, but in dry areas some irrigation must be applied, the actual amount depending upon the rainfall. Apply 2 in (9 gal per square yard) at a time under the trees, starting in early July. Use a hose and keep the water on the ground rather than on the foliage, irrigating over the rooting area, which is roughly equivalent to the spread of the tree.

Fruit thinning The main purpose of fruit thinning is to obtain larger and better quality fruits. In heavy cropping years if the fruits are not thinned, the resultant crop will consist of small, poor quality apples or pears and, as with lack of water, the strain imposed upon the tree might put it into a biennial habit.

Manuring

1 In January apply sulphate of potash at the recommended rates. In late February apply sulphate of ammonia or nitro-chalk.

Colour yellow-green with pronounced red flush and red dots. Cropping regular, growth strong upright. Season October. Blossom fairly frost-tolerant. **'Beurré Hardy'** Good flavour, sweet, excellent quality. Flesh white and juicy. Fruits medium to large, conical and uneven. Yellow-green, almost covered with a fine brown russet and occasional

carmine flush. Sometimes a shy cropper and slow to start bearing. Growth vigorous and upright. Season mid- to late October. Pick when hard and ripen in store. **'Conference'** Pleasant flavour, sweet, flesh firm, creamy white, very juicy. Fruits medium, long and thin, skin dark olive-green with brown russet. Cropping

heavy. Growth moderately vigorous. Season mid-October to late November. Suitable for the north. A reliable pear. ★ **'Seckle'** Excellent flavour, flesh yellow-white, tender, honey sweet and juicy. Fruit small, skin red-brown with prominent white dots. Cropping only moderate, weak growth, making an upright tree. Season October to November.

Much depends upon the condition of the trees: trees with healthy foliage and a strong framework can carry more fruit than can weaker trees. Young trees should not be allowed to crop so heavily that the branches are bowed down and the tree cannot make the essential strong growth needed for its framework.

Some cultivars naturally shed some of their fruitlets in late June or early July which is called the June drop, but this may not be sufficient. Start lightly thinning before this in mid-June by removing the malformed fruits, and then complete the task after the June drop in about mid-July.

Culinary cultivars should be thinned harder than the dessert fruits.

Use sharp scissors or press the fruitlet off with the thumb and finger, leaving the stalk behind. In the final thinning, dessert apples should be spaced on average 4–6 in apart with about one fruit per cluster and occasionally two where there is a good show of supporting leaves. Culinary apples should be spaced on average 6–9 in apart.

With apples, sometimes the "king" or "crown" fruit produced in the centre of a cluster is virtually stalkless and malformed. If this is the case, remove it, but if the apple is well shaped, leave it because the king fruit can be the best in the cluster.

Pears need less thinning than do apples. Start thinning after the natural drop in late June, but not until the fruitlets turn downwards. Thin to two fruits per cluster and occasionally to one where the foliage is poor or sparse.

Supporting heavily laden branches Prop up heavily laden branches well before there is a risk of the branches breaking. Use forked poles or stakes but place a cushion of soft material such as a piece or rubber tyre between the prop and the branch.

Weak branches can be tied to stronger ones with rope or webbing. Small trees can be supported by "maypoling". This involves driving a tall stake into the ground near the stem of the tree and tying rope or thick string from its top to each branch needing support (see page 125 for illustration).

Mulching

2 In early March, mulch newly planted and young trees with a 2 in layer of well-rotted manure or compost over a radius of 18 in.

Watering

3 In summer, apply 4 gal per square yard every ten days in dry periods.

Apples and pears 13

'Packham's Triumph' Good musky flavour, sweet, flesh white, melting and very juicy. Fruits medium, conical and irregular, ribbing on the surface. Skin green with fine russeting, ripening to yellow with orange flush. Good cropper, weak growth. Season November to December.

Blossom fairly frost-tolerant.

Protection from wasps and birds

Apples and pears (especially the early cultivars) sometimes need protection against wasps and birds. The trees can be netted or collars placed around the fruit stalks against birds (see page 33) but wasps are more difficult to combat. One remedy is to find and destroy the wasps' nests. They can also be trapped in jam jars partly filled with beer and sugar. However, these two methods guarantee only partial control, and the most positive (if tedious) protection against wasps is to enclose each fruit, or cluster of fruits, in a muslin bag or piece of nylon stocking.

Harvesting and storing

The time for picking apples and pears varies according to the season and the locality so it is not possible to give exact picking dates. As a guide, in southern Britain the earliest cultivars of apples are ready for picking in late July to early August.

Apples A good test for ripeness is to lift the fruit in the palm of the hand and if it leaves the spur easily with its stalk intact, it is ready.

Another sign is the first windfalls (discounting drops from strong winds and codling moth attack). With the later ripening cultivars, the colour of the pips is an indication. They should be beginning to change colour from white to straw-coloured and eventually to brown. With dessert apples in particular the skin of the fruits becomes more brightly coloured.

Early cultivars are best picked when slightly immature because they soon go mealy. Pick those apples that have coloured rather than clearing all the apples in one go. Usually those apples in full sun are ready first and those in the middle of the tree last. Handle the fruits very gently because bruised fruits do not keep. Put the fruits carefully into a picking container lined with a soft material and transfer them just as gently into their final container.

Late apples reach maturity in storage sometime after picking, depending upon the cultivar. Most should be off the tree by the third week in October in Britain, but there are a few cultivars which keep better and

Thinning

4 In mid-June, thin the fruits using sharp scissors or press the fruitlets off with the thumb and forefinger, leaving the stalk behind.

In mid-July, thin again to leave one or two dessert apples per cluster 4–6 in apart; culinary apples 6–9 in apart. Pears need less thinning; leave two fruits per cluster.

★ **'Thompsons'** Delicious flavour, flesh white, melting and juicy. Fruits medium to large ribbed. Skin golden-yellow with red flush and russet marking. Cropping moderate. Habit medium vigour, upright. Season October to November.

★ **'Doyenné du Comice'** Excellent flavour, flesh white, melting and juicy.

Fruits medium to large. Skin green-yellow with a brown-red flush. Sometimes a shy cropper. Habit vigorous, fairly upright tree. Season late October to late November. Susceptible to scab Requires a warm and sheltered site.

★ **'Winter Nelis'** Sweet delicately perfumed flavour, flesh green-white,

transparent, very juicy. Fruits small to medium. Skin dull green with dark brown russet, mainly around the eye. Cropping heavy, growth moderate. Season November to January. Blossom fairly frost-tolerant. One of the best winter pears.

---

acquire more flavour if left on as long as possible, birds and winter gales permitting. These include 'Granny Smith' 'D'Arcy Spice', 'Sturmer Pippin', 'Idared', 'Wagner' and 'French Crab'.

Store only sound fruits (see page 178 for details of storage).

Pears The correct time for picking pears is harder to assess than it is for apples. The best test for readiness is to lift the pear in the palm of the hand and with a slight twist and tug, it should leave the spur with its stalk intact. There is also an almost imperceptible change in the ground colour of the skin from dark green to lighter green.

Early and early mid-season pears (August to September in Britain) must not be left on the tree until they are fully ripe otherwise they may go sleepy, that is very soft, mealy and brown at the centre. Pick them when they are almost ready but still firm, and then let them mellow in the storage house. Their storage life can be extended by keeping them under cool conditions (3°–7°C/37°–45°F).

Late pears should be left on the tree until

they leave the spur easily; the first sign of windfalls is an indication. The fruits are hard at this stage but will mellow in storage. Keep them under cold conditions and bring the pears into room temperature to finish ripening whenever required. (See page 178 for details of storage).

Pest and diseases

Apples The most troublesome diseases are scab, mildew and canker and the most troublesome pests are aphids, leaf-eating caterpillars, sawfly and codling moth larvae.

Scab and mildew can be controlled by regular spraying with suitable fungicides (see page 28) starting at bud burst and finishing in July. If canker occurs, cut out the rotting wood and paint the clean wounds with a canker paint. In bad attacks also apply copper sprays after harvest and at 50 per cent leaf-fall, and the following year at bud burst. Check that the soil is not badly drained (see pages 18–19).

Use a systemic insecticide against aphids and fenitrothion or permethrin against caterpillars.

Maypoling

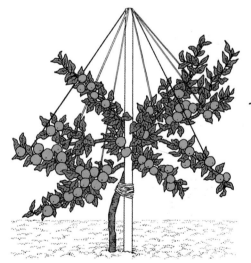

5 On small trees, to support branches with a heavy crop, drive a tall stake into the ground near the stem of the tree. Tie a rope from its top to each branch.

Grassing down the orchard

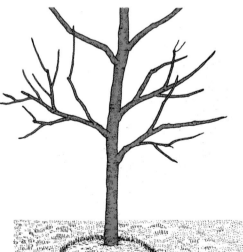

6 After four or five years, grass down the orchard. Sow a fine lawn mixture at 2 oz per square yard, leaving a grass-free area of 2 ft radius around the base of each tree.

125

Apples and pears 14

Spraying with permethrin, pirimiphos-methyl or fenitrothion one week after petal-fall controls sawfly larvae. Use fenitrothion or permethrin against codling moth caterpillars in mid-June and again in early July.

Pears The most troublesome disease of pears is scab and the most troublesome pests are aphids and leaf-eating caterpillars.

For scab spray with carbendazim, mancozeb or bupirimate at bud burst, repeating every two weeks until late July.

A systemic insecticide controls aphids and fenitrothion or permethrin controls leaf-eating caterpillars.

Propagation

Apples and pears do not come true from seed nor are they satisfactory from cuttings, so they are propagated by budding or grafting on to suitable rootstocks, a task normally performed by the fruit tree nursery.

Biennial bearing

Biennial bearing, or the carrying of a heavy crop one year and little or none in the next, is a common problem with apples and pears. Certain cultivars are prone to it, 'Laxton's Superb', 'Bramley's Seedling' and 'Blenheim Orange' for example, although almost any cultivar can fall into this habit. It is more likely to happen to trees which are starved or receiving insufficient moisture, which makes them unable to carry a heavy crop and at the same time develop fruit buds for the following year. Frost destroying the blossom one spring can sometimes be the start of biennial bearing. Once the tree is into this cropping pattern it is difficult to correct, although there are certain techniques the gardener can try which sometimes improve the situation.

In early spring before an expected heavy crop year, half to three-quarters of the fruit buds are rubbed off the spurs, leaving about one or two per spur. This lessens the burden of too heavy a crop in that year and hopefully enables the tree to develop fruit buds for the next year.

In conjunction with bud rubbing, a policy of more generous feeding and watering should be adopted in "on" and "off" years. First, clear away grass or weeds from the base of the tree over a radius of at least 2 ft. Each

BIENNIAL BEARING

1 In spring, before a heavy crop year, rub one-half to three-quarters of the fruit buds from the spurs, leaving one or two per spur.

February apply a compound fertilizer such as a brand of Growmore at 4 oz per square yard and sulphate of ammonia (or nitro-chalk) at 2 oz per square yard. Small trees should also be mulched with well-rotted manure or compost to a depth of 2 in over a radius of 2 ft but keep the material clear of the stem.

In late August apply a further 2 oz per square yard of sulphate of ammonia (or nitro-chalk). Throughout the growing season, whenever the conditions are dry, the tree should be irrigated copiously by applying at least 1 in of water (4½ gal per square yard) over the rooting area every ten days until rain restores the balance.

If bud rubbing does not work, an alternative technique is to induce the tree to crop biennially over half the tree by removing half the blossom. Alternate branches are selected and marked in some way. Half the branches

★'Joséphine de Malines' Excellent flavour, flesh pink-white, tender, juicy. Fruits small. Skin green-yellow with russet around the stalk. Reliable cropper. Growth weak, moderate, rather weeping. A tip-bearer. Season December to January. Blossom fairly frost-tolerant.

CULINARY PEARS
'Catillac' One of the best pears for stewing, when cooked becoming a deep red. Flesh white, firm and acid. Fruits large and round, skin brown-red flush over dull green, ripening to yellow. Cropping heavy, but irregular. Growth vigorous, spreading. Season

December to April. Should be left on the tree as long as possible. Triploid. Blossom fairly frost-tolerant.

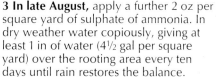

2 Each February, apply 4 oz per square yard of a compound fertilizer, such as a brand of Growmore, and sulphate of ammonia at 2 oz per square yard. Mulch small trees with a 2 in layer of well-rotted manure over a radius of 2 ft.

3 In late August, apply a further 2 oz per square yard of sulphate of ammonia. In dry weather water copiously, giving at least 1 in of water (4½ gal per square yard) over the rooting area every ten days until rain restores the balance.

are designated to crop in the even years (1992, 1994, and so on) and half the branches are designated to crop in the odd years (1993, 1995, and so on). Each spring, those branches not selected to crop in that particular year must be rigorously de-blossomed. At first this de-blossoming represents quite a task, especially with a large tree, but after the third or fourth year it should be found that the branches have accepted this alternate pattern and very little blossom removal is necessary. However, a careful watch should be kept to see that the tree does not slip back into the full biennial cropping. As with the first technique, generous feeding is recommended.

Grassing down the orchard
After four or five years, grass down the orchard. Grass checks the vigour of the trees and promotes colour in the fruits, so grass down dessert fruits, but not culinary apples or culinary pears for which size is more important than colour. Delay grassing down if the trees are growing poorly. Once the sward is sown, maintain a grass-free area of 2 ft radius around the base of each tree. Over-vigorous trees should have a smaller area of clean land, but do not grass right up to the stem because the vegetation might encourage the disease collar rot. Where trees are closely planted (cordons, for example), maintain a grass- and weed-free band 3 ft wide down the row.

Sow a fairly fine lawn mixture (but not rye grass because this tends to restrict the growth too much) at 2 oz per square yard. Poor soils should have wild white clover added to the mixture at ¼ oz over 10 square yards because it adds nitrogen to the soil.

Plums 1

Listed in order of ripening.

DESSERT PLUMS
'Early Laxton' Fair flavour. Fruits small,
oval, yellow with pink flush. Flesh golden
and juicy. Ripens late July to early August.
Heavy cropper. Dwarfish growth.
'Opal' Excellent flavour, sweet and juicy,
medium sized, reddish purple fruit.

Plums and gages
The origins of the European plum (*Prunus domestica*) are obscure. It is thought to have arisen from hybridization between the sloe (*P. spinosa*) and the cherry plum (*P. cerasifera* or the closely related *P. divaricata*). It may have come from the Caucasus, where these species and hybrids between them occur.

The plum is a deciduous tree, ranging in height from 15–30 ft when mature. The gage is a sweeter, more refined type of dessert plum. Both are usually grown in bush, half-standard or standard forms, or fan-trained against a wall or fence. They may also be grown as pyramids – a very good form for the small garden. They are not suited to such restricted forms as the cordon or espalier.

Damsons and bullaces
The damson (*Prunus domestica* sub-species *insititia*) is a hardier, less vigorous type of plum used mainly for culinary purposes. The fruits are oval, usually blue-black and have a unique, rich flavour. The bullace and the Mirabelle plum also belong to this sub-species. Bullaces are very small, round or oval and may be blue, black, yellow or white. Mirabelle plums are round, small, sweet and golden yellow. All make small, compact, deciduous trees of 10–20 ft in height and spread. They can be grown as bushes, half-standards, standards or pyramids.

Myrobalan plums
The cherry or Myrobalan plum (*P. cerasifera*) is used mainly for hedges and as a rootstock for plums, although when grown as a fruiting tree, it gives a useful yield of small, red or yellow, cherry-like plums that are excellent for jam-making. On its own roots it makes a large tree 20–30 ft in height and spread.

Cultivation
The cultivation of plums, gages, damsons, bullaces and Mirabelles is generally the same so, unless indicated otherwise, text references to plums apply to all these fruits.
Yield A good average yield from a plum tree in the open ranges from 30–120 lb and from a fan 20–30 lb.

1 In autumn, prepare the ground, clearing away perennial weeds. Lightly fork in 3 oz of a balanced fertilizer and 2 oz of bonemeal per square yard.

2 For trees in the open, drive in a stake. For fan-trained trees construct a system of wires on the wall. Plant the tree and tie it to the stake or to the wall wires.

Ripens early August. Moderate vigour. Crops well.
'Victoria' Fairly good flavour. Fruits large, oval, pale red and mottled. Flesh green-yellow and juicy. Ripens late August to early September. Very heavy cropper, sometimes irregular. Moderate growth. Self-compatible. Also suitable for cooking.

'Coe's Golden Drop' Excellent, very sweet flavour. Fruits large, oval, pale yellow with red-brown spots. Flesh golden and very juicy. Ripens late September. Light, irregular cropper. Moderate growth.

GAGES
'Oullin's Golden Gage' Moderate, fairly sweet flavour. Fruits large, round, yellow with green dots. Flesh pale yellow and transparent. Ripens mid-August. Slow to bear. Vigorous growth. Self-compatible.
'Count Althann's Gage' Rich flavour. Fruits large, round, dark crimson. Flesh golden and juicy. Ripens mid- to late August. Good cropper. Moderate growth.
'Early Transparent Gage' Excellent flavour. Fruits small to medium, round,

---

Soil and situation Plums require a deep, moisture-retentive, well-drained soil with a pH range 6.5–7.2. The plum grows best in clean soil. Control grass and weeds around the tree by shallow hoeing. Avoid deep cultivation because this encourages suckering. Plum varieties on vigorous stocks can be grassed down, but maintain a clean area 2 ft square around the tree.

Plums, particularly the Myrobalan plum, flower early so a sheltered, frost-free site is essential to avoid irregular cropping. Gages and dessert plums need a warm, sunny position to acquire their full flavour. Gages particularly are good plants for a south- or west-facing wall, but they can be grown in the open in milder areas. Culinary plums will tolerate some shade. They can also be grown against an east-facing wall and a few early cultivars will grow on a north-facing wall. Damsons are fairly hardy and will crop satisfactorily in regions too cool for plums.

Plums and gages are hardy in zones 4–8; damsons, Myrobalan plums and bullaces in zones 3–8; and Mirabelles in zones 4–8.

Selecting the tree The most suitable rootstock for the garden, both for trees in the open and on walls, is the semi-dwarfing rootstock St Julien A. The relatively new stock Pixy is more dwarfing but it is hard to obtain because propagation is difficult. Rootstocks Brompton and Myrobalan B are too vigorous for all but the largest gardens.

For bush, standard or fan-trained trees, buy a maiden tree or a two- to three-year-old tree already partly trained by the nursery. Plum pyramids are best obtained as maiden trees. A plum on St Julien A or Pixy usually begins cropping in the third to sixth year.

Soil preparation In early autumn, prepare the ground, thoroughly clearing away perennial weeds over an area 3 ft square. Just before planting, fork in a balanced fertilizer such as a brand of Growmore, at 3 oz per square yard and bonemeal at 2 oz per square yard. If the soil is light, also fork in well-rotted manure or compost at one 2 gal bucketful per two square feet.

Planting and spacing Plant in the dormant season from November to March. Trees in

Thinning

3 In February, apply a balanced fertilizer at 4 oz per square yard. One month later, apply sulphate of ammonia at 1 oz per square yard. Mulch the tree with a 1–2 in layer of compost or manure.

4 Thin the fruits when they are the size of hazelnuts and once the stones have formed within the fruits. Repeat when the fruits are twice this size to leave them 2–3 in apart on the branches.

Plums 2

pale yellow with crimson dots. Flesh golden, transparent and juicy. Ripens mid- to late August. Good cropper. Moderate growth. Self-compatible.
'Denniston's Superb' Good flavour. Fruits large, round, green-yellow with dark green streaks. Flesh yellow-green, transparent and juicy. Ripens late August. Heavy cropper. Vigorous growth.

containers can be planted at any time. Dig a hole wide and deep enough to take the roots fully extended. For trees in the open, before planting drive in a stake to reach just below the lowest branches. For fan-trained trees, construct a system of supporting, horizontal wires spaced 6 in apart (see pages 14–17).

Plant the tree to the same depth as it was at the nursery. Return the soil and firm it well. Tie to the stake with a tree tie and cushion or tie in the branches of a fan to the wall wires. Water well.

Trees in the open require staking for the first five or six years. If the site is exposed they require permanent support and a heavy-headed standard needs two stakes and a crossbar.

Space bush, half-standard, standard and fan-trained plum and gage trees on Brompton or Myrobalan B rootstocks 18–20 ft apart and on St Julien A rootstocks 12–15 ft apart. Space bush trees on Pixy rootstocks 10–12 ft apart. Space plum pyramids on either St Julien A or Pixy, 10–12 ft apart. Use the smaller spacing also for damsons and bullaces.

Pruning

Never prune plums in winter because of the risk of silver leaf disease. Always protect the cuts with a wound paint.

Pruning bush, half-standard and standard trees The pruning methods for all these forms are basically the same except that in the first year after planting, the maiden half-standard or standard is cut back to a greater height.

The first year In late February to early March, just as the buds start to break, cut back the central stem of the maiden tree to a bud at 3 ft for a bush, at 4½ ft for a half-standard, and at 6 ft for a standard. It may be necessary to grow the tree on for a further year to acquire the necessary height for a standard before cutting it back. Shorten all laterals to about 3 in to help thicken the stem.

In July or August, select four or five evenly spaced primary branches around the stem at the top. Pinch out the growing points of all others at four or five leaves, including those lower down the main stem.

The second year In late February to early March, select four branches that have formed

The pyramid plum: the first year

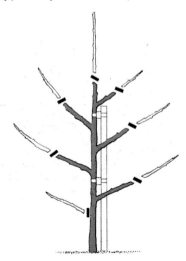

1 In March, cut back the leader to 5 ft. Cut back to the stem all laterals up to 18 in from the ground. Cut back the remaining laterals by one-half.

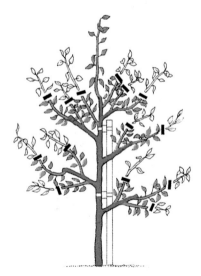

2 In late July, shorten the new growth of the branch leaders to 8 in to downward-facing buds. Shorten the current season's laterals on the branches to 6 in. Do not prune the central leader.

Self-compatible.
'Cambridge Gage' Very similar to 'Old Green Gage'.
'Old Green Gage' Excellent flavour. Fruits small, round, yellow-green with slight red flush and russet dots. Flesh yellow-green and very juicy. Ripens late August to early September. Fair cropper. Vigorous growth.
'Jefferson' Excellent flavour. Fruits large, round, green with russet dots and pink flush. Flesh pale yellow-green and very juicy. Ripens late August to early September. Moderate cropper. Vigorous compact growth.

MYROBALAN PLUM
Cherry Plum Good flavour. Fruits very small, round, red. Flesh yellow. Ripens late July. Flowers very early. Self-compatible. There is a yellow form.

CULINARY PLUMS
'Early Rivers' Good flavour. Fruits small, round or oval, purple-blue. Flesh golden and very juicy. Ripens late July to early August. Good cropper. Moderate growth.

---

wide angles with the stem. Cut back each leader of those selected by one-half to outward-facing buds. Remove the remainder, including the lower laterals left the previous year to thicken the stem.

In the summer, remove any suckers that appear from the ground and remove shoots on the main stem below the head.

The third year Repeat the procedures adopted in the previous spring and summer but allow more secondary branches to develop to fill the increased space, allowing up to eight strong and well-placed, outward-growing branches. From late February to early March, cut these back by one-half to two-thirds of the maiden growth to outward-facing buds. Leave shoots on the outer parts of the head not required for leaders. Prune back unpruned laterals on the inside of the tree to 3–4 in.

Little pruning is necessary in subsequent years. The leading shoots of weaker cultivars such as 'Early Laxton', may need cutting back for a further one to two years in February to early March. Otherwise, all that is necessary is to cut out dead, broken, rubbing and crossing branches and to thin out the head when it becomes too crowded; do this between June and the end of August.

Pruning a fan-trained tree Starting with a maiden tree, the framework of a fan-trained plum is built up in exactly the same way as a fan-trained peach (see pages 146–53). Thereafter the pruning is different because the plum fruits on short spurs on two-, three- and four-year-old wood as well as on growth made in the previous summer. However, the older wood tends to become bare with age and because of damage by frost or bullfinches. The aim in pruning is to encourage spur formation and, when necessary, to replace worn-out branches.

In the early years, extend the framework, as with the peach, to fill in the wall space, then follow the illustrated steps below.

In later years, in the spring, cut out a proportion of the old wood back to young replacement branches. Paint the wounds.

Feeding and watering In February, apply a balanced fertilizer, such as Growmore, at

Second and subsequent years

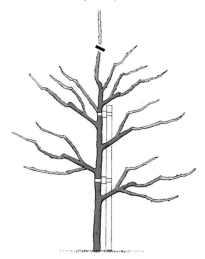

3 In March, shorten the central leader by two-thirds of the previous summer's growth until the tree has reached about 9 ft, then shorten the central leader to 1 in each May to keep the tree at this height.

4 In late July, shorten the current season's growth of each branch leader to eight leaves. Shorten the laterals to six leaves. Cut out any vigorous shoots at the top of the tree.

Plums 3

'**Czar**' Good, acid flavour. Fruits medium, round or oval, dark purple. Flesh yellow-green and very juicy. Ripens early August. Heavy cropper. Moderate growth. Self-compatible. Hardy.
'**Pershore**' ('Yellow Egg') Fair flavour. Fruits medium, oval, golden. Flesh yellow. Ripens mid-August. Heavy cropper. Moderate growth. Self-compatible.

4 oz per square yard. In late March, apply sulphate of ammonia, or nitro-chalk if the soil is acid, at 1 oz per square yard. Mulch young trees with 1–2 in layer of well-rotted manure or compost over a radius of 18 in, keeping the mulch clear of the stem.

Water well and regularly in dry weather during the growing season, applying 1 in (4½ gal per square yard) every ten days until rain redresses the balance. Avoid irregular heavy watering which can split the fruits, especially near the ripening stage.

Frost protection
Protect plums on walls and, where it is practicable, trees in the open against frost at blossom time by draping with hessian or bird netting (see pages 12–13).

Pollination
Plums are one of the earliest tree fruits to flower and those on walls flower about seven to ten days earlier than those in the open when there may be few insects about, so hand pollination is worth while (see page 95).

Some plums and gages are self-compatible (see cultivar lists above) and can be planted singly, but others require cross-pollination (see pollination tables pages 96–7). Most damsons, bullaces and Mirabelle plums are self-compatible. The Myrobalan plum is self-compatible.

Thinning the fruits
Thin the fruits (if the tree carries a heavy crop) after the stones have formed within the fruits to avoid loss of flavour and the possibility of a biennial pattern of bearing. Thin once when the fruits are about the size of hazelnuts and again when they are about twice this size. Those left on the tree to ripen should be 2–3 in apart, or 4 in for large cultivars. Do not tug the fruits off because this might tear away the following year's fruit buds, but cut the fruit stalk with scissors or secateurs.

Supporting the branches
Support for heavily laden branches is essential because they may break and spoil the shape of the tree and increase the risk of

The plum fan

1 For the first three years, follow the formative pruning steps for the peach fan (see pages 146–53), extending the framework to fill in the wall space. Prune only in spring or summer.

Fourth and subsequent years

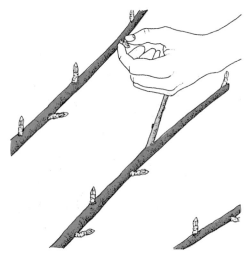

2 Each spring, as growth begins, rub out shoots growing directly towards the wall and breastwood.

Hardy. There is also a purple variety.
'Victoria' See Dessert plums.
'Monarch' Fair flavour. Fruits large, oval, purple-red with russet dots. Flesh pale yellow. Ripens end September. Moderate cropper. Vigorous. Self-compatible.
'Marjorie's Seedling' Good flavour. Fruit large, oval, purple-blue. Flesh yellow and juicy. Ripens late September to early

October. Very good cropper. Vigorous upright growth. Self-compatible.

DAMSONS
'Prune' ('Shropshire Damson') Excellent flavour. Fruits small, oval, blue-black. Flesh green-yellow. Ripens September to October. Moderate cropper. Dwarfish growth.

BULLACES
'Langley' Good flavour. Fruits large, oval, blue-black. Flesh green. Ripens late October. Heavy cropper. Vigorous.

MIRABELLES
'Mirabelle Petite' Excellent flavour. Fruits small, round, golden. Flesh golden, dry. Ripens mid-August. Fair cropper. Dwarfish.

---

silver leaf or bacterial canker infection. Support individual branches with a clothes prop or forked stake driven into the ground at an angle. Wrap the branch with sacking where it meets the crotch. Alternatively, support laden branches with thin ropes tied to the top of a tall central stake in the form of a maypole (see page 125).

Protection against birds
The fruit buds of plums are susceptible to bird damage in winter and the ripe fruit is also at risk in the summer. Where practicable protect the tree with netting (see page 33).

Harvesting and storing
Plums ripen from late July to November, depending on the cultivar and locality. They do not ripen simultaneously and it is necessary to go over the tree two or three times. Pick fruits intended for bottling, jam-making and cooking when slightly underripe. Pick all fruits with the stalks intact.

Plums cannot be stored for prolonged periods, but if picked when a little underripe

they will keep for two to three weeks in a cool place, at about 6°–7°C/42°–45°F.

Propagation
Plums are propagated by budding or grafting – a task normally carried out by the nursery.

Pests and diseases
Control aphids with tar oil in the winter and by spraying with dimethoate or heptenophos in the growing season. Spray with fenitrothion or permethrin against caterpillars. Grease banding also helps to reduce infestations. If plum sawfly maggots are troublesome, spray the trees with fenitrothion, pirimiphos-methyl or permethrin 7–10 days after petal-fall.

Cut back branches affected by silver leaf to healthy wood as soon as the disease is noticed. Paint the cuts immediately with a wound paint. Spray with bordeaux mixture or copper oxychloride in mid-August, mid-September and mid-October against bacterial canker, if this has been troublesome in previous years. Remove branches dying back with canker. Pick off and burn fruits infected with brown rot.

3 From late June to late July, as new shoots are made, pinch out the growing points of shoots not wanted for the framework when they have made six or seven leaves. This begins to form the fruit-bearing spur system.

4 After cropping, between mid-August and mid-September, cut back the pinched-out shoots to three leaves to encourage fruit buds to form at the bases of the pinched-out shoots the following year.

Sweet and Duke cherries 1

The cultivated sweet or dessert cherry is basically derived from *Prunus avium*. It is a hardy deciduous tree which is cultivated in many areas of Europe and western Asia. It bears clusters of attractive, white flowers in spring and bears fruits, ranging in colour from yellow and pink to almost jet black, from June onwards in cool temperate areas.

The Duke cherry is thought to be a cross between the sweet and acid cherry and it is intermediate in character between the two.

Cultivation

Although this delicious fruit merits a place in any garden, it has one serious drawback – its extreme vigour. Despite the introduction of increasingly dwarfing rootstocks, the cherry remains quite vigorous and is therefore not suitable for a small garden. It is usually grown as a fan on a wall, but the wall must be fairly high. In the open it is grown as a standard and occasionally as a bush or half-standard. By using the less vigorous rootstock Colt, it could be grown as a pyramid (see the plum pyramid pages 130–33). For cultural purposes, treat Duke cherries in the same way as sweet cherries.

Yield The yield from different kinds of cherry can vary enormously depending, of course, on the size, age and form of the tree and the climate. A good average from a fan is about 30 lb and from a well-grown standard 100 lb.

Soil and situation Cherries grow in any good, well drained soil but it should be deep, ideally a loam more than 2 ft deep. Nevertheless light, sandy soils are acceptable and produce smaller trees but more generous feeding, mulching, and at times irrigation, are necessary.

Cherry blossom is susceptible to frost and young trees to wind damage so the site should be sheltered from winds, in full sun and not in a frost pocket.

Soil preparation In early autumn clear away weeds over an area 3 ft square, single digging clear ground and double digging weedy ground. Just before planting, fork in a balanced fertilizer such as a brand of Growmore at the rate of 3 oz per square yard with bonemeal at 2 oz per square yard.

Planting and spacing Plant in the dormant

1 From November to March, prepare the soil. Dig a hole wide and deep enough to take the roots fully extended. Plant the tree against a wired wall for fan-training (or with two stakes and a crossbar for standards).

2 Each February, apply a top dressing of balanced fertilizer at a rate of 3 oz per square yard over the rooting area. Mulch with a 2–3 in layer of well-rotted manure over a radius of 18 in.

season from November to March. Container-grown trees can be planted at any time. Dig a hole wide and deep enough to take the roots fully extended. For trees in the open, before planting drive in a stake to reach just below the lowest branches. Standard cherries require two stakes and a crossbar. For fan-trained trees, erect a system of horizontal wires on the wall using gauge 14 wire and spaced 6 in or two brick courses apart (see pages 14–17).

Plant the tree to the same depth as it was at the nursery. Return the soil and firm it well. Tie to the stake with a tree tie and cushion, or tie in the branches of a fan to the wall wires.

On Malling F12/1 (vigorous) space fan-trees 18–25 ft apart; half-standards and standards at 30–40 ft apart; and bushes 25–35 ft apart. On the rootstock Colt (semi-vigorous), space fans and bushes 15 ft apart and pyramids 12–15 ft apart.

Pruning the fan-trained tree

The sweet cherry fan is pruned as shown in the step-by-step instructions below. Prune in

spring as the buds burst and not in winter because of the risk of bacterial canker. If the maiden tree is well feathered use two strong laterals, one to the left and one to the right at the first wire to form the initial ribs. Tie these to canes fixed to the wires at 35 degrees.

Pruning bushes, half-standards or standards
The first year: the maiden tree Prune in the early spring just as the buds begin to open. The head is formed by cutting back to three or four suitably placed buds in the same way as for the apple (see pages 104–5). The objective is to obtain three or four well-placed primary branches by the end of the summer. Pinch out any flowers that are produced. Shoots lower down on the main stem should be pinched back to four leaves. These help to stiffen the stem and should not be removed until the cherry is four years old.
The second year In spring, prune each leader by one-half to an outward-facing bud. Summer prune the pinched-back shoots on the main stem by pinching out the growing points.

Pruning the fan-trained tree: the first year

The second year

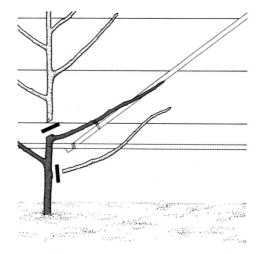

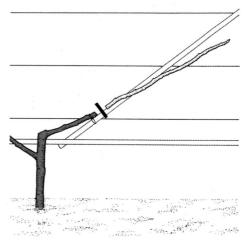

1 In spring, tie two strong laterals to canes fixed to wires at 35 degrees. Head the centre stem back to the uppermost of the selected laterals. Remove all other laterals and protect the cuts.

2 In spring, select suitable buds and shorten each leader to about 12 in. This encourages shoots to develop in the summer which are used as the ribs of the fan.

Sweet and Duke cherries 2

The third year By the third spring six to nine well-spaced leaders should have been formed. Prune them lightly, leaving about 24 in of the previous summer's growth. Prune laterals competing with the leaders back to three buds. Upright laterals in the centre should be cut out because these may grow too vigorously and spoil the shape of the tree. Where there is room, leave other laterals unpruned.

Fourth and fifth years No more leader pruning should be necessary. In the fourth spring clean up the trunk by removing the pinched-back shoots. Protect the wounds.

Pruning an established tree
Very little pruning is necessary while the tree is well furnished with cropping wood and of manageable height. Each year cut out dead, broken, crowded or crossing branches, cutting them flush to avoid any snags. Prune in the spring and protect the wounds.

Grassing down For the first four or five years the soil around trained trees must be kept clear by maintaining a 3 ft wide border along the length of the wall over the spread of the tree. The border may then be grassed down, if the tree is growing satisfactorily.

Bush and standard trees should also be grassed down after five years. For the grass mixture see page 125. Keep the grass clear of the trunk of the tree.

Feeding and watering In February apply a balanced general fertilizer, such as a brand of Growmore, at 3 oz per square yard as a top dressing over the rooting area. Young trees, both fan-trained and in the open, should also be mulched to a depth of 2–3 in over a radius of 18 in.

Cherries against walls require watering in dry spells during the growing season. Once a good set of cherries has been achieved, water the border soil copiously in times of drought. Apply 1 in (4½ gal per square yard) over the rooting area every seven days (ten for the acid cherry) until rain falls. Keep the tree accustomed to moist soil conditions. Do not suddenly give heavy applications of water after the soil has become dry because this may cause the fruits to split.

The third year

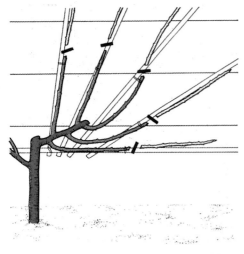

3 In spring, cut back all leaders to suitable buds, leaving 18–21 in of new growth.

Fourth and subsequent years

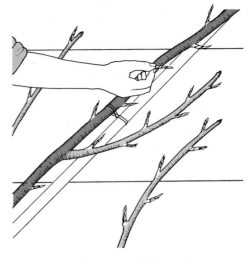

4 In spring, when most of the wall space has been filled, rub or cut out any breastwood or laterals growing directly towards the wall.

'Cristalina' Fair quality. Medium sized blackish red cherry. Ripens mid to late July. Moderate cropper. Tree vigorous, upright with some resistance to frost at flowering time. Self fertile.

'Summer Sun' Excellent quality. Dark red medium sized fruits. Ripens late July. Hardy and reliable. Cropping fair. Moderate vigour. Self fertile.

'Celeste' Good quality. Large, juicy black fruits. Ripens late July. Moderate cropper. Tree very compact with good resistance to black fly. Self fertile.

'Bradbourne Black' Rich, dark crimson cherry. Fruits large, round with dark red flesh. Ripens late July. Heavy cropper. Vigorous, drooping habit. Self infertile.

'Merton Favourite' Excellent flavour. Fruits large, round, black with dark red flesh. Ripens late July. Good cropper. Tree vigorous but compact. Self infertile.

'Van' Sweet flavour. Fruits large, bright red, shiny. Firm dark red flesh. Ripens late July. Regular cropper. Very vigorous. Self incompatible.

'Lapins' ('Cherokee') Excellent quality. Large, black, juicy, firm fruits. Tree vigorous and upright, crops well. Ripens early August. Self fertile.

Pollination
With one or two exceptions (eg the cultivar 'Stella') sweet cherries are not self-compatible, in fact, cross-incompatibility occurs. Most Duke cherries are self-compatible and can be planted singly but a few are not, so before making the final selection of varieties, refer to the pollination tables on pages 96–7.

Protection against frost and birds
It is feasible to protect the blossom of a fan-trained tree against frost, but hardly practicable with a tall standard. Drape the fan with hessian or netting (see pages 12–13). Birds, particularly bullfinches, destroy the buds in the winter and starlings and blackbirds eat the ripe fruits in summer. Where practicable, the best solution is to protect the tree with netting.

Harvesting
Leave the cherries on the tree until ripe unless they start cracking. Pick with the stalk on using scissors or secateurs: if fruits are pulled off and the stalk is left hanging it encourages brown rot. Cherries should be eaten as soon as possible after picking.

Propagation
Cherries are propagated by budding, or by grafting on to rootstocks, tasks normally carried out by the nursery but which can be done by keen amateurs.

Pests and diseases
Cherry blackfly is the most troublesome pest and occasionally caterpillars attack the foliage. Spray with tar oil in December or use dimethoate or heptenophos whenever black-fly occurs. Apply fenitrothion or permethrin against caterpillars, except at flowering.

Bacterial canker is the most serious disease, but silver leaf also occurs. Brown rot can affect the fruits. Spray with bordeaux mixture or copper oxychloride against bacterial canker, in mid-August, in mid-September and finally in mid-October. There is no cure for silver leaf, as yet. Cut the diseased branches back to healthy wood. Fruits affected by brown rot should be picked and burnt as soon as possible.

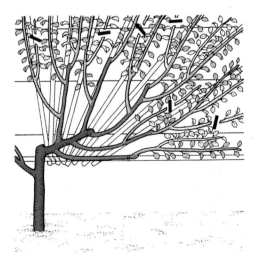

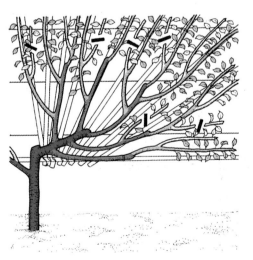

5 In late July, cut back to six leaves any laterals not wanted for the framework. When growth reaches the top of the wall, cut back to a weak lateral just below. Or, bend and tie down the shoots.

6 At the end of September, cut back to three leaves the laterals that were pinched out in July. This encourages fruit buds to form at the base of the shoots in the following year.

Acid cherries

The acid cherry is a culinary fruit derived from *Prunus cerasus*. It is a hardy deciduous tree that is much less vigorous than the sweet cherry and can be grown in a small garden. There are two types of acid cherry: the Morello with dark red, almost black fruits and red juice; and the Amarelle, with red fruits and colourless juice. Both are self-compatible and can be planted singly.

Cultivation

Usually grown as a fan on a wall, or as a bush tree in the open, the acid cherry can also be grown as a central-leader tree in pyramid form.

The acid cherry begins to bear fruit in its third or fourth year. A maiden tree can be planted but a few years are gained if a two- or three-year-old tree already partly shaped by the nursery is obtained.

Soil and situation Provided the soil is well drained, the acid cherry is tolerant of a wide range of soils but it prefers one that is neutral to slightly alkaline (pH 7.0).

The acid cherry flowers early in spring and so should not be planted in a frost pocket. It will tolerate partial shade and can be grown as a fan on a north-facing wall.

Planting and spacing Plant the tree at any time in the dormant season from November to March. Prepare the soil and plant, stake and tie as for the sweet cherry (see pages 134–5). Bush and central-leader trees should be staked for the first four or five years. For fan-trained trees, erect a support system of horizontal wires on the wall before planting. Use gauge 14 wire and stretch the wires at every 6 in or two brick courses (see pages 16–17).

Space bush trees, fans and pyramids on the vigorous rootstock F12/1 15–18 ft apart. On the Colt rootstock, which is less vigorous, space them 12–15 ft apart.

Control weeds and grass by shallow hoeing or use weedkillers (see pages 32–3). Leave a border of uncultivated soil around the tree.

Pruning the fan-trained tree

The formative pruning and training is the same as for a peach fan (see pages 148–53), taking care to cut the leaders back hard in the first three years of training so that densely ribbed head is formed.

Pruning the cropping tree is based on the fact that the acid cherry fruits almost solely on the growths made in the previous summer. As with the peach, the aim is to obtain a constant supply of strong new shoots to carry the next season's cherries.

In spring and early summer, thin out the new shoots to about 4–6 in apart along the framework branches. Leave one replacement shoot at the base of each fruit-carrying lateral. Tie the young shoots to the wires while they are still flexible. Do not pinch out the growing points of the young shoots, but let them extend where there is room.

After harvesting in late August, cut out the laterals that have fruited back to the young replacement shoots.

Some acid cherries are relatively weak growing and the fruiting laterals do not readily produce replacement shoots near the base. If these fruiting laterals are left unpruned and no replacements form, they become extremely long with the base and centre of the fan bare and the crop carried only on the perimeter. When this happens, in March, cut out a proportion of the three- and four-year-old branches back to younger laterals to stimulate new growth.

Pruning the bush and pyramid

The initial training for these forms is the same as for the open-centred bush and pyramid plum (see pages 130–2). The leaders are cut back in early spring as growth begins to establish the framework.

Mature trees bear fruit along young wood formed in the previous season. In March cut back a proportion of the older shoots to one-year-old laterals or young shoots so that old growth is continually replaced.

As the trees become older, the centre may become bare and unproductive. Each August after harvesting, cut back one-third of the main branches to within about 3 ft of the head to produce vigorous young replacement branches. Protect the cuts with a wound paint to avoid infection.

Routine cultivation

For feeding, watering, protection, thinning, harvesting, propagation, pests and diseases see Sweet and Duke cherries (pages 134–7).

Morello By far the most widely planted and regarded as being synonymous with the acid cherry. Juicy with a bittersweet flavour when fully ripe. Flesh soft, dark red. Fruits large, round, very dark red. Crops heavily and regularly. Moderately vigorous on good soils. Ripens August to September. The clone 'Wye Morello' is grown for making cherry brandy.

'Kentish Red' An Amarelle type. Flavour slightly bitter, acid, juicy. Flesh yellow, softish. Fruits small to medium, round, slightly tapering. Skin shiny, bright transparent, scarlet, cropping moderate. Medium vigour. Ripens early July or into August on a north-facing wall. Good resistance to bacterial canker.

Fan-trained tree

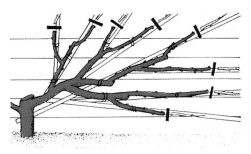

1 For the first three years, follow the steps for formative pruning of a peach fan (see pages 150–3), cutting the leaders back hard.

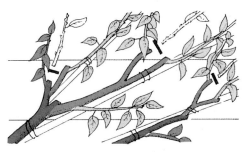

3 After harvesting, in late August, cut out the laterals that have fruited back to the young replacement shoots.

The mature tree

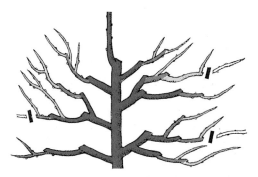

2 In spring and early summer, thin out new shoots to 4–6 in apart along the framework branches. Tie in young shoots to the wires.

Fourth and subsequent years

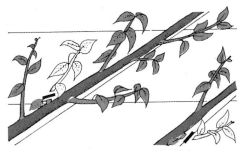

2 In March, cut back some of the older shoots to one-year-old laterals or young shoots to replace the older growth.

Pyramid tree

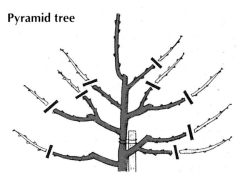

1 For the first three years, follow the steps for the initial pruning of a pyramid plum (see page 130). Cut back the leaders in early spring.

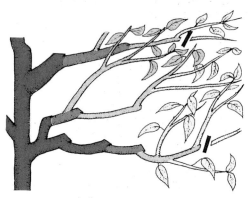

3 After harvesting, if the tree is bare and unproductive, cut back one-third of the main branches to within 3 ft of the head.

Figs 1

Figs in the open

The fig (*Ficus carica*) is a deciduous tree considered to be native to the area ranging from Afghanistan to Syria. It has since spread and is now widely grown, and sometimes naturalized, in all the tropical, sub-tropical and warm temperate regions of the world.

The figs grown in cool temperate regions are parthenocarpic – that is, they will develop fruit without fertilization, so single trees can be grown.

Cultivation

In the Tropics the fig can yield three crops a year, in sub-tropical regions two, and in cool temperate areas only one.

Soil and situation The fig is tolerant of a wide range of soils provided they are well drained. Root restriction is necessary, however, to prevent the tree becoming over-large and vigorous at the expense of fruitfulness. This restriction is provided either by planting the fig in a container, or by planting in a narrow border about 1½–2 ft wide between a wall and a concrete path. The size of the container influences the eventual size of the tree.

The fig is usually hardy in zones 9 and 10 and half-hardy in zone 8. It does, however, require warmth to ripen and, in the cool temperate regions (zone 8), the tree must be planted in the sunniest position possible. This means, for preference, on a south- or south-west-facing wall as a fan. It may also be grown as a bush in a sunny corner bounded by walls or in the open as a half-standard but only in warm areas, for example where the sea has a modifying influence. The fig is susceptible to winter damage to its fruit-bearing shoots and where very hard winters are experienced it is best grown under glass (see pages 144–5).

Preparing the site Before planting, fork into weed-free ground 2–3 oz per square yard of a compound fertilizer, such as a brand of Growmore.

Planting the fan-trained fig Prepare the site for planting by digging a trough about 6 ft long, 2 ft wide by 2 ft deep. This will allow the tree to cover an 8 ft wall with a spread of 15 ft. Make a 2 ft square box if the tree is to cover a 6 ft high by 10–12 ft wide fence. Paving slabs 2 ft square are ideal for the purpose. The

Fan-trained figs

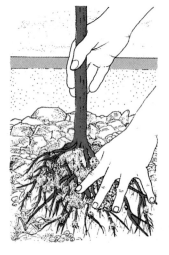

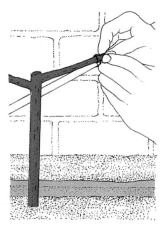

1 From November to March, dig a trough and line it with concrete slabs. Tightly pack the base with broken bricks to a depth of 9 in. Fill it in with good loam.

2 Plant the tree to the same depth as it was at the nursery, spreading the roots well out. Firm the soil. If grown against a wall, plant it 9 in away from the wall.

1 Construct a system of horizontal wire supports on the wall 12 in apart. Tie the branches to the wires with 4-ply fillis string.

'Brown Turkey' Flesh red, rich and sweet. Fruits large, oval. Skin brownish-red with blue bloom. August to September. Reliable and widely grown. Hardy. Prolific cropper.
'Brunswick' Flesh yellow, red near centre, sweet and rich. Fruits very large, oval. Skin green-yellow, brown flushed.

Mid-August. Hardy. Cropping moderate.
'White Marseilles' Flesh practically transparent, sweet and rich. Fruits large, pear-shaped. Skin pale green-white. August to September. Hardy. Reliable, crops well.

---

slabs of the sides of the container should protrude 1 in above the surrounding soil. For good soil drainage leave the base of the trough open but, to prevent the fig forming strong tap roots, tightly pack the bottom with broken bricks, mortar rubble or lumpy chalk to a depth of 9 in; then fill it up with a good fertile loam.

Plant the tree in the dormant season from November to March (see pages 98–9), 9 in away from the wall.

To support the branches construct a system of horizontal wire supports on the wall using galvanized gauge 14 wire, spaced 12 in apart. Tie the branches to the wires with 4-ply fillis string.

Planting a bush or tree in the open In a small garden a bush tree is best but root restriction is necessary to keep it small. Construct a 2½ ft square container with an open base, and fill it in as described above. The half-standard and standard are more suitable for the large garden. Where possible buy a two- or three-year-old tree with the framework partly formed by the nursery.

Standard and half-standard trees should be planted to a stake. Drive in the stake, then plant the tree to the same depth as it was at the nursery (see pages 98-9). Secure the tree to the stake with a tree tie and cushion.

Feeding and watering To maintain fruitfulness, each spring apply 2 oz of a compound fertilizer, such as a brand of Growmore, as a top dressing over one square yard around the tree base, followed by a light mulch of stable manure, rotted compost or peat. With root-restricted figs, give a liquid feed every fortnight once the fruits have developed.

Irrigation is important because a fig growing under root-restricted conditions can quickly become short of water. This is a frequent cause of fruitlet drop in the spring.

Pruning a cropping tree It is important to understand the cropping habit of the fig grown in cool temperate areas because this governs the pruning. The fig bears two crops but only one ripens. The fruits that are successfully harvested are those which develop at the apex of the previous summer's shoots and extend back 6–12 in from the tip. They are carried over the winter as embryo fruits about the size of peas. Provided the

Formative pruning

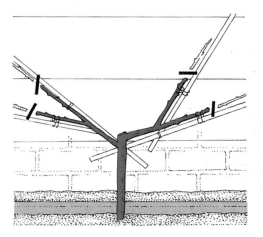

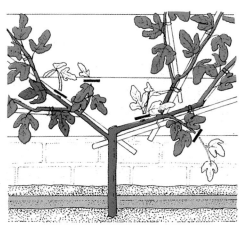

2 From February to March, prune back the leaders by about one-half to a bud. This encourages some of the remaining buds to break and produce more shoots for framework branches.

3 From June to July, select and tie in those shoots growing parallel with the wall so that they radiate out from the centre like a fan. Rub out shoots growing towards the wall. Pinch back breastwood to three leaves.

Figs 2

embryo figs are not destroyed by cold, they develop in the following spring and summer to ripen in August and September. The second crop is produced on the growth made in the current season. These fruits develop throughout the summer but, because the season is not long or hot enough, they are still green by the autumn. They should then be removed. Their removal helps to divert the energies of the plant into developing embryo figs for the next summer.

Fan-trained tree: formative pruning

In the formative years the fig is pruned in the same way as the peach (see pages 148–53), and the aim is to fill in the wall space with strong framework branches. When the hardest frosts are over, from February to March, prune back each leader – there may be five or six – by about one-half to a bud. This is repeated every year until the wall is covered, which should take three or four years. Thereafter prune as for the cropping tree.

Pruning a mature fan-trained tree The aim is to produce each year a plentiful supply of shoots and embryo figs by the autumn.

At the end of June pinch out the growing points of every other young shoot carried by the main framework branches. This encourages the lower buds to break and produce more shoots which will be hardy and produce their own embryo figs by the autumn. As the shoots develop, tie them to the wires. In November prune back to 1 in half the shoots that carried fruits. This encourages new growth from the base in the following spring. All the remaining shoots should be tied in parallel with the wall. Aim for a 9–12 in spacing between the shoots, cutting back to source any growth in between. Do not overcrowd the framework because it is important that plenty of sunlight reaches the young growth, as well as the figs, in summer.

Bush, standard or half-standard tree: formative pruning

The first year With a very young tree where the framework branches have not been formed, select and leave one stout shoot to form the main stem, cutting the remainder back to their point of origin in February. In the following growing season, train the chosen

Pruning a mature fan-trained tree

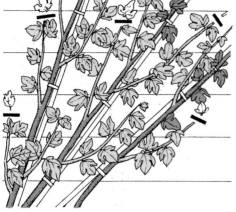

4 At the end of June, pinch out the growing points of about one-half of the young shoots carried by the main framework branches. As the shoots develop, tie them to the wires.

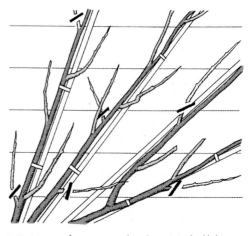

5 In November, prune back to 1 in half the shoots that carried fruits. This encourages new growth from the base in the following spring. All the remaining shoots should be tied in parallel with the wall 9–12 in apart. Cut back to source any growth in between.

shoot up a stout cane driven into the ground 2 in away from the stem.

Next February cut the shoot to a bud at about 4½ ft for a half-standard and 6 ft for a standard. With the latter, it may be necessary to grow it on for a further year before this height is reached.

As a result of heading back, the lower buds should break to form the primary framework branches the following spring. Retain 4–6 well-spaced shoots close to the apex of the stem to form the framework. Cut out any shoots that appear below this.

The third year (or the first year if planting a two- or three-year-old with the framework partly formed) In February cut back the leader of each branch by about one-half to an outward-facing bud.

Subsequent pruning Very little pruning is necessary after the main framework has formed except to remove any badly placed branches. To rejuvenate an old fig where the branches have become rather gaunt and bare, each February cut out a proportion of the older wood back to a young shoot where these exist. In their absence leave a 1 in stub

from which new growth will spring the following season.

Winter protection
Without protection the young shoots and embryo figs are likely to be damaged by frost. Protect them by thatching them loosely in bracken or material of a similar open nature. Use 6 in square plastic netting to retain the thatch. Remove the protection after the last of the hard frosts (see pages 12–3).

Harvesting
The fig is ripe when it is very soft to the touch and hangs downwards. Slight splits in the skin and sometimes a drop of nectar exuding from the eye are signs that the fig is ready for picking. Picked carefully and kept cool (but not in a refrigerator), figs will keep for 2–3 weeks but they are best eaten fresh.

Pests and diseases
The fig is generally trouble-free, but occasionally suffers from the disease coral spot – dead twigs covered in pink pustules. Cut diseased twigs back to a healthy bud. Burn prunings.

**Bush, standard and half-standard trees
The first year**

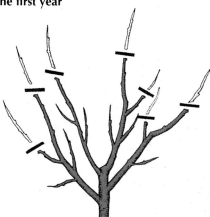

1 In February, on a two- or three-year-old tree, cut back the leader of each branch by one-half to an outward-facing bud.

Subsequent pruning

2 Thereafter, little pruning is necessary after the main framework has formed except to remove any badly placed branches. Where the branches have become gaunt and bare, each February cut out a proportion of the older wood back to a young shoot.

Figs 3

Figs in the greenhouse

Although the fig does produce a reasonable crop when grown in the open in cool temperate areas, it produces heavier crops of higher quality fruit under glass. In addition, if artificial heat is available, more than one crop a year can be expected. Figs can be grown as bushes or fans. Fans require an area of not less than 8–10 ft to allow proper development of the branch system. The back wall of a lean-to greenhouse is most suitable. It can be grown under the roof glass like grapes and peaches but the big leaves cast a dense shade and need extra roof space to develop properly. In a smaller, free-standing greenhouse, grow figs as small bushes in pots (see pages 174–7).

Cultivation

For the best results the greenhouse should receive uninterrupted sunshine for at least half of each day in summer.

Soil Any free-draining soil is suitable but the root run should be restricted to prevent over-exuberant, unfruitful growth.

Planting Take out a hole 3–4 ft square, and 2–3 ft deep. Line with bricks or concrete and proceed in the same way as for figs planted in the open (see pages 140–1). Alternatively, grow the fig in 12 in pots filled with John Innes potting compost No. 1.

Fans require supporting wires, whether trained on the wall or under the glass. For wall wires see pages 16–17. For training against glass, the wires must be suspended about 12 in under the glass to allow room for leaf development. Planting or potting is best done in autumn or winter but it may be delayed until spring if the new plants are pot-grown.

Temperature and watering To get two or more crops of fruit each year, a minimum temperature of 13°C/55°F must be maintained from mid-winter onwards. Ventilation of the greenhouse is only required when the temperature tops 21°–24°C/70°–75°F. On days when the temperature reaches 15°C/59°F, spray the stems and foliage and damp down the floor, preferably with rainwater. Spraying is particularly important in summer because it helps to discourage red spider mite.

However, if one crop of figs is enough, then it is not necessary to provide artificial heat.

When the last fruits have been gathered in autumn, the greenhouse should be left open until it is time to start the trees into growth again. Like peaches and nectarines, the fig needs a cool resting period with the temperature dropping to at least 4°–10°C/40°–50°F at night. During severe frosty weather, the greenhouse is best closed, particularly at night.

As the root system is largely confined to a small area, particularly if in pots, watering must never be neglected. In brick- or concrete-lined beds, water twice a week.

Pruning and feeding Once the main framework of branches has been built up (see pages 140–43), pruning is aimed at providing a supply of young replacement stems upon which the fruit will be borne. Under warm conditions this will consist of thinning out about one-half of the old fruiting stems, cutting them back to two leaves once the first crop of fruits is picked. This is repeated after the second crop, and again if enough warmth is maintained and a third crop matures.

Under cold greenhouse conditions pinch out lateral shoots at the fourth leaf in June, and thin out unfruitful stems in July. The June pinching is optional for mature fans. Thinning is important to prevent congested growth and to allow air and light to penetrate.

Fan-trained trees should be top-dressed each winter with rotted manure or compost, and two or three handfuls of bonemeal. If subsequent growth is not vigorous or is yellow-green, apply 2–3 oz of a general fertilizer, such as a brand of Growmore, to each tree in spring or early summer.

Harvesting and storing

Figs must ripen on the tree before picking (see page 143).

Pests and diseases

Red spider mite is the main pest and mealybugs and scale insects can sometimes be troublesome. Control them by using an insecticidal soap or biological control. The only serious disease is fig virus but it is rarely encountered. Infected trees still grow and crop fairly well but are best replaced if possible.

FIGS IN THE GREENHOUSE
'Bourjasotte Grise' One of the sweetest and
most richly flavoured. Fruits rounded and
somewhat flattened, medium to large. Skin
pale green, suffused purple.
'Brown Turkey' ('Everbearing') See page
141 for description.
'White Marseilles' See page 141 for
description.

1 In autumn or winter, in the prepared
border soil, dig a hole 3–4 ft square and
2–3 ft deep. Line with bricks or concrete
and fill with rubble and soil.

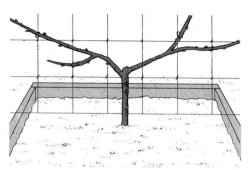

2 Plant the tree as described on pages
140–1. Then, construct a system of wire
supports on the wall or hang 6 in wire
netting 12 in away from the glass.

Pruning the cropping tree

3 In summer, water the plants twice a
week. When the temperature reaches
15°C/59°F spray the plants and damp down
the floor daily.

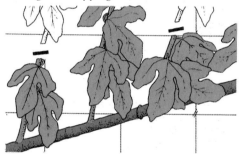

4 In the heated greenhouse, once the first
crop of fruits is picked, cut back about one-
half of the old fruiting stems to two leaves.
Repeat after every crop.

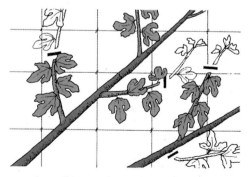

5 In the cold greenhouse, in June, pinch out
lateral shoots at the fourth leaf. In July, thin
out unfruitful stems.

6 Each winter, apply a top dressing of
rotted manure or compost and two or three
handfuls of bonemeal.

Peaches and almonds 1

Peaches, nectarines and almonds (outdoors)

The peach (*Prunus persica*) is a small deciduous tree with long, tapering light green leaves and attractive pink flowers borne singly in the early spring. Despite its name, the peach did not originate in Persia, but almost certainly in China where it was cultivated for many centuries before being introduced to Europe. The peach is grown throughout the warm temperate regions of the world (zones 8–10).

The nectarine is a smooth-skinned sport, or mutation, of the peach. Generally the fruits are smaller than peaches and often considered to have a better flavour. For most cultural purposes, however, it is treated in exactly the same way as the peach although it is slightly less hardy.

The almond tree is similar in size, habit, leaf form and flower to the peach, but it blossoms even earlier and therefore in cooler areas the blooms are frequently destroyed by frost or affected by cold. For this reason in northern latitudes it is grown largely more for its beautiful blossom than its fruit, nevertheless in frost-free springs moderate yields can be gathered.

There are two types of almond, the sweet almond (*Prunus dulcis dulcis*) and the bitter almond (*Prunus amygdalus amara*). In areas where almonds are grown commercially, there are named varieties, but in Britain it is sold as the flowering almond. It is usually grown either as a bush, half-standard or standard and is grafted on to the same rootstocks as the peach.

The ornamental flowering almonds are closely related and their nuts are edible to a greater or lesser degree, depending upon the amount of hydrocyanic acid in the nut. If growing it for its fruit, choose from the two species mentioned (above).

Cultivation

The peach and the nectarine are self-compatible and single trees can be planted. The almond is only partly self-compatible.

Yield The yield from a peach or a nectarine can vary enormously depending upon the size of the tree and the environment. A good average yield from a fan is about 30 lb and from a bush 30–100 lb.

Planting

1 Before planting, fork in 3 oz per square yard of a balanced fertilizer, such as a brand of Growmore, with 3 oz bonemeal. Repeat every February.

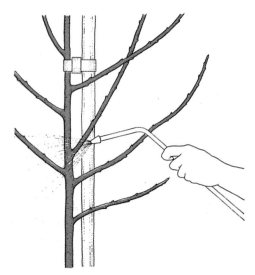

4 At the end of January, in February and at leaf-fall every year, spray with a copper fungicide against peach leaf curl.

PEACHES

Listed in order of ripening, which is based on fruit on a wall in southern England.

'Amsden June' Good flavour, flesh creamy white. Fruits medium, round, green-white with red flush. Crop moderate. Ripens mid-July. Suitable for growing under glass or in the open.

'Duke of York' Good flavour, flesh tender, pale yellow. Fruits large, rich, crimson. Crops well. Ripens mid-July. Suitable for growing under glass or trained against a wall.

'Hale's Early' Good flavour, flesh soft, pale yellow. Fruits medium, yellow with red mottling and flush. Crops well but needs rigorous thinning. Ripens mid- to end July.

Hardy, suitable for growing under glass or on a wall.

'Peregrine' Excellent flavour, flesh firm, juicy, green-white. Fruits large, round, crimson. Crops well, ripens early to mid-August. Suitable for growing under glass, on a wall or out in the open in warmer areas. A good garden cultivar.

2 From November to March, plant during the dormant season. A fan should be 6–9 in away from the wall or fence with the stem inclined towards it.

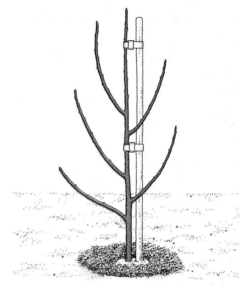

3 After planting, mulch to a depth of 2–3 in with manure or compost for 18 in around the tree. Replenish every year in February.

Thinning

5 From early May to August, give the tree 1 gal of diluted high-potassium liquid feed every 14 days. Thin the fruits, starting when they are the size of large peas.

Harvesting

6 From August onwards, pick the fruit when the flesh feels soft at the stalk end. Hold the fruit in the palm of the hand, lift and twist it slightly.

Peaches and almonds 2

Rootstocks and spacing Three rootstocks are widely used for peaches and nectarines: plum stock St Julien A (semi-vigorous); plum stock Brompton (vigorous) and occasionally peach seedling stock (vigorous). For most gardens St Julien A is adequate.

Fans on St Julien A should be spaced 12–15 ft apart and on Brompton or peach seedling 18–24 ft apart. Space bush trees on St Julien A 15–18 ft and standards on Brompton 18–24 ft apart.

Soil and situation The peach is tolerant of a wide range of soils but it is essential that they are well drained. To improve the drainage of a heavy soil, place brick rubble and chopped up turves in the bottom of the planting hole. The ideal soil is a medium to heavy, moderately limy loam, not less than 18 in in depth with a pH of 6.7–7.0.

The peach is quite hardy, preferring a cold winter and a sunny dry spring rather than a warm, wet winter which causes the buds to open only to be damaged by subsequent frosts. The site must be in full sun and sheltered from cold winds and ideally not in a frost pocket. The peach flowers very early so it is best grown as a fan on a wall or fence with a southerly aspect, where it can be protected against frost at flowering time and benefit from the warmth of the structure. In southern England and further south it can also be grown in the open, usually as a bush and sometimes as a full or half-standard.

Soil preparation Where there are poor soils at the base of a wall, it is worth while preparing the border specially (see page 98).

On good soils, however, it is sufficient to fork in a balanced fertilizer such as a brand of Growmore at the rate of 3 oz per square yard with sterilized bonemeal at 3 oz per square yard over an area of two square yards.

Selecting the tree For a bush tree buy a well-feathered maiden tree. For a fan, obtain a fan already partly formed by the nursery, choosing one with 5–12 shoots (depending upon the age of the tree) that are evenly spaced to form the first ribs of the fan.

Planting Plant during the dormant season from November to March. If planting a container-grown tree, it can be planted at any time. In the prepared soil, dig a hole wide and deep enough to take the roots fully spread out. Plant the tree to the same depth as it was at the nursery.

A fan must be planted 6–9 in away from the wall or fence to allow for growth, with the stem inclined slightly towards its support structure (see page 99).

After planting, apply a 2–3 in mulch of well-rotted manure, compost, peat or mushroom compost for 18 in around the tree.

A system of horizontal wires is necessary to support the fan. Fix the wires to the wall or fence every 6 in or two brick courses apart, starting at 12 in above the ground (see pages 15–17). Tie canes to the wires where needed with thin wire.

Pruning and training

Stone fruits such as the peach are never pruned in the winter because of the risk of silver leaf disease and bacterial canker. They should be pruned while the sap is rising, from February onwards.

The fan-trained tree

The first year In February, starting with the feathered maiden tree, cut back to a lateral at about 24 in above the ground, ensuring that there are two good buds, or laterals, beneath it, one to the left and one to the right. Cut all remaining laterals to one bud. If there is no suitable lateral, cut back to a wood bud which is slender and pointed. If in doubt, cut to a triple bud which consists of two round flower buds and one wood bud.

In the early summer select three strong shoots. Train the topmost shoot vertically and of the other two, train one to the left and one to the right, choosing those that come from just below the bottom wire. Remove all other buds or shoots entirely.

As the two side-shoots lengthen, tie them to canes at an angle of 45 degrees. When both these shoots are about 18 in long, in June or July, cut out the central shoot entirely. Protect the wound with a wound paint.

The second year In February, cut back the two side-shoots to a wood or triple bud at 12–18 in from the main stem. This will induce new shoots in the coming summer. Protect the cuts with wound paint.

In summer, select four strong shoots from

'Redhaven' Good flavour, flesh firm, yellow, reddening near the stone. Fruits medium, round, deep red over yellow. Crops well. Season mid-August. Suitable for growing under glass, on a wall or in the open in warmer areas.

'Rochester' Fair flavour, flesh firm, yellow and juicy. Fruits medium, yellow with a deep crimson flush. Crops well. Ripens early August. Hardy, suitable for growing under glass, on walls or out in the open as a bush. The best all-round cultivar.
'Royal George' Rich and highly flavoured, flesh firm, pale yellow, very red at the stone. Fruits large round, pale yellow with deep red flush. Crops well. Ripens late August to early September. Suitable for growing under glass or on a wall.
'Bellegarde' Richly flavoured, firm flesh. Fruits large, golden-yellow, almost covered dark crimson with darker mottling. Crops well. Ripens early to mid-September. Suitable for growing under glass or on a wall.

each arm. One to extend the existing rib, two equally spaced on the upper side and one on the lower side of the branch to give the tree a total of eight ribs by the end of the season. Pinch back all other shoots as they develop to one leaf.

Carefully train each new shoot to a cane to extend the wings of the fan. Keep the centre open at this stage.

The third year In February shorten each leader by about one-third, cutting to a downward-pointing wood bud. Protect the cuts with a wound paint.

In the summer, allow the leading shoot on each of the eight ribs to extend. Also select three more shoots on each branch and train these outwards, tying them to canes on the wires, to fill in the remaining space on the wall or fence. Rub out buds growing directly towards the structure and breastwood. Of the remaining buds, allow young shoots to grow every 4 in on the upper and lower sides of the ribs. Pinch back to one leaf any surplus shoots. Repeat this process as and when necessary throughout the summer. When the selected laterals have made 18 in of growth, pinch out the growing points, unless they are required as part of the framework. In late summer tie them to canes on the wires. Fruit will be borne on these laterals in the following summer.

Fourth and subsequent years From this point onwards the tree must be regarded as a cropping tree. The wall or fence should now be more or less completely covered with framework branches on which every 4 in are fruit-bearing laterals.

The peach carries its fruits on shoots made during the previous summer so pruning is aimed at a constant and annual renewal of young shoots. It follows also that the shoots which have borne fruits are cut out to make room for the new young ones.

Each late spring, about May, remove shoots growing directly towards and away from the wall or fence but leave one or two leaves on shoots which have flower buds at the base. Next deal with the previous summer's laterals which should be carrying both blossom and side-shoots. Select one side-shoot at the base as the replacement, one in the middle as a reserve and one at the tip to extend the fruit-carrying lateral. Pinch back the remaining side-shoots to two leaves. When the basal side-shoot and the reserve lateral are 18 in long and the fruit-carrying extension lateral has six leaves, pinch out the growing points of each.

Pruning the bush tree The formative pruning is the same as for a bush apple (see pages 104–5) except that the pruning is done in the spring and a few branches in the centre of the tree can be left.

In the cropping years the objective is to encourage plenty of strong new growth each year to carry fruit in the next summer. This pruning should be done in the spring as the young shoots appear. It is occasionally necessary to cut back to young healthy replacements some of the older wood which has become bare. Avoid, however, making large wounds because these encourage bacterial canker to which peaches and nectarines are susceptible.

Feeding and watering In February each year, apply a balanced fertilizer such as a brand of Growmore at the rate of 3 oz per square yard as a top dressing over the rooting area. Replenish the mulch if necessary.

In May start giving a liquid feed every 14 days diluted in a gallon of water at a time, but stop in August when the fruits start to ripen. Use a high-potassium feed such as that sold for tomatoes.

The base of a south-facing wall can become very dry. Once a good set has been achieved, water copiously during dry weather. Apply 1 in, or 4½ gal per square yard, every ten days until rainfall restores the balance. Keep the tree accustomed to moist soil conditions and do not suddenly apply a lot of water near ripening time because there is the risk of splitting the fruits.

Pollination and frost protection

The peach flowers early when there are few pollinating insects about, so it is worth while pollinating the flowers by hand to ensure a full set (see page 95).

Protection of the blossom against frost is also essential from pink bud stage until the danger of frost has passed. Drape the tree with hessian or bird netting (see pages 10–13). Remove it during the day.

Peaches and almonds 3

Thinning
To obtain good-sized fruits it is essential to thin the fruits. Thin over a period, starting when the fruitlets are the size of large peas and stopping when they are the size of walnuts. Peaches should be 9 in apart and nectarines 6 in apart after the final thinning.

Harvesting peaches and nectarines
The fruit is ripe when it has a reddish flush and the flesh feels soft near the stalk end. Hold the peach in the palm of the hand, lift and twist it slightly. It should part easily from the tree. Store the fruits in a cool place until they are to be eaten. They will keep for up to a week only and for long-term storage they must be bottled or frozen without the stones.

Pruning the fan-trained tree after harvesting
Immediately after cropping, not later than the end of September, cut out the laterals which carried the fruits back to the replacement shoots. Tie in the young shoots and cut out any dead or broken branches.

Once the peach has reached the required height and spread, remove any unwanted extension growth by cutting to a lateral further back along the branch. Cut out bare wood back to strong young replacements. Protect the wounds with a wound paint.

Harvesting and storage of almonds
Harvest the nuts in early October when they fall naturally and the husks split. Remove the nuts from the husks and dry them thoroughly in well-ventilated conditions: in sunshine is ideal, or in an airing cupboard. Keep the nuts off the ground by laying them on wire netting to allow air circulation. Once dry they should be kept in cool and dry conditions.

If squirrels are troublesome, harvest the nuts slightly earlier and dry both husk and nut initially before splitting them open.

Propagation
Peaches, nectarines and almonds are propagated by budding or grafting, a task normally carried out by the nursery, but it can be performed by the keen amateur.

Pests and diseases
The most troublesome pest is glasshouse red spider mite, especially on warm walls. This can be controlled by applying bifenthrin, dimethoate or pirimiphos-methyl. Alternatively, use the predacious mite, *Phytoseiulus persimilis*. Occasionally aphids infest the young shoots; control these by spraying with a systemic insecticide as necessary.

The most devastating disease on outdoor peaches and almonds is peach leaf curl. To prevent it, dust or spray thoroughly with bordeaux mixture or spray with copper oxychloride at leaf-fall, end of January and in mid-February. A good alternative to spraying an outdoor fan-trained tree is to cover it with clear plastic to keep the tree's branches and buds dry from early December until after the danger of frost has passed in May or June. Keep the plastic away from the leaves and flowers with canes (see diagram page 13) or better still construct a wooden frame to hold the plastic.

Cultivars
Under glass any of the cultivars listed above will ripen. Outdoors it is best to choose those ripening not later than early September in the south and early August in the north.

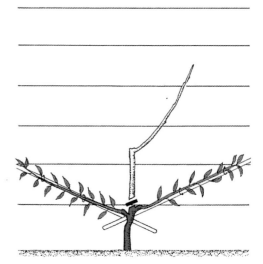

3 In June or July, tie the lengthening side-shoots to canes set at an angle of 45 degrees. Later that summer, cut out the central shoot and protect the cut with wound paint.

'Dymond' Richly flavoured, flesh firm and melting. Fruits large, pale yellow with deep red flush and mottling. Cropping moderate. Ripens mid- to end September.

NECTARINES
'Early Rivers' Rich juicy flavour. Pale yellow flesh. Fruits large, yellow with red streaks. Ripens end July. Suitable for growing under

glass or on a wall.
'Lord Napier' Rich flavour. Flesh white. Fruits large, yellow-orange with a crimson flush. Heavy cropper. Ripens early August. Suitable for under glass or on a wall.
'Humboldt' Rich flavour. Golden-coloured flesh. Fruits medium to large, yellow-orange with a deep crimson flush. Heavy cropper. Ripens mid-August.

'Elruge' Good flavour. Green-white flesh, red near the stone. Fruits medium, round to oval, pale green with a dark purple flush. Ripens end August. Suitable for growing under glass or on a wall.
'Pine Apple' Excellent rich flavour. Yellow flesh. Fruits medium to large, rich crimson red. Ripens early September. Suitable for growing under glass.

The fan-trained tree: the first year

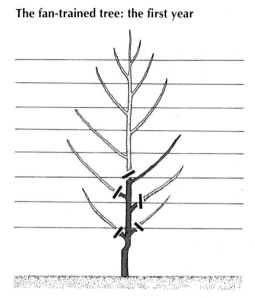

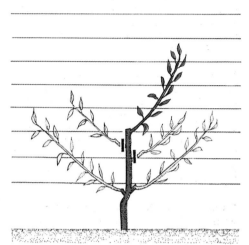

1 In February, cut back a feathered maiden peach to a lateral about 24 in above the ground, leaving one good bud on each side beneath it. Cut remaining laterals to one bud.

2 In early summer, select three shoots. Train the topmost vertically, and one to the left and one to the right. Remove all other buds or shoots.

The second year

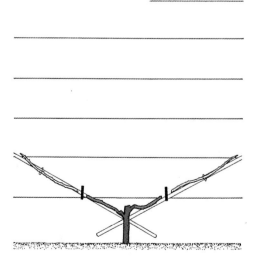

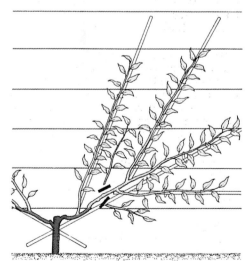

4 In February, cut back the two side-shoots to a wood or triple bud at 12–18 in from the main stem. Protect the cuts with wound paint.

5 In summer, select four shoots on each arm, one to extend the existing rib, two spaced equally on the upper side and one on the lower. Stop other shoots at one leaf.

151

Peaches and almonds 4

The third year

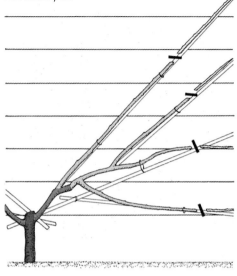

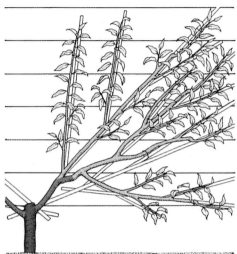

6 In February, shorten each leader by one-third by cutting to a downward-pointing wood bud. Protect the cuts against silver leaf.

7 In summer, allow the leading shoots on each rib to extend. Train three shoots on each branch outwards, tying them to canes. Allow shoots to grow every 4 in.

Fourth and subsequent years

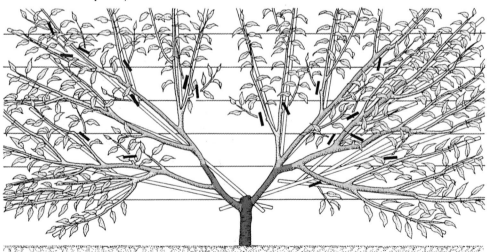

9 Each year in about May, remove shoots growing directly towards and away from the wall or fence. Leave shoots with flower buds at their base one or two leaves.

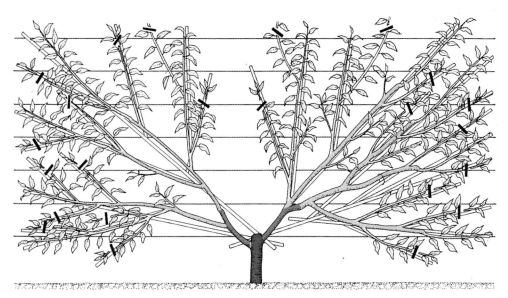

8 In late summer, when the selected laterals have made 18 in of new growth, pinch out the growing points of each and tie them to canes on the wires. These laterals will bear fruit the following summer.

10 Select two replacement laterals on each leader: one at the base and a reserve in the middle. Allow a lateral to extend the fruit-carrying lateral. When the basal and reserve laterals are 18 in long and the extension has six leaves, pinch out the growing points. After harvesting, cut the fruited laterals back to their replacements.

Peaches and almonds 5

Peaches and nectarines in the greenhouse
Owing to the often cool, rainy summers and frosts in Britain, peaches and nectarines do not always mature satisfactorily outside with the result that a tradition of growing them under glass has arisen. In warmer countries they are almost always grown outside.

Fan-trained trees are used for growing under glass and may be grown on the back wall of a lean-to greenhouse or under the roof of a single or double span structure. An area of not less than 10 ft × 7 ft is needed for each tree and 15 ft × 10 ft is ideal.

Peach and nectarine cultivars are propagated by budding on to a seedling peach, cherry plum (Myrobalan) or a form of the common plum rootstock St Julien A. The latter rootstock is ideal for greenhouse culture because it has a semi-dwarfing effect and restricts the peach's vigorous nature.

Cultivation
The greenhouse should receive sunlight for at least half of each day in summer.
Soil preparation Growth is more satisfactory if the plants are rooted into the soil base of the greenhouse. See also Fruit in tubs and pots (pages 174–7). Any well-drained, fertile soil is suitable. If the soil is poor, work in plenty of organic matter. Alternatively, re-soil the border with a fibrous chalky loam, if possible made from turves stacked for six months before use. Add to the loam rubble in the ratio ten soil to one rubble. Two weeks before planting mix in John Innes base fertilizer at the rate of 8 oz per 2 gal bucketful of soil. For one tree the planting site should be at least 3 ft square. For several trees, make a border at least 3 ft wide by the eventual spread of the trees.

Planting and spacing If two or more trees are to be grown, they should be planted 10–15 ft apart. Erect supporting wires as described for wall-trained trees outside (see page 148). Where trees are to be trained under the roof, use long-shanked eye-bolts (vine-eyes) to keep the stems 6–9 in clear of the glass. Plant the tree as described for Peaches and almonds outdoors (see page 148).

Temperature and watering For really early peaches, a minimum temperature of 7°C/45°F should be maintained from late winter until the fruits are formed. Artificial heat is not, however, essential and temperatures can be raised to initiate early flowering by closing the greenhouse from late January or early February. From then on, ventilate only when the temperature rises above 18°C/65°F. Damp

1 Before planting, re-soil the border with a fibrous loam mixed with rubble. Mix in John Innes base fertilizer at the rate of 8 oz per 2 gal bucketful of soil.

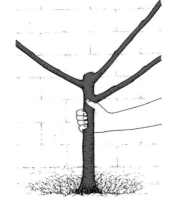

2 From November to March, plant the tree in the prepared border 6–9 in away from the wall or glass. Construct wire supports spaced 6 in apart.

3 From late winter until the fruits form maintain a temperature of at least 7°C/45°F. Ventilate at 18°C/65°F. Spray the foliage with water on sunny days.

down on sunny days until the flowers open and resume when the fruitlets form.

As soon as the foliage starts to expand, spray the trees daily with clean water to create humidity and deter red spider mites. From the time the flower buds begin to swell to leaf-fall, make sure that the plants never lack water. In summer the beds need a soaking at least twice a week, and during hot spells perhaps every other day.

Once the fruits have been picked, leave all the ventilators open until it is time to start the trees into growth again. The peach needs a cool, dormant season although temperatures need not go below 5°–7°C/42°–45°F. Frost will not harm dormant trees.

Feeding In early summer mulch with well-rotted manure or garden compost. Or, use peat and a general fertilizer such as a brand of Growmore at 2–3 oz per square yard. In addition, apply a proprietary liquid feed suitable for tomatoes every ten days from bud burst until the fruits begin to ripen.

Pruning The formative pruning of the fan peach and nectarine in the greenhouse is the same as the peach outdoors (see pages 148–53).

Pollination
Peaches and nectarines are self-fertile but need insects to transfer the pollen. Trees under glass must therefore be pollinated by hand (see page 95).

Thinning
When the fruitlets are about ½ in long, thin them out to about two per cluster. When the fruits are about 1 in long, thin again so that fruits are evenly spaced at 8–10 in apart each way on the branches.

Harvesting
See Peaches and almonds 3 (page 150).

Pests and diseases
Red spider mite is the primary pest under glass, causing mottling of leaves and premature leaf-fall. Aphids may also attack young shoots. Control both pests as on page 150.

Peach leaf curl is seldom troublesome under glass (see Peaches and almonds 3, page 150). Mildew may occur. Dust the tree with sulphur as soon as mildew is noticed repeating every 14 days until it is controlled. Increase the ventilation.

Varieties
Any of the varieties listed on pages 146–51 can be grown in the greenhouse.

4 When the fruitlets are about ½ in long, thin them out to about two per cluster. When the fruits are about 1 in long, thin again, so that the fruits are evenly spaced at 8–10 in apart each way on the branches.

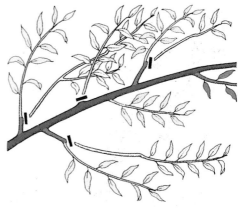

5 After harvesting, cut back the fruiting stems to just above the selected basal shoots. Thin out the crowded growth. Tie in young leafy stems 3–4 in apart to replace those cut out. Ventilate the greenhouse and maintain at a cool temperature.

Apricots

'**Alfred**' Good flavour. Fruit medium to large, round and flattened, orange with pink flush; flesh orange and juicy. Ripens late July to early August. Tends to biennial cropping. Flowers early. Vigorous tree.
'**Breda**' Good, sub-acid flavour and aromatic. Fruit medium to large, squarish, orange with dark red flush and

The apricot (*Prunus armeniaca*) is a hardy deciduous tree. It is a native of China and is widely grown in California, around the Mediterranean and in Australia. With care, it can be grown in zones 6–8.

Cultivation

A dwarf tree is best for the garden where space is limited. Even this can reach a height of 8 ft and a span of 15 ft. Buy a two- or three-year-old tree, already partly formed by the nursery, grafted on to a plum rootstock (such as St Julien A) which is less vigorous than other available rootstocks.

Soil and situation The apricot needs a well-drained but moisture-retentive and slightly alkaline soil with a pH range of 6.5–8.0. Light, sandy soils are not suitable.

Warmth in summer is essential and, although the apricot can be grown in the open in warm temperate areas, it thrives best fan-trained against a south- or west-facing wall in the cooler regions. It can also be grown successfully in containers (see pages 174–7).

Shelter the tree from frost and wind to encourage pollinating insects and to protect the ripening fruit. Keep the soil around the tree clear of weeds and grass so that ample moisture can reach the roots.

Planting In mid-autumn, prepare the ground, clearing away perennial weeds over an area 3 ft square. Dig in well-rotted manure or compost at a rate of one 2-gal bucketful per square yard. Plant the tree (see page 98). Water well and mulch lightly with well-rotted leaf-mould or compost.

Plant fan-trained trees 15 ft apart and 6 in from the wall or fence. Plant bush trees 15–20 ft apart.

Formative pruning and training The formative pruning of the fan-trained apricot is the same as that of the fan-trained peach (see pages 148–53). The formative pruning of the bush apricot is the same as that of the bush plum, but prune it in early spring as growth begins (see pages 130–3).

Pruning the cropping tree Mature fan-trained apricots are pruned in the same way as are fan-trained plums (see pages 130–3). Mature bush apricots are pruned in the same way as acid cherries (see pages 138–9).

The apricot carries the best quality and most abundant crops on short spurs on two- and three-year-old wood. Extensive pruning is not necessary because it results in a poor crop. Every four to six years, cut out the older shoots that have fruited to make room for new young ones. This means cutting out some of the lateral and sub-lateral branches of a fan-trained tree. Retain and tie in the same number of new shoots to replace them. Do not prune or pinch back these shoots until the second season and then only if required.

Thinning Thin the fruits at intervals from the time they are the size of cherries until they are almost full size. First remove misshapen fruits and those growing towards the·wall. Later, thin pairs and clusters so that those left to ripen have 3–4 in between them.

Feeding Root dryness is a common problem with wall-trained trees. Water generously until the root area is soaked, especially if the weather is dry when the fruit is setting or when it starts to swell.

In late winter, sprinkle nitro-chalk around the tree at a rate of 1 oz per square yard and apply a general fertilizer, such as a brand of Growmore, at a rate of 2 oz per square yard. Every four years, if necessary, apply lime to maintain the pH at a little above 7.0. In late spring, mulch the root area to a depth of 1 in with leaf-mould or compost.

Pollination Apricots are self-compatible but, because the flowers open early in spring when few insects are about, hand pollination is sometimes necessary (see page 95).

Protecting the blossom The apricot is highly susceptible to frost damage. Protect it with polythene or netting (see pages 10–13).

Harvesting

Depending on the cultivar, apricots ripen from midsummer to early autumn. The fruits are ripe about one week after they have stopped swelling and reached their full colour. Pick the ripe fruit carefully and try not to break the skin. It should come away easily in the hand.

Pests and diseases

Major diseases are silver leaf bacterial canker and apricot die-back (see page 26); major pests are aphids and red spider mite. See peaches and nectarines (page 150) for details.

brown and red dots; flesh orange, moderately firm and juicy. Ripens mid-August against walls and September in the open. Heavy cropping but tends to be short-lived. Flowers mid-early to late. Moderately vigorous tree.

'Early Moorpark' Rich flavour. Fruit round to oval, yellow with crimson flush and darker mottling; flesh deep orange and

juicy. Ripens late July. Heavy cropping. Vigorous when young.

'Farmingdale' Very good flavour. Fruit medium, roundish, orange-yellow with red flush; flesh orange and moderately juicy. Ripens late July. Heavy cropper. Vigorous, fairly disease-resistant tree.

'Hemskerk' Good, very sweet, rich flavour. Fruit large, conical, yellow with red

patches; flesh golden yellow. Ripens early August. Good cropper. Moderately vigorous tree.

'Moorpark' Very popular cultivar. Rich sweet flavour. Fruit large, uneven round, pale yellow with reddish-brown flush and dots; flesh orange, firm and juicy. Ripens late August. Regular cropper. Moderately vigorous growth. Prone to die-back.

1 In mid-autumn, in prepared ground dig a hole large enough for the roots. Plant at the same depth as at the nursery. Mulch well.

A three-year-old fan-trained tree

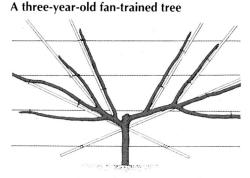

2 Erect supporting horizontal wires 9 in apart on the wall or fence. Tie in the young branches to the canes on the wall wires.

The first year

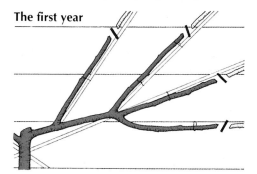

3 In February, shorten each leader by one-third, leaving about 30 in of growth.

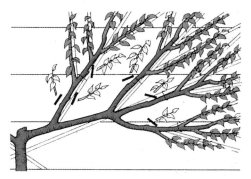

4 In July/August, select and tie in three additional shoots from each pruned leader. Pinch out all remaining shoots.

The second and subsequent years

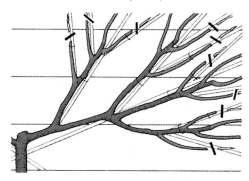

5 In spring, rub out buds pointing towards or away from the wall or fence. Prune the leaders by one-quarter.

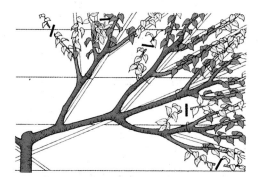

6 Early in July, pinch off the tips of side-shoots at six leaves. After cropping, cut back these laterals by one-half.

Mulberries

The common or large black mulberry (*Morus nigra*) is a deciduous tree native to western Asia, now grown throughout Europe. The red-black fruits resemble loganberries and have a sharp but sweet flavour.

Cultivation

The mulberry is long-lived and decorative. It is self-compatible and so will fruit if grown as a single plant. When mature it reaches a height of 20–30 ft.

Soil and situation The mulberry is tolerant of a variety of soils but thrives best planted in rich, fertile well-drained but moisture-retentive soil with a pH of 5.5–7.0.

It is hardy in zones 5–8 and should be planted in a sheltered, warm and sunny position. In colder areas it is best grown against a south-facing wall or fence.

Planting Between November and March, prepare the ground thoroughly, clearing away perennial weeds over an area 3 ft square. For planting in the open, drive in a stake to reach just below the lowest branches. For wall- or fence-trained trees, construct a system of supporting horizontal wires spaced every 9 in (see pages 15–17).

Dig a hole wide and deep enough to take the roots fully extended. The roots are brittle and so take care not to damage them at planting. Never dig near a mulberry tree.

Plant the tree to the same depth as in the nursery, spreading the roots out well. Return the soil and firm it carefully. Tie the tree to the stake with a tree tie and cushion. For wall-trained trees, tie in the branches to the wall wires. Water well and mulch with well-rotted manure or compost.

Pruning and training The mulberry is slow growing, taking eight to ten years to begin cropping, so a three- to five-year-old tree already shaped at the nursery is best.

Prune mulberries grown in the open in winter. Cut back to four or five buds any strong laterals longer than 12 in that are not required as framework branches. Remove or shorten any which spoil the shape of the head. Protect the cuts with a wound paint.

Trees in the open

1 In autumn, clear the ground of perennial weeds. Dig a hole wide and deep enough to take the roots. Drive in a stake.

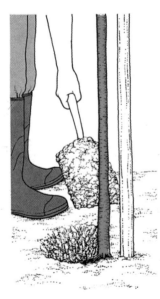

2 Plant the tree, spreading the roots out. Return and firm the soil. Tie the tree to the stake. Water well. Mulch with manure or compost.

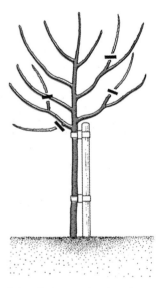

3 In winter, cut back to four or five buds laterals longer than 12 in not required for the framework. Cut out branches spoiling the head.

Prune wall-trained mulberries in summer. Train in the main branches 15–18 in apart to cover the wall. Tie down the leaders at the end of the summer and once they have reached the required length stop them by cutting back each leader to one bud on the previous year's growth in April. Prune side-shoots to four or five leaves in late July to encourage fruit spurs to form.

The branches of mature trees become crooked and brittle and may need supporting with a forked stake. Wrap the branch with sacking where it meets the crotch.

Watering and feeding Watering is necessary in extremely dry weather.

In February, apply a balanced fertilizer, such as a brand of Growmore, at a rate of 2 oz per square yard. In spring, mulch with well-rotted manure or compost.

Propagation

Propagate from cuttings. In early October, after leaf-fall, remove a one-year-old stem with all the year's growth. Make a sloping cut just above the proposed top bud and a horizontal cut about 6 in below it. Dip the basal cut only in rooting hormone. Heel in several cuttings, in bundles of ten, into a sandbox almost to their full depth. Label them and leave for the winter.

Just before the dormant buds break in spring, dig the propagation bed thoroughly. Make a furrow 5 in deep. Lift the cuttings and plant vertically 4–6 in apart. Firm back the soil leaving about 1 in of the cutting exposed. The following autumn, lift and transplant the rooted cutting.

Harvesting

The fruit ripens from late August over a period of about three weeks. Pick fruit for cooking when it is slightly unripe. Dessert fruit is almost black and comes off easily.

Pests and diseases

The mulberry is generally free of pests and diseases but protect the ripening fruit against birds (see page 33).

Wall-trained trees

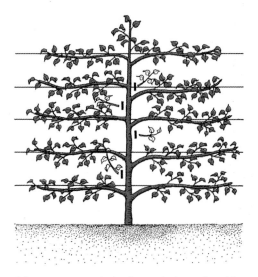

1 In summer, train in the main branches 15–18 in apart. Tie down the leaders at the end of summer. Cut out breastwood and any branches growing into the wall.

2 In April, once the leaders have reached the required length, stop them by cutting back to one bud on the previous year's growth. In late July, prune the side-shoots to four or five leaves.

Elderberries

The common elder (*Sambucus nigra*) is a deciduous tree native to Europe, western Asia and parts of northern Africa and now grows wild over much of the USA and Canada. The shiny purple-black berries are widely used in preserves, and both the fruit and flowers are popular for making wine. The plant grows as a large shrub or small tree and is often considered too wild and vigorous for the garden. Its new woody growth gives off an unpleasant smell and was used in the past as a fly-repellent. In the northern USA, the American or sweet elder (*S. canadensis*) is widely grown and several improved clones are available.

Cultivation
Only elders with black berries are grown for their fruit. The red-fruited kinds are inedible.
Soil and situation The elder is tolerant of a wide variety of soils, including those with bad drainage, and a wide range of soil pH. It is lime-tolerant.

The elder will grow in most situations but it fruits most freely in a sunny position. Common elder is hardy in zone 6; *S. canadensis* in zone 4.

Planting The elder may be grown as a standard on a single stem but it is more usually grown as a large rounded bush with a number of branches from near ground level.

Plant a one- or two-year-old tree in mild weather between October and March. Four weeks before planting prepare the ground, clearing away perennial weeds over an area 3 ft square. Fork in a balanced fertilizer, such as a brand of Growmore, at a rate of 3 oz per square yard.

Dig a hole wide and deep enough to take the roots fully extended. For standards, drive in a stake to reach just below the lowest branches. Place the plant in the hole at the same depth as at the nursery and then fill in the soil gradually, firming it at the same time. Tie the standard to the stake with a tree tie and cushion. The stooled bush does not need staking or tying.

The American elder is not self-compatible – that is, it will not set fruit with its own pollen. For cross-pollination to occur there should be a minimum of two varieties, planted about 10 ft apart.

Pruning After planting, cut out weak and damaged growth and cut back main shoots by a few inches to a good, outward-facing bud. This ensures that during the first growing season the plant's energy is concentrated on producing a strong basic framework of branches. Cut back any unwanted suckers to ground level. Little flower is produced in the first year of growth.

In subsequent years, in winter, cut out dead and congested branches to maintain a good shape. Cut out about a quarter of the old wood back to base each year to encourage new growth. Cut back unwanted suckers to ground level and protect the cuts with a good coating of wound paint.

Feeding In dry spring and summer weather water well and mulch the root area with well-rotted manure or compost. If growth is weak or slow, feed with a general fertilizer, such as a brand of Growmore, at a rate of 2 oz per square yard in April.

Propagation
In late October take a 9–12 in cutting from a sturdy one-year-old stem. Plant in open ground 6 in deep. Alternatively, in July, take 4–6 in cuttings of semi-hard wood stems. Insert them 2 in deep in a cold frame 4–6 in apart. In October in the following year, lift the rooted cuttings and carefully replant them in a permanent position.

Harvesting
The fruit ripens from mid-August to early September. Pick when it is dark in colour with a noticeable bloom. It keeps well in a refrigerator for about two weeks.

Pests and diseases
The elder is generally free of pests and diseases. Aphids can sometimes be troublesome. If so, spray with dimethoate or heptenophos in spring (see pages 26–31). Birds may take the ripening fruit.

Cultivars
In Britain there are no specially named cultivars for fruit but in Europe, where elderberries are grown commercially, there are a number including 'Korser' and 'Sambu', which are both excellent croppers.

'Adams' Very large clusters and berries. Ripens early August. Strong, vigorous bush. Productive.
'Kent' Large clusters and berries. Ripens about ten days earlier than 'Adams'. Vigorous and productive plant.

'Nova' Sweet flavour. Large fruit. Ripens early and uniformly in the cluster. Produces suckers easily.
'York' The largest fruit, in heavy clusters. Very large, productive plant.

The first year

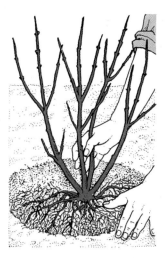
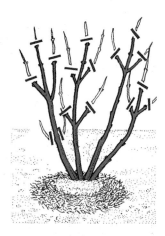

1 Four weeks before planting, clear away weeds over an area 3 ft square. Fork in a general fertilizer at 3 oz per square yard.

2 Between October and March, plant the elder at the same depth as it was in the nursery, spreading the roots out. Firm the soil. Water well.

3 After planting, cut out all weak growth and cut back the main shoots a few inches to a good outward-facing bud. Mulch well.

Second and subsequent years

4 In April, if growth is slow, feed with a compound fertilizer, such as a brand of Growmore, at a rate of 2 oz per square yard.

5 In winter, cut out dead and congested branches. Cut out about a quarter of the old wood back to base. Seal the cuts with a wound paint.

Quinces and medlars 1

The true quince (*Cydonia oblonga*) is a native of central to south-western Asia. It has been cultivated since ancient times and is now naturalized in southern Europe. It is related to the pear, for which it is often used as a root-stock to induce a more dwarfing effect on the vigour of the pear tree. The true quince is often confused with its distant relatives the oriental quinces (*Chaenomeles* spp), referred to as "Japonicas", which are grown as garden shrubs. "Japonicas" have light pink to deep red flowers, spines and edible fruits.

The true quince is a low, deciduous, thornless tree with a crooked irregular mode of growth. When fully grown it is about 12 ft in height and spread, although it can be half as tall again on fertile soils. It may also be grown as a fan against a warm wall in much the same way as a pear. This method is particularly suitable for more northerly areas.

The tree's natural form is attractive and it can serve an ornamental purpose in the garden. It often lives to a great age and, once established, requires little attention. It comes into cropping in the fourth to fifth year. The flowers are large (1½–2 in), solitary, white to very light pink and most attractive, resembling the wild dog-rose. It has a pale grey bark and dark green oval leaves with downy white undersides.

Quince fruits are apple- or pear-shaped, mostly with a greyish-white down on the skin; when ripe they are pale or deep, clear, golden-yellow. The flavour is acid and astringent, and the texture rather gritty – they are too harsh, in fact, to be eaten raw when grown in northern climates. When grown in warmer, sunnier areas (such as Turkey), the fruits become much sweeter and are eaten raw. Quinces are not grown commercially in cool temperate areas, but they can be cultivated fairly easily by the amateur, providing an interesting alternative to the more conventional tree fruits.

Quinces make a delicious orange-coloured jelly, marmalade or preserve; and a slice or two of quince in an apple pie provides a subtle aromatic taste to the dish.

Cultivation

The tree is hardy in zones 4–7, but, as mentioned above, warmth is necessary for the fruits to ripen properly. Quinces can be raised from seed but this is a lengthy process so buy a plant from a nursery.

Soil and situation The quince succeeds in most soils but grows best in a deep, light, fertile and moisture-retentive soil.

It does well planted near a pond or stream. In warmer areas, it can be grown in the open, but in a sunny, sheltered position. In more northerly areas, extra protection is needed, the best situation being a sunny corner where two walls meet, with the plant grown as a fan or bush tree.

Planting and spacing Since it has a rather crooked mode of growth, the quince tree needs support for the first three or four years of its life until the stem has acquired sufficient strength to support the head.

Plant at any time during the dormant period from November to March. Container-grown plants can be planted at any time of the year. Prepare the ground thoroughly in the autumn before planting, clearing away perennial weeds over an area 3 ft square. Fork in 4 oz per square yard of a compound fertilizer such as a brand of Growmore and a

Planting the tree

1 Between November and March, prepare the ground, clearing away perennial weeds over an area 3 ft sq. Fork in 4 oz of a compound fertilizer such as a brand of Growmore and a handful of bonemeal.

'Bereczcki' Very similar to 'Vranja'.
'Champion' Fruits pear-shaped, 4 in dia., yellow; flavour delicate. Tree very productive, starting to bear freely when young.
'Lusitanica' (Portugal) Fruits pear-shaped, 5–7 in long; skin deep yellow covered with grey down; juicy, excellent for cooking and preserving. The tree is taller and more vigorous than other cultivated varieties, but less hardy. The best quince, but suited to warmer areas.
'Maliformis' (Apple-shaped quince) Fruits 2½ in dia., of a rich golden colour. Very productive, ripens in a colder climate.
'Meech's prolific' Fruits fairly large, 5–7 in long, pear-shaped. Flavour excellent. Colour bright golden-yellow, skin smooth. Flowers very large. Growth vigorous; early into cropping.
'Vranja' This was introduced from the Vranja region of southern Serbia, Yugoslavia, where it has been grown for many years. The fruits are pear-shaped, 5–7 in long, very fragrant, of a clear shining gold. Fine flavour. Growth vigorous. A precocious cropper.

---

handful of bonemeal. Drive the supporting stake in first so that it will just clear the lowest branches. Dig a hole deep and wide enough to take the whole root system with the roots spread well out. Plant with the main stem about 2 in away from the stake and the tree at the same depth as it was in the nursery, ensuring that the union between the rootstock and scion (grafted stem) is not less than 4 in above soil level. Firm the soil well. Tie the tree to the stake with a tree tie and cushion.

Bush trees should be spaced 10–12 ft apart, half-standards at 15 ft, and standards 20 ft apart.

Pruning and feeding The quince is a difficult tree to train in the first year, and so it is best to obtain a tree already partly shaped by the nursery. Buy a two-year-old for a bush tree or a three- or four-year-old for a full or half-standard.

The aim is to achieve a goblet-shaped tree with an open but by no means barren centre. Prune during winter for the first three or four years by cutting back the leaders of the main framework branches by one-half the previous summer's growth, to an outward-facing bud. Prune back to two or three buds any side-shoots that compete with the leaders and those crowding the centre. Leave other side-shoots unpruned to fill in the framework where there is room. Twist off any suckers around the base and cut off unwanted shoots on the main stem back to their point of origin. After the fourth year, little pruning is necessary apart from the removal of shoots that cause crowding, low-lying branches, or suckers at the base. The quince bears its fruit on spurs and on the tips of the previous summer's growth, therefore prune only to keep the head tidy. Cut back any vigorous or badly placed laterals but do not prune every lateral otherwise a large number of fruit buds will be lost.

Each February apply a general fertilizer such as a brand of Growmore at 3 oz per square yard, and in late March apply sulphate of ammonia at 1 oz per square yard. On poor soils, mulch the trees in the early spring with well-rotted manure or compost. Maintain a weed-free area over an 18 in radius around the base of the tree.

2 Drive a prepared stake about 1½–2 ft into the ground and dig out a hole deep and wide enough to take the root system with the roots spread out well.

3 Then, plant the tree to the same depth as it was at the nursery, about 2 in away from the stake, firming well during planting. Level off and rake the surface clean. Tie to the stake using a tree tie and cushion.

Quinces and medlars 2

Harvesting and storing

The fruits should be left on the tree as long as possible to develop their full characteristic flavour, provided there is no danger of frosts. They usually ripen from the middle of October to the beginning of November, depending on the locality. Once gathered, they should be stored in trays or apple boxes in a cool dark place and allowed to mellow for about a month before use. Quinces are strongly aromatic and should be stored by themselves because their aroma will affect the taste of any other stored fruits nearby.

Pests and diseases

Many of the insect pests such as aphids, codling moth, slugworm and various caterpillars that attack apples and pears also attack quinces. If these pests prove troublesome, a spray programme similar to that for apples and pears may be used.

The only diseases that may occur are leaf blight (*Entomosporium maculatum*) and brown rot of the fruit. To prevent them, spray with bordeaux mixture in mid-June and again two or three weeks later.

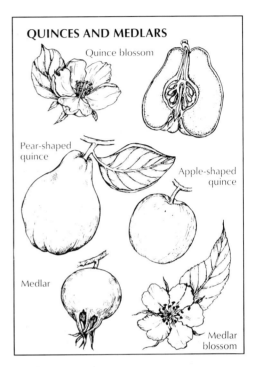

QUINCES AND MEDLARS

Quince blossom

Pear-shaped quince

Apple-shaped quince

Medlar

Medlar blossom

The first winter after planting

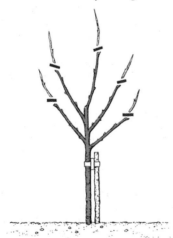

4 Cut back the leaders of the main framework branches by about one-third of the previous summer's growth, pruning each to an outward-facing bud. Cut back to 2–3 buds weak and badly placed lateral shoots.

In the second and third years

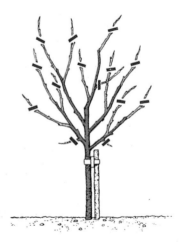

5 In winter, cut back the leaders of the main framework branches by about one-third of the previous summer's growth to an outward-facing bud. Cut back weak and badly placed lateral shoots to 2–3 buds.

'Dutch' A handsome tree, flat-headed and rather weeping. Flowers late May. Fruits are 2–2½ in dia., russet brown. Flavour fair.
'Nottingham' A more upright tree than 'Dutch'; growth straggly. Flowers late May. Fruits small, about 1½ in dia. Flavour good.

'Royal' A moderately upright tree of good habit. Flowers late May. Fruits 1½–2 in dia. Flavour and cropping good.

Medlars

The medlar (*Mespilus germanica*) is related to the quince, hawthorn and other rosaceous plants. It is a native of south-eastern Europe and Asia Minor, although it is widely naturalized throughout a large part of northern Europe. It is a deciduous long-lived tree armed with thorns, but these are often lacking in the cultivated varieties. Medlars have an attractive, tortuous weeping habit and are admirably suited to the ornamental part of an average-sized garden. They are slow-growing and when mature may reach from 12–20 ft in height, depending upon the environment and variety. The leaves are oval or spear-shaped, dull green and downy, changing to a reddish-brown in the autumn. The white or pink-tinged flowers resemble those of the quince, and are 1–1½ in in diameter, borne singly in May or June at the ends of short stubby shoots.

Medlars are self-fertile and fruit freely without cross-fertilization. When ripe, the fruits are russet-brown and vary in size from 1–2 in in diameter, depending on the cultivar. In shape, the medlar fruit resembles a large flattish rose hip with a russet skin. Embedded in the flesh are five stone-like carpels containing the seeds.

The flavour is by no means to everyone's taste. The fruits are eaten when they reach a point of incipient decay, a process called "bletting". Medlars can also be used to make a bright, orange jelly with a distinctive flavour not unlike that of quince.

Cultivation

The medlar is tolerant of a wide range of soils provided that they are well drained.
Situation The tree is hardy in zones 4–7. The site should be sunny and yet sheltered, because the leaves and flowers are easily damaged by strong winds.
Planting and spacing Usually a tree supplied by a nursery is two or three years old, full or half-standard. If more than one is planted, space them not less than 15 ft apart. Staking in the early years is essential, especially for those cultivars with a weeping habit, because the head needs support. Plant in the dormant season from November to March. Prepare the ground thoroughly in the autumn before planting, clearing away any perennial weeds over an area 3 ft square. Fork in 4 oz of a compound fertilizer such as a brand of Growmore and a handful of bonemeal. Drive a stake in first so that it will just clear the lowest branches and then dig out a hole deep and wide enough to take the whole root system with the roots well spread out. Plant with the stem about 2 in away from the stake, ensuring that the base of the tree is at the same depth as it was in the nursery. Ensure the union between stock and scion is at least 4 in above soil level. Tie to the stake using a tree tie and cushion. Firm the soil during planting, level it off and rake the top surface clean. If the soil is light, apply a 3 in layer of well-rotted manure or compost as a mulch around the base of the tree, keeping it just clear of the stem. The mulch helps to keep the soil cool and moist.
Pruning and feeding Each winter for the first three or four years, cut back the leaders of the main framework branches by about one-third of the previous summer's growth, pruning to an outward-facing bud. Cut back to two or three buds any badly placed shoots that cross over the centre. Other shoots may be left unpruned to fill in the framework where there is room. Thereafter, pruning should be light, just sufficient to keep the head in good shape. Prune out overcrowded growth and dead wood.

In March each year apply a compound fertilizer, such as a brand of Growmore, at 3 oz per square yard as a top dressing.

Harvesting and storing

Medlars are ready for picking in late October or early November when they part from the shoot easily. Pick the fruits when the weather is dry and dip the stalks in a strong salt solution to inhibit rotting. They are unpalatable at this stage and should be "bletted". To do this, store them in a cool, dry place, eye downwards and not touching each other, for two to three weeks until the flesh softens and turns brown.

Pests and diseases

Relatively trouble-free, but occasionally attacked by leaf-eating caterpillars. Control as for apples, see page 125–6.

Cobnuts and filberts

Cobnuts and filberts are derived from two European species of *Corylus*. They are both bushy trees that bear separate clusters of male and female flowers on the same tree. The cobnut (*C. avellana*) has soft yellow male catkins. The filbert (*C. maxima*) bears decorative male catkins that range in colour from yellow-green to claret-red. Its nut is longer and proportionately narrower than that of the cobnut and its long, tapering husk totally envelops it.

In the USA, *C. avellana* is known as the filbert and *C. maxima* as the giant filbert.

Cultivation

The cultivation of cobnuts and filberts is identical.

Soil and situation The trees will grow on almost any soil from light gravel to heavy loam, but they require moderately good drainage. They are lime-tolerant and do best on a medium loam over limestone with a pH of 7.5–8.0. Rich soils tend to cause vigorous leafy growth at the expense of the nut yield.

As these are woodland plants by nature, they tolerate light shade but usually produce heavier crops in an open sunny position.

Plant them where they are protected from cold, wet winds because the flowers, which open from the end of January to early February, are susceptible to wind damage. They are hardy in zones 6–9.

For good crops, keep the ground clean between the trees. Fork the soil in autumn and hoe regularly in spring and summer.

Planting Plant two- or three-year-old trees from late November to early March.

Four weeks before planting, prepare the ground thoroughly, clearing away perennial weeds over an area 3 ft square. Lightly fork in lime at the rate of 7 oz per square yard.

Dig a hole wide and deep enough to take the roots fully extended. Drive in a stake to reach just below the lowest branch. Plant the tree to the same depth as at the nursery. Return the soil, and firm it in. Tie the tree to the stake with a tree tie and cushion and water well. If planting more than one tree, allow 15 ft between them.

Pruning Both the cobnut and filbert are best grown in bush tree form with a 15 in tall stem and six or seven good main branches, giving an open cup or goblet shape.

Prune in late February during the latter

The first four to six years

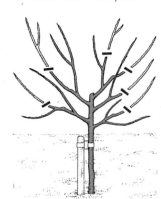

1 In autumn, after preparing the soil, dig a hole large enough to take the roots spread out well. Drive in a stake. Plant the tree, firming the soil. Tie the tree to the stake.

2 In late February, cut back the leaders by about half to an outward-facing bud. Cut back vigorous laterals to three or four buds. Twist and pull out suckers.

3 In January, apply a compound fertiliser at a rate of 3 oz per square yard. Every third winter, on acid soils, to keep the soil alkaline, fork in lime at a rate of 7 oz per square yard.

COBNUTS

'Cosford' Good flavour. Large, oblong nut with a short husk. Catkins numerous, bright yellow. Good pollinator. Heavy cropper. Vigorous tree.

'Nottingham Cob' Good flavour. Small to medium, flattened round nut. Catkins prolific, pale yellow. Good pollinator. Good cropper. Dwarfish growth.

FILBERTS

'Kentish Cob' ('Lambert's Filbert') Good flavour. Very long, large nut. Catkins sparingly produced, short, yellow-green. Abundant cropper. Moderately vigorous, upright growth. Widely planted.

'Purple Filbert' Excellent flavour. Medium nuts in purple-red husk. Long, dark red catkins. Moderate cropper.

Vigorous and ornamental tree.

'Red Filbert' Excellent flavour. Small, long and narrow nut with a reddish husk. Catkins sparse, long, claret-red. Moderate cropper. Vigorous and ornamental tree. Requires a pollinator.

'White Filbert' Similar to 'Red Filbert' but with a white husk over the nut.

---

part of flowering. For the first four to six years, cut back the leaders by about half to an outward-facing bud. Keep the trees at a height of 6–7 ft and, if necessary, cut back to a lateral at the required height. Cut back vigorous laterals to three or four buds. Do not prune the laterals that bear the tiny red female flowers (these are usually carried on the weaker shoots). Twist and pull out suckers around the base. Cut out any dead and crowded branches.

In August, break off by hand strong lateral growths to about half their length (six to eight leaves from the base) and leave them hanging. This is called "brutting" and allows air and light into the tree to help ripen fruit buds. It is the brutted side-shoots which are usually shortened back a further 2–3 in in winter.

Feeding In January, apply a compound fertilizer, such as a brand of Growmore, at a rate of 3 oz per square yard. In late February, apply nitro-chalk to old trees making poor growth, at a rate of 1 oz per square yard.

In autumn, on light soils, lightly fork in well-rotted manure or compost at the rate of one 2 gal bucketful per square yard.

Every third winter, on acid soils, to keep the soil alkaline, lightly fork in lime at a rate of 7 oz per square yard.

Pollination Disturbance of pollen by pruning at pollination time is highly beneficial, so leave winter pruning until late February or early March.

Propagation

The most usual methods are by layering or by removing suckers.

For layering, select a young vigorous stem in spring and mark its position on the soil 9 in behind its tip. Dig a hole with one straight side 4–6 in deep. Peg the stem down against the straight side, and return and firm the soil. Keep the soil moist.

In late autumn, after leaf-fall, sever the layered stem from the parent plant. Four weeks later, cut off the growing tip. Lift and transplant the layered stem.

Pests and diseases

Aphids, winter moth caterpillars and nut weevil can occur but seldom cause significant problems. The trees are generally free of disease.

In subsequent years

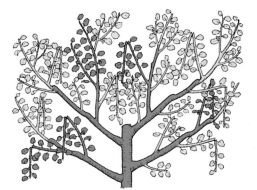

4 In August, break off by hand strong lateral growths to about half their length (six to eight leaves from the base) and leave them hanging. This allows air and light into the tree and helps the fruit buds to ripen.

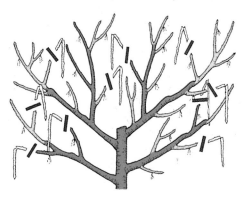

5 In February, cut back previously brutted laterals to three or four buds. Do not prune laterals carrying female flowers. Twist out suckers around the base and cut out dead and crowded growths.

Sweet chestnuts and walnuts

Sweet (Spanish) Chestnuts

A native of southern Europe and North Africa, the sweet, or Spanish, chestnut (*Castanea sativa*) is now widely cultivated throughout Europe. It is hardy in zones 5–9. In southern areas the sweet chestnut is grown for both nuts and timber, but in northern areas it tends to be grown more for effect as a single tree or for coppicing. Grown as a central-leader standard, it reaches a height of about 35 ft in 20 years and may eventually grow to 70–100 ft so it is not suitable for small gardens.

Cultivation

There are two types of chestnut, the marron and the domestic. Marrons are the most important if the tree is cultivated for its nuts, because they are large and sweet.

Soil and situation The sweet chestnut does well in sandy soils and sandy loams with a pH of 5.5–6.5 and it is the ideal tree for dry soils. Shallow, clay, waterlogged and alkaline soils are not suitable. It grows well in an open sunny but sheltered position.

Planting Purchase a one- or two-year-old tree. In autumn, prepare the ground thoroughly, clearing away perennial weeds over an area 4–5 ft square. Dig in well-rotted manure or compost at a rate of one 2 gal bucketful per square yard.

Dig a hole wide and deep enough to take the roots fully extended. Drive in a tall stake to leave about 6–7 ft above the ground. Plant the tree to the same depth as at the nursery, spreading out the roots well. Return the soil. Tie the tree to the stake. Water it well.

Pruning In the first year, cut back by half the laterals produced during the first growing season when they reach 9–12 in. A few of the upper laterals produced later in the season may be left unpruned. In late autumn or early winter, cut back the pruned laterals flush with the stem. Repeat this process each year until the required length of clear stem has been produced and then allow the top four or five laterals to form the primary branches.

Little pruning is required after the main branch system has been formed. Where there is congestion, cut out thin shoots in summer. If growth is excessive, lightly prune the roots in winter.

Pests and diseases

The sweet chestnut is relatively free of pests and diseases. If leaf spot occurs, spray with zineb (see pages 27–8).

Walnuts

The common, English or Persian walnut (*Juglans regia*) is native to China, Iran, the

The first year	Second and third years

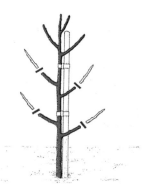

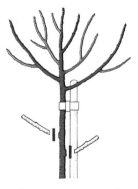

1 In prepared ground, dig a hole large enough for the extended roots. Drive in a stake and plant the tree. Tie it to the stake.

2 Cut back by half all lower laterals produced during the first growing season when they reach 9–12 in.

3 In late autumn or early winter, cut back the pruned laterals flush with the stem.

SWEET (SPANISH) CHESTNUT
'Doré du Lyons' Excellent flavour. Large, round, light-coloured nuts. Ripens October.

WALNUTS
'Bijou' Good flavour. Large nuts with rough skins and thin shells. Ripens October to November. Nuts lose flavour in storage. Tends to be a very tall tree.
'Broadview' Good quality, large nuts, fruits at an early age. Ripens November.

'Franquette' Good sweet flavour. Large, oval nuts with moderately thick shells. Ripens October to November. Late flowering. Vigorous, spreading tree.
'Mayette' Delicate flavour reminiscent of a hazelnut. Large, round, tapering nuts. Ripens November. Late flowering. Vigorous, spreading tree.

Himalayas and south-western Europe. It is hardy in zones 5–8, although it can be killed by a bad winter in zone 5.

The eastern black walnut (*J. nigra*) is widely grown in eastern and central USA. It is hardier and bigger than the English walnut. It does not bear such good fruit but is faster growing and yields a beautiful and valuable timber.

Cultivation

Usually grown as a central-leader standard, the walnut reaches a height of about 25 ft in 20 years and a final height of 60–70 ft. It is therefore suited only to large gardens. It is slow to crop, taking five to ten years before beginning to bear fruit.

Soil and situation The walnut grows well on a wide variety of soils provided they are deep, fertile and well drained. The ideal soil is a heavy loam, at least 2 ft deep, over limestone, with a pH of 7.5–8.0.

An open position with shelter from spring frosts is best because both the young growths and the flowers are susceptible to frost damage. Temperatures below −2°C/27°F will kill most of the female flowers.

Planting For fruiting purposes, it is best to obtain a three- or four-year-old grafted tree of a named cultivar. It will be supplied as a full or half-standard with the head partly formed.

In subsequent years

4 In summer, once the head has been formed little pruning is needed. Where there is congestion cut out thin shoots. Protect the cuts with a wound paint.

Two months before planting, lightly fork in ground lime at a rate of 7 oz per square yard on acid soils. In early autumn, clear away perennial weeds over an area 4–5 ft square. Then, fork in a compound fertilizer, such as a proprietary brand of Growmore, at the rate of 3 oz per square yard.

Dig a hole wide and deep enough to take the roots fully extended. Drive in a stake to reach just below the lowest branches. Plant the tree at the same depth as at the nursery. Return the soil. Tie the tree to the stake with a tree tie and cushion. Water well.

If planting more than one tree, allow a space of 40–50 ft between them.

Pruning Once the head of the tree has formed, very little pruning is required. Cut out any dead or awkwardly placed branches in August. Protect the cuts with a wound paint.

Pests and diseases

Spray with mancozeb in spring if there is evidence of leaf blotch. The walnut is also susceptible to honey fungus. If this occurs dig up the tree with as much of the root system as can be found and burn it. Change the soil completely before replanting (see pages 26–31).

HARVESTING AND STORING NUTS

Pick up walnuts and sweet chestnuts from the ground as soon after they fall as possible and de-husk them. If left, the husks turn black and are difficult to remove. Scrub walnuts with a soft brush to remove all the fibres. Pick cobnuts and filberts when the shells are quite brown and hard.

Spread the nuts out in a warm place to dry, turning them every two or three days. De-husk cobnuts and filberts. When the nuts are thoroughly dry, pack them in barrels or earthenware jars. Pack walnuts with alternate layers of equal parts dry peat and salt. Pack cobnuts and filberts with alternate layers of salt. Pack sweet chestnuts with alternate layers of sand. The nuts can then be stored in a cool, dry, frost-free place for up to six months.

Renovation of neglected trees 1

Neglected or mutilated fruit trees are common and many gardeners inherit them when moving to a new house and garden.

Apart from its untidy appearance, a neglected tree may produce many small or misshapen fruits or it may be unfruitful; it may also be stunted or, conversely, over-vigorous. If the tree is very old (say over 30 years old) and producing little or no fruit, it might not be worth taking a lot of trouble to restore it, especially if it is also suffering from such diseases as silver leaf, canker and collar rot, which can destroy many branches or even kill the whole tree. It is better to dig it up and plant a new young tree.

However, most gardeners are unwilling to give in without a struggle and, provided the tree's basic framework is sound, with time and care a neglected tree can be restored to a fruitful and healthy condition.

Neglect A tree that has not been pruned at all may produce plenty of blossom but the fruit is often small and disease- or pest-ridden. First of all, of course, treat any pests or diseases present (see pages 26–31). Then carry out remedial pruning. Remove all dead, diseased and damaged wood completely. Cut any crossing or rubbing branches and any that spoil the shape of the tree. Finally, thin out overcrowded side-shoots on the main branches. Feed and mulch well.

The stunted tree

If the tree is unfruitful and stunted it may be because of starvation resulting from poor feeding, competition for nutrients and water from weeds or neighbouring trees, unsuitable soil conditions, damage to roots through wind-rock, excessive shade or weakening by pests and diseases.

To remedy starvation, remove weeds and other vegetation, including grass, over an area 4 ft square around the tree. Remove overhanging branches if possible. Mulch the tree heavily with well-rotted manure or compost to a depth of 3 in over a 2 ft radius, keeping the material clear of the trunk. To help to prevent root breakage during gales, drive in a stake to reach just below the lowest branch and tie the tree to it with a tree tie and cushion. Check the soil depth and drainage and, if necessary, install a drainage system

(see pages 18–19). Control pests and diseases.

There is usually very little new wood to prune but if the tree bears a dense mass of complex spur systems, thin these out and severely shorten any maiden wood. This admits light and air to the remaining spurs and encourages the formation of shoots which will replace the old framework.

For one or two years, thin out the fruitlets or, preferably, remove them all. This relieves the tree of the strain of reproduction.

Once the balance of the tree is restored, maintain it by correct pruning, feeding and mulching, and control of pests and diseases.

The over-vigorous and unfruitful tree

An extremely vigorous tree is usually the result of severe pruning over a number of winters, or of being grafted on to a vigorous rootstock. There are other causes; the soil may be very fertile, the tree may have been given too much nitrogen, or scion rooting may have occurred which destroys the dwarfing effect of the rootstock.

The first step is to grass down the orchard (see page 125) and moderate the supply of

The stunted tree

1 Remove weeds and grasses over an area 4 ft square around the tree. Mulch with well-rotted manure or compost. Drive in a stake and tie the tree to it with a tree tie.

Bark-ringing apples and pears

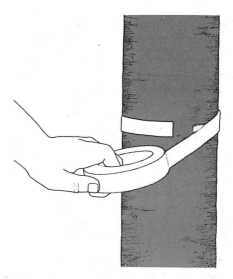

1 In May, mark out a ring ¼ in wide on the trunk. Remove a nearly complete circle of bark using a sharp knife. Leave 1 in of the ring uncut.

2 Then, cover the wound immediately with several overlapping circles of adhesive tape. Smear petroleum jelly on the edges of the tape to exclude air, pests and diseases.

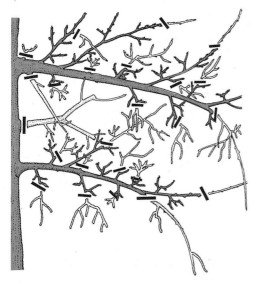

2 In winter, thin out overcrowded spurs and severly shorten any maiden wood.

3 In spring, for a year or two, remove most or all of the fruitlets. Feed with fertilizers and mulch well annually. Control pests and diseases.

171

Renovation of neglected trees 2

nitrogenous fertilizers until the tree is once again fruitful.

More drastic methods of reducing the vigour are by bark-ringing or root-pruning. Root-pruning is recommended for stone fruits such as plums which cannot be bark-ringed because of the risk of silver leaf disease. Surface root-pruning may be necessary for the tree that has scion rooted.

Renovation of severely pruned apple and pear trees The most common cause of over-vigorous growth is severe over-pruning. The tree becomes out of balance and over-vegetative, and simply cutting back branches only perpetuates the problem. Renovation treatment must be spread over a period of two or three winters in order to minimize the shock to the tree.

From November to March, thin out crossing, broken, diseased and congested branches. Leave healthy, well-placed branches which are spaced 2–3 ft apart. Over a period of two or three years, unpruned branches will produce flower buds and eventually fruit.

When taking off a limb, always cut back to the point of origin or to a replacement branch not less than half the diameter of the sawn-off branch. Never leave a stub, because this might lead to die-back, with subsequent canker. Where it is necessary to remove a heavy branch, undercut it first and then complete the cut from the top so that when it parts, the branch does not tear the bark. Protect all pruning cuts larger than ½ in dia.

Winter pruning stimulates growth but summer pruning checks it. Starting with the longer laterals in early August and finishing in late September, cut back to five leaves any unwanted laterals of the current season's growth that have become woody at the base and are longer than 12 in.

Shoots growing horizontally tend to be fruitful, whereas those growing vertically tend not to be. Avoid, where possible, cutting horizontally-inclined shoots and branches. Tie down young upright shoots or loop one over another to form arches, which encourages the production of fruit-bearing spurs.

Bark-ringing apple and pear trees In May, mark out a ring ¼ in wide on the main trunk. With a sharp knife, remove almost a complete circle of bark but leave 1 in of the ring uncut.

Cover the wound immediately with several overlapping circles of adhesive tape. Smear petroleum jelly on the edges of the tape to exclude air, pests and diseases. Bark-ringing temporarily interrupts the passage of foodstuffs to the roots and encourages a better crop of fruit. Remove the tape in the autumn, when the wound should have callused over.

Scion rooting Sometimes the soil becomes heaped up around the trunk, burying the union with the rootstock, which results in the scion rooting and vigorous growth. To establish if this is the case, remove the soil, weeds and other vegetation for a 4 ft square around the tree. Inspect the trunk and sever any

---

RENOVATION OF PLUMS & DAMSONS

Old, neglected plum and damson trees, especially those on vigorous rootstocks, are particularly likely to become unkempt and unmanageable. However, plums are not as tolerant of poor growing conditions as are apples and pears so renovation is not always successful. If the tree is badly infected with silver leaf, it is best to dig it up and burn it.

The first year

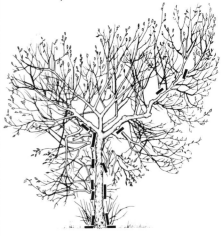

1 In June to August, cut out any large branches that upset the symmetry. Cut out any dead or damaged wood. Remove suckers and twiggy growths on the trunk.

roots coming from above the union. Paint the wounds. If the union is below ground level or not visible at all (and this may be difficult to detect in old, knotty trunks) drastic action such as bark-ringing may be needed on over-vigorous apple and pear trees (see above).

Root-pruning The roots are pruned to reduce the vigour of the tree and to encourage fruit buds to form. In November or December, mark out and dig a trench around the tree about 5 ft from the trunk (further away if the tree is large). Fold back the thin fibrous roots to expose the thicker woody roots. Cut back the thicker roots with a pruning saw. Retain the thinner fibrous roots and spread them

back into the trench. Cover the soil and firm the ground. Drive in a supporting stake to reach just below the bottom branch. Tie the tree to the stake with a tree tie and cushion. Mulch the root area with well-rotted manure or compost. Water well during the summer.

If the tree is old and very badly neglected, spread this process over two winters.

An over-vigorous tree less than five years old may be lifted to prune the roots. In winter, dig up the tree and cut back the deeper and wider-ranging roots. Replant it in the same position or in a different, more suitable site if appropriate. Support the replanted tree with a stake. Water in dry weather in summer.

First, clear the ground, removing weeds and other vegetation over an area 4 ft square around the tree and mulch heavily. Treat the tree for any pests and diseases present (see pages 26–31).

Avoid severe pruning and spread the renovation process over three years. The principles of pruning are basically the same as for a neglected apple or pear tree. The main

difference is that plums and damsons are pruned in July to August when the danger of infection by silver leaf is small. The aim is to return to a tree with a more or less symmetrical branch system.

Once the tree has been restored to a healthy fruitful condition, maintain it with correct pruning, feeding, and control of pests and diseases (see pages 128–33).

Second and subsequent years

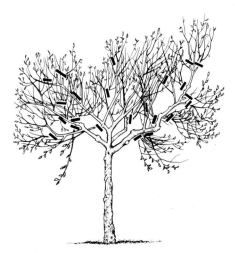

2 At the same time, thin out lateral branches and twigs where they are overcrowded. Protect all cut surfaces with a wound paint.

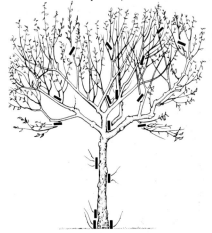

3 In June to August, remove any over-vigorous growth that spoils the symmetry. Thin out remaining overcrowded branch systems. Cut out any suckers.

Fruit in tubs and pots 1

Lack of space to grow fruit trees and bushes can be turned from a drawback into an advantage. Most fruits can be grown in containers such as pots, tubs, boxes and troughs.

Pot-grown fruits can be more easily protected against frost, high winds and birds and given the exact type of soil they prefer and need. Although container-grown fruits never give very large yields per tree or bush – their small size sees to that – the quality of the fruit can be very high because extra attention can be given.

Types and sizes of container

The container must have good drainage and be of a shape and construction to allow the plant to be removed when required. Within these constraints, the choice of material and shape is considerable. Remember, however, that it is not worth investing in an expensive pot until the plant has reached its final size. Strawberries, for example, can be grown in perforated barrels or specially designed containers.

The tree's first pot must be large enough to accommodate the root system, and up to 3 in wider but no larger. This usually means a container 9–12 in in diameter and depth.

Cultivation

The principle behind container growing is to limit the size of the plant by constricting the root system. Starting with a maiden, a two- or a three-year-old tree, the gardener adjusts the pot size, repotting until the tree reaches the required size. Maiden trees are preferable if the gardener wishes to train the tree in a particular way.

Site Container-grown fruits should be sited in a sunny corner where they are protected from high winds, which can damage plants by battering and by cold. Beware of eddies produced by walls and fences. Temporary shelter with plastic sheeting or netting can be erected at such critical times as blossoming and fruit formation or, better still, take the containers into a greenhouse or conservatory if possible. Avoid frost pockets.

In cool climates, south-facing walls provide an extra source of radiated heat – excellent for the warm temperate fruits. The reflected warmth from the stone or brick often creates a warmer microclimate than the open ground. Walls also cause a rain shadow effect which helps to protect plants from storms, but containers in such rain shadows need extra watering.

Soil An advantage of container growing is that the soil can be more easily tailored to each plant's needs. Stone fruits, for example, thrive best in a slightly alkaline soil whereas pip fruits, such as apples, need a slightly acid soil. The compost can be modified to suit the plant concerned. John Innes potting compost No. 2 for soft fruits and No. 3 for tree fruits are good basic container soils.

Soilless composts (generally peat-based with the necessary nutrients added) are useful for short-term crops such as strawberries. They are light and clean to handle but there is little buffer action against excessive salts, so feeding and watering are more critical. They are not suitable for long-term fruit such as apples or peaches.

Potting If the plant is bare-rooted, soak the roots of the tree for one hour before planting. If the tree is already container-grown, the existing root ball should be retained but

Planting

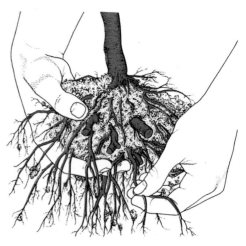

1 Soak bare-rooted plants for one hour before planting. Gently tease out the perimeter roots on container-grown plants. Cut back any large thong-like or broken roots using a clean sloping cut.

Black currants: All cultivars, but 'Baldwin' is especially compact.

Cherries: 'Stella'.

Culinary apples: 'Lord Derby' with 'Lane's Prince Albert', 'Rev. W. Wilks' with 'George Neal'.

Dessert apples: 'Discovery' with 'Sunset', 'Ellison's Orange' with 'Golden Delicious'.

Figs: 'Brown Turkey'.

Gooseberries: 'Careless', 'Lancer', 'Leveller', 'May Duke'.

gently tease the perimeter roots outwards to avoid any pot-bound effect. Whatever the age of the tree, large thong-like roots should be cut back so that the root ball fits the pot. Trim broken roots using a clean sloping cut with the face of the wound downwards. This trimming induces the tree to create a more fibrous root system. Crock clay pots to ensure good drainage. Plastic pots are usually well equipped with drainage holes, but if there is any doubt crock these also.

Place the plant in the centre of the pot at the same depth as it was previously. Fill the container, firming the soil well as filling proceeds; very firm planting is essential. Level off 1 in below the rim to leave room for watering. Stand the container on bricks so that drainage is not impeded. Water well and leave the pots in a cool but frost-free place for the winter.

Watering and feeding Fruit plants in pots must be watered carefully, avoiding the two extremes of waterlogging and desiccation. The former causes root death and both result in fruitlet drop. Check the top inch of soil regularly: it should be damp but not sodden.

Daily watering is necessary during hot sunny spells. In really hot weather, place moist sacking around the pots to protect the roots. Little watering is necessary in the winter.

No matter how good the potting compost, liquid feeding is necessary in the growing season. A pot-grown plant cannot seek out nutrients as can a plant in open ground. Most fruit trees require a high-potassium feed, particularly when they are carrying a good fruit crop. Apply a proprietary liquid fertilizer to the manufacturer's instructions once a fortnight when the plant begins to grow and every 7–10 days when it is in full leaf. Stop liquid feeding when the fruits begin to ripen.

Repotting In the late autumn gently knock the plant out of its pot. Trim the roots by about one-tenth, particularly any thong-like roots. Cut the aerial parts of the plant by an equivalent amount to balance the root loss. Tease out the perimeter roots to avoid the fruit becoming pot-bound. Take a little of the old soil out of the root ball. Repot into a larger container each year while the plant is growing to its final size. Remember the larger the container, the bigger the tree will grow.

2 Crock the pot. Place the plant in the pot to the same depth as it was previously. Fill the container, firming well. Level off 1 in below the rim. Water well and stand on bricks to allow excess water to drain away.

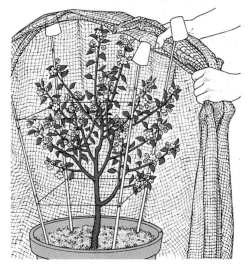

3 In spring, give the plants a top dressing of a 1 in layer of peat or well-rotted manure. Replace each year. Protect blossom from frost with netting over a framework of canes or wire.

Fruit in tubs and pots 2

As a guide, gooseberries grow quite satisfactorily in a final pot of 15 in diameter, black currants in an 18 in pot, and trees in an 18–20 in diameter container. Thereafter plants can stay in the same container, except for a change of compost each autumn. An easier but less efficient technique is to leave the plant undisturbed and merely to change the top 4–6 in of compost each autumn.

Protection In the spring, to protect the blossom against frost, cover the plants with netting or take them inside. Keep the netting off the blossoms by inserting canes or a wire framework into the pot around the plant. Netting should be used to keep birds away from the buds in the winter and from the fruit in the summer.

As with all early-flowering fruit trees, frost is a greater danger in spring than in winter, but container-grown fruits are also sensitive to heavy frosts that can freeze the entire root system and kill the tree. In winter, the container should be buried in well-drained ground up to its rim, or moved to a sheltered position. If this is not possible, wrap the container with hessian or sacking.

Top-dressing In the spring, just as growth commences, the plants should be top-dressed with a 1 in layer of peat or well-rotted stable manure. This helps to conserve soil moisture. Trees requiring extra nitrogen (for example, stone fruits) should be given a dressing of dried blood $\frac{1}{2}$–1 oz at a time, first when the buds burst, second after the stones have formed and finally when the fruits have reached full size, but well before ripening. Replace the mulch each year.

Training and pruning

Container-grown fruit trees can be trained to any of the tree forms (see page 15). They are particularly suitable for single cordon training, that is, growing a single stem at a 45 degree angle against a wall or fence. Single cordons make the best use of restricted space. Bear in mind that such trees as citrus that need to be moved into shelter during the winter should be trained in a self-supporting round form such as bush or pyramid. Apples, pears, cherries, plums and apricots respond well to training in the dwarf pyramid form.

4 When the plant begins to grow, feed with a liquid fertilizer high in potassium once a fortnight. When it is in full leaf, feed every 7–10 days. Stop the feed when the fruits begin to ripen.

5 During the formative years, remove some of the blossom to prevent heavy fruiting. Thin the fruits to leave about 6–9 on three-year-old apple, pear or peach trees; leave about 20 on a plum tree.

Grapes: 'Black Hamburgh', 'Buckland Sweetwater', 'Chasselas d'Or'.

Hybrid berries: Loganberry L654, Tayberry.

Peaches and nectarines: 'Peregrine' (peach), 'Pine Apple' and 'Early Rivers' (nectarine).

Pears: 'Conference' and 'William's Bon Chrétien'.

Plums: 'Denniston's Superb', 'Oullin's Golden Gage' and 'Victoria'.

Red currants: 'Jonkheer van Tets' and 'Red Lake'.

Apart from training the fruit tree, during its formative years it should be prevented from fruiting too heavily by removing some of the blossoms. Three-year-old apple, pear and peach trees in 10–12 in pots can carry about 6–9 fruits. Plums should be limited to 20 on a three-year-old tree. More fruits can be obtained if the trees are in larger pots or tubs. When mature, all pot-grown fruits should be discouraged from producing too much fruit by thinning at intervals. Provided they are well fed and watered, the final spacing of fruit can be a little closer than that recommended for outdoor trees. The final thinning of stone fruits should not take place until after the stone has formed.

Cultivars

The number of cultivars suitable for pot growing is legion. The main criterion is that they should not be triploids, because these are too vigorous and they are poor pollinators. Self-incompatibles trees need a partner (see pages 94–7). The cultivars on pages 175–7 represent only a few of the many suitable for pot growing.

Repotting

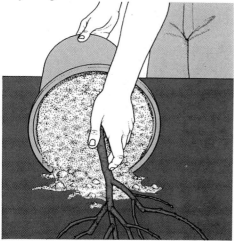

6 In late autumn, gently knock the plant out of its pot. Trim the roots by about one-tenth, particularly any thong-like roots. Tease out perimeter roots. Remove a little old soil. Replant with new soil.

GRAPE VINES IN POTS

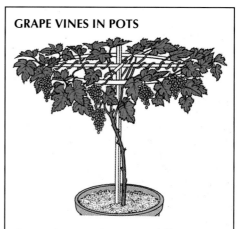

Grape vines can be successfully grown in pots in a small greenhouse or on a patio where a large greenhouse is not available. (For full details of growing grapes see pages 74–81.)

A vine can be bought as a one-year-old rooted cutting. In the first season, grow it in a 7 in pot. When the vine is in its second season, transfer it to a 12–15 in pot in November.

Allow the vine to produce one good rod during this second summer, which should be stopped at about 6 ft. Support the rod with a cane.

In the second winter, prune off the unripe wood. Insert three or four canes into the soil around the pot rim, or insert the kind of wood or metal frame used for supporting weeping standard roses. Tie in the vine rod to this to form a circle. When the circle is complete, stop the vine. Remove the lower side-shoots to create a clear stem up to the ring.

Allow the vine to produce a token crop of two bunches during the second season. In later years, allow the vine to produce progressively larger crops, but no more than one bunch per spur at 12 in apart, making a total of 5–8 bunches.

Prune the vine by the rod and spur method (see pages 79–80).

Water and feed as described for other pot-grown fruits (opposite). Repot or pot on each winter using fresh compost.

Fruit storage

In the past fruit could be stored in the home in two basic ways. Apples, pears and quinces were stored in the traditional winter store-house for three to eight months, which is still a popular method; other fruit could be stored only by bottling in jams and jellies, or by drying, all of which affect the basic taste and texture. With the advent of the home freezer, almost all fruits can now be eaten at any time of the year virtually in prime condition.

Traditional storage

The procedure for storing hard fruit such as apples, pears and quinces varies little. Store them separately because the strong aroma of quinces, in particular, can affect other fruit.

Early apples and pears are best eaten from the tree and will keep for only a few weeks. Mid-season cultivars generally keep for one to two months, but do not store them with late cultivars because the gases given off will hasten the maturity of the later ones. Store late varieties, that mature from late September onwards, for three to eight months.

Picking for storage Pick apples and pears when they are fully sized and when they leave the spur easily with the stalk intact. Very late apples are picked when still unripe; ripeness for eating develops in storage.

Handle the fruit carefully. Bruising can allow fungus spores to enter and rot the damaged fruit. Do not pick the fruit when it

Wrapping the fruit

1 Place each fruit in the centre of a square of paper. Oiled or waxed wraps can prolong storage life.

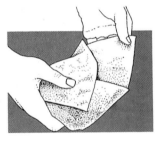

2 Fold the bottom point to the middle. Then fold in the two side points to form a firm parcel.

3 Fold down the fourth point and gently place the apple "parcel", folded side down, in the box.

STORAGE BOXES AND TRAYS

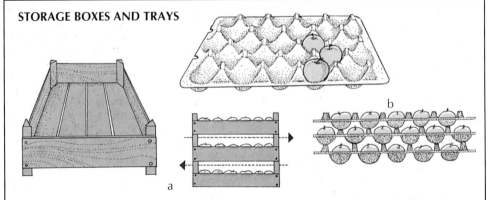

Orchard boxes (a) have slatted sides and corner posts to allow air to circulate and the slats have rounded edges to protect the fruit. Do not wrap fruit packed in polystyrene or fibre trays (b) because the compartments separate the fruit.

is raining because dampness encourages mould. It is best to pick by hand and put the fruit gently into a lined basket or soft bag. Use a fruit picker for the highest fruit (see page 23).

The storehouse If there is a regular and sizeable harvest it may be worth building a special storehouse. However, a cellar, cool attic or shed is also suitable.

Ideally, the store should be kept at an even temperature from 3°–4°C/37°–40°F, but this requires refrigeration equipment. Most gardeners have to be satisfied with maintaining the store at a temperature of about 4°–7°C/40°–45°F during the winter months. Air must circulate freely. To achieve this, fit ventilators at each end covered with wire mesh to keep out birds. The atmosphere must not be too dry or the fruit will shrivel. Damp down the floor occasionally if it is soil, stone or concrete. Keep the storage area clean and remove containers of paint and creosote, which could taint the fruit.

A soil floor is ideal because it can be kept moist but fine mesh wire netting must be laid about 1 ft below soil level to keep out rats and mice. The floor should be firmed down and cleaned each year.

Storage boxes and trays Apples and pears can be stored on slatted shelves inside the storehouse, although wooden orchard boxes and trays, and fibre or polystyrene trays are more convenient because they stack on top of each other. They must have corner posts for air to circulate. A thin sheet of polythene laid loosely over the fruit helps to delay shrivelling. After use, clean the containers with soapy water and disinfectant.

Preparing the fruit for storage Using only undamaged fruit, store pears unwrapped in single layers on trays. Wrap and pack apples in layers in boxes or in trays. Using special oiled wraps extends the storage life but 8 in squares of newspaper are an alternative for cooking apples. Some gardeners let apples sweat for one to two weeks before storing them, to prevent later condensation and thus possible rotting while in store.

Polythene bags Clear polythene bags have been tried recently for storing apples and pears and they are particulary successful with cultivars that tend to shrivel. Store no more than 4–5 lb of fruit to a bag.

After picking leave the fruit to cool completely before packing to avoid condensation in the bag. When the bag is packed, fold the top over and place it so that the fold is underneath. Do not exclude all the air from the bag. Make two small holes for every 1 lb of fruit. Alternatively, cut off the bottom two corners of each bag. Store the bags in the same way as boxes at the coolest temperature possible but not below 3°C/37°F.

Storage problems Generally, problems are the result of storing damaged or contaminated fruit, lack of ventilation, or of fluctuations in temperature in the storehouse. Check all fruit regularly and remove any showing signs of disease or rotting. The most common diseases are brown rot fungus, scald and bitter pit (see pages 26–31). Set mouse traps and check them regularly.

Freezing

Almost all fruits freeze well, except strawberries and most type of dessert pears. Berry fruits (currants and gooseberries) are particularly suitable. Freeze all fruits as soon after picking as possible.

Drying

Drying is a successful method for storing apples, pears, plums and grapes to be used later for cooking.

Peel and quarter apples and pears, or cut apples into rings 1/4 in thick. Plums may be left whole or halved and stoned. Leave grapes whole. Arrange the fruit on clean muslin or mesh trays or wooden frames so that it is not touching. Hang apple rings on sticks or bamboo canes across the oven. It is essential to dry fruit slowly or it hardens and whole plums burst their skins. An airing cupboard or an oven that can be heated to low temperature is ideal. Dry for one hour at 49°C/120°F and then increase the temperature to 60°C/140°F. Leave the fruit at this heat for three to six hours depending on the size. When the fruit is dry, it should be soft and pliable with no excess moisture.

Spread out the fruit on clean paper to cool. Cover with paper or muslin and leave at room temperature for 12 hours. Store in a dry place in boxes lined with waxed paper.

Warm temperate fruits

Introduction

The fruits in this section are tender and need warm or hot summers and mild winters to thrive and crop satisfactorily. Apart from the various sorts of citrus fruits, the Cape gooseberry, Chinese gooseberry and passion fruit are not widely known or grown in Britain. But none of these is difficult to grow and so they are worth trying at least once. Even if the fruits do not appeal, all are attractive plants.

This collection of tender fruits embraces a wide range of habits. The various kinds of citrus fruits are evergreen shrubs or small trees. The Chinese gooseberry and passion fruit are vigorous climbers, the former deciduous, the latter evergreen. The Cape gooseberry is a semi-erect, herbaceous perennial often grown as an annual.

Chinese gooseberries

The Chinese gooseberry, or Kiwi fruit (*Actinidia chinensis*), was discovered in China and Japan by the European plant-hunters of the nineteenth century, since when it has been cultivated in Europe, the USA and in New Zealand (hence its alternative name). Until relatively recently horticultural fashion valued this plant more for its leaves and flowers than for its fruit, and so there are few named varieties available for fruiting.

The Chinese gooseberry is a hardy perennial climber, with large heart-shaped leaves and creamy flowers. The fruits are furry brown outside, green inside, 1½ in across by 3–4 in long and are usually eaten fresh.

Cultivation

The Chinese gooseberry is a rampant climber which will occupy a large amount of space if allowed to grow unchecked. It is hardy outdoors up to zone 8, but it really needs long warm summers for the fruits to mature. The young shoots carrying the flowers are extremely vulnerable to frosts and need protection in the spring (see pages 12–13). In borderline areas of zone 7, choose a sunny site such as a south- or west-facing wall. When dormant, the Chinese gooseberry can withstand relatively hard winter frosts, but in cold zones a greenhouse with enough heat to keep out the worst frost is necessary.

Soil The Chinese gooseberry grows best in a deep sandy loam rich in organic matter but it will grow in a wide soil range, provided the soil is well drained. It tolerates a range of pH, but neutral (pH 7.0) is ideal.

If the plants are grown in pots inside a greenhouse, any good proprietary potting compost can be used. Apply a liquid fertilizer at weekly intervals once the foliage has expanded and during the growing season.

Selecting the plants Although plants can be grown from seed they are extremely variable and this is not recommended. Where possible buy one-year-old rooted cuttings or grafted plants of a named variety.

Planting and support Plants should be spaced 10–15 ft apart. If grown in pots, plant the vines as described on pages 174–7. If grown in the greenhouse border, plant them in the same way as a grape vine (see pages 74–5). The Chinese gooseberry entwines itself around any support available, so provide a flat-topped pergola, a strong fence or a trellis. A system of posts and wire supports such as that used for blackberries is suitable (see pages 58–61).

After planting, prune the vines to 12 in above the ground to promote vigorous growth. When the plants fill the available space, pinch out the growing points.

Pollination Take care to provide one male plant for up to seven females to ensure pollination. Plants in greenhouses should be pollinated by hand (see page 95). Outdoors, insects should do the job adequately.

3 In summer, train canes along the wires, one to each. Stop them by pinching out the tips when space is filled. Stop any laterals at five leaves.

CHINESE GOOSEBERRIES

'Abbott' Fruits medium size, oblong; densely covered with soft long hairs. Vigorous. Flowers early, so susceptible to frost. Crops well.

'Bruno' Fruits large, elongated, dark brown; densely covered with short bristly hairs. Flowers later than 'Abbott'.

'Hayward' Large, oval fruits. Pale green-brown skin covered with fine silky hairs. Late flowering. Moderate vigour. Cropping moderate, but has the best flavour of the three cultivars. Recommended.

Pruning Young plants are pruned to just above the top wire of the support to encourage the growth of lateral canes. These canes are trained horizontally along the wires, one to each wire, and stopped by pinching out the tips when the allocated space is filled. Then, young fruit-carrying shoots are regularly pinched back to seven leaves beyond the last fruit and barren laterals are pinched back to five leaves when necessary throughout the summer. Also remove any subsequent sub-laterals that may form behind the pinched-back shoots. This summer pruning encourages the initiation and formation of fruiting spurs.

In later years, congested growth is thinned out during the winter. The three-year-old fruiting laterals are cut back to a dormant bud near the main cane to renew the fruiting laterals.

Harvesting

The fruit is usually ripe in October, but it needs 4–6 weeks in store before the fullest flavour is attained. To store, spread the fruit out in trays in single layers.

Propagation

Named cultivars are reproduced by cuttings in late summer or by layering in spring.

Pests and diseases

The plant is not usually troubled by any pest or disease.

First and second years

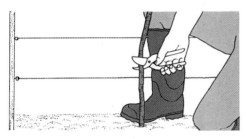

1 From November to March, plant the vines in the prepared border 10-15 ft apart. Erect a system of posts and wire supports. Cut the vines back to 12 in above the ground.

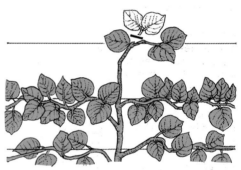

2 In early summer, when the new growth has passed the top vine of the support, cut back the tips to promote the growth of lateral canes.

The third year

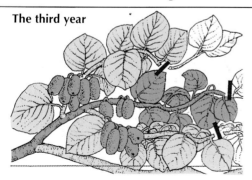

4 During the growing season, fruit is produced on laterals on the main framework. Pinch back young fruits to seven leaves beyond the last fruit.

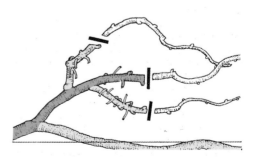

5 In winter, cut back laterals to two buds beyond where the last fruit was borne. On older vines, cut back some three-year-old laterals to a dormant bud.

Cape gooseberries

The Cape gooseberry, or golden berry (*Physalis pruinosa* [syn. *P. peruviana* or *P. edulis*), comes from Peru, although it is now widely cultivated in many areas of the world, particularly in South Africa. A tall perennial, it is related to the ornamental Chinese lantern plant (*P. alkekengi*), which also has edible but indifferent-tasting fruits.

The distinctive feature of this fruit is its lantern-like calyx or husk which conceals the golden, cherry-sized fruit. The husk protects the berry from birds and insects, aids the storage of the fruit, and is attractive, as are the small yellow-white blossoms with their purple-black markings. The leaves are large and slightly heart-shaped. The fruit of the Cape gooseberry is sweet with a distinctive taste. It can be eaten raw, cooked or preserved. It has a high vitamin C content. Each plant will produce about 1–12 lb of fruit.

Cultivation

The Cape gooseberry is a half-hardy perennial usually grown as an annual. It can be grown in the open in sheltered areas, or under glass or in pots where the summers are cool. It responds to much the same treatment as its relative the tomato.

Soil and situation Do not grow the Cape gooseberry in ground just used for tomatoes or potatoes, because it is subject to the same pests and diseases, which may still be present in the soil. A sandy, well-drained soil of pH 6.5 is ideal but it will tolerate a wide range of soils, including chalky soil if well laced with humus. It should be planted in a sunny, sheltered position.

Propagation The Cape gooseberry can be grown from seed under glass, or from cuttings taken from mature plants. The seeds should be sown in gentle heat in early spring. Sow the seeds individually, ¼ in deep, in seed trays filled with any proprietary seed compost such as John Innes seed compost. The seed trays should be covered with glass. A temperature of 18°C/65°F is necessary for good germination. A propagator is an alternative to a heated greenhouse. When the seeds germinate in 10–14 days remove the glass. When the seedlings are large enough to grip, prick them out into 3 in pots filled with John Innes potting compost No. 1.

Planting and staking Prepare the site, which should be cultivated to a fine tilth. No extra fertilizer is needed unless the soil is poor, when a 2 gal bucketful of well-rotted manure should be applied per square yard. An alternative to manure is a dressing of compound fertilizer such as a brand of Growmore at 2–3 oz per square yard.

Plant out in late April to early May, setting the plants 2½ ft apart. Protect the young plants with cloches or tunnels until the danger of frosts and cold winds is past. If cloches are not available, keep the seedlings in a cold frame until the end of May and plant out when the danger of frosts is past. Plants can be stunted by a cold wind as late as early summer so provide shelter in the form of screens when necessary.

The plants should be supported with individual stakes 3 ft high or with a network of posts and wire. If the plants have not produced flowers by the time they are 12 in high, pinch out the growing points to induce branching, and thereafter regular stopping and pinching is not needed. Watering should be carefully regulated, for if the plants are given too much moisture they produce growth at the expense of fruit. Give a liquid feed sparingly only after the first flowers appear. Tomato fertlizers are suitable, as are compound fertilizers, which should be applied at the maker's recommended rates.

Growing under glass In areas where the frost-free season is less than about 80 days, or summers are cool, protection is essential. There are two methods: cultivate in a greenhouse for the whole season, with plants growing in beds and trained up a wall or stakes, or growing the plants in pots which can spend the early and ripening stages inside and the summer in the open.

Seed should be sown in the same way as for outdoor plants. Instead of planting out, the plants should be potted on into 10 in pots filled with John Innes potting compost No. 2 or an equivalent all-peat compost. Plants should be staked individually. Or, if stood outside, the stakes should be secured to a wire stretched between stronger stakes driven into the soil. Greenhouse plants need to be gently tapped or shaken at flowering time to assist pollination. Cape gooseberries grown under glass need full ventilation on hot days and more water than outdoor plants.

Although plants can be retained for the following year and potted on into larger containers, it is recommended that new seeds are sown each year and the plants discarded after fruiting because thereafter they do not crop so heavily.

Harvesting
Fruits grown outdoors may not be ripe by the time of the first frosts. Pot-grown plants can be put back under glass to ripen. The fruits are ready to pick when they turn golden-yellow and the husks have a papery texture. Ripe fruits can be left on the plants for several weeks, the peak of flavour being reached 2–3

weeks after ripening. If frost threatens outdoor plants, gather all those berries that have a hint of yellow colour. They will go on ripening if laid in their husks on a sunny windowsill. The fruits can be stored, unwrapped, often until December, providing the husks are quite dry. They should be stored in a dry place at a temperature of 10°–15°C/50°–59°F.

Pests and diseases
Outdoor plants should be regularly inspected for aphids, which may gather on the shoot tips. If seen, spray with dimethoate, heptenophos or pirimicarb. Greenhouse plants may suffer from greenfly and whitefly. Spray with permethrin insecticide when seen. Repeat at four-day intervals as necessary.

1 In early spring, sow seeds ¼ in deep in seed trays filled with a proprietary seed compost. Cover the seed trays with glass. Maintain a temperature of 18°C/65°F.

2 In 10–14 days, when the seeds germinate, remove the glass. When the seedlings are large enough to grip, prick out into 3 in pots.

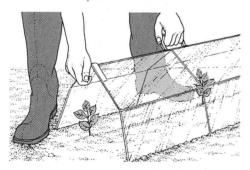

3 In late April to early May, plant out the seedlings 2½ ft apart and protect them with cloches. Remove the cloches when the danger of frosts is past.

4 During the growing season, provide support for the plants. When 12 in high, if they have no flowers, pinch out the growing points. When flowers appear, feed sparingly.

Passion fruit

The passion fruit (*Passiflora edulis*) is ·a native of southern Brazil, but now well distributed throughout the Tropics. It is a vigorous, evergreen climber with deep glossy green leaves and white fragrant flowers. The fruits (technically berries) are 1½–2½ in long and oval in shape. Although basically a sweetish fruit, when eaten fresh it has a pleasant, somewhat aromatic tartness. Two forms are recognized: *P. edulis edulis* with deep purple fruits and *P. edulis flavicarpa* with deep yellow fruits.

Cultivation

The two passion fruit forms need cool or temperate greenhouse culture in northern temperate regions, with a minimum winter temperature of 7°–10°C/45°–50°F. The best results are obtained from plants grown in greenhouse borders, in a fertile, moist, but well-drained soil. Some root restriction may be necessary in rich soils to avoid over-vigorous growths at the expense of flowers and fruit.

Planting and spacing The young plants raised either from seed in the same way as Cape gooseberries, or from cuttings, should be planted in the prepared border in early spring. Support is essential so provide a system of wires as described for grapes (on pages 78-9) or 2 in mesh plastic netting, which should be suspended about 6 in beneath the roof glass.

Training and general cultivation If the plants are single-stemmed, remove their tips to promote branching. Train two leaders on to the supports and allow the plants to develop naturally, gently guiding in any wayward growths to the support system. If, however, the main stems have not produced laterals by the time they are 2–3 ft long, then pinch out their tips. Little or no fruit is produced during the first year. In winter during subsequent years, after the main framework of branches has been built up, cut back the current season's growth (which bore fruit) close to other framework stems. In spring, new growth is produced and it is guided into position initially and then allowed to develop naturally. Care must be taken not to overfeed or hard-prune established plants because this encourages vigorous growths and few flowers or fruits. Established plants should be given a dressing of a compound fertilizer such as John Innes Base at a rate of 3 oz per square yard in late winter.

Pollination

Passion fruit raised from seed may be self-sterile. If possible obtain clones of the

1 In spring or early summer, plant two seedlings 2 ft apart in the prepared border. Pinch out the growing tip.

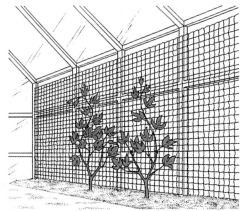

2 During the summer, hang 2 in mesh plastic netting 6 in beneath the roof glass. Train two leaders on to the supports and allow the plants to develop naturally.

CULTIVATION OF POT-GROWN PLANTS

Passion fruit can be grown successfully in large pots (not less than 10 in dia.) or tubs. For this method a good proprietary compost is recommended, ideally John Innes potting compost No. 3.

Support the plants in the same way as plants grown in the greenhouse border. Alternatively, wind them spirally around three or four 6–8 ft canes pushed into the compost near the edge of the pot or tub 3–4 in apart. Tie the stems to the canes.

Pot-grown plants benefit from an annual top dressing of fresh potting compost. During the period from flowering until the fruit begins to ripen, give a high potash liquid fertilizer at 14 day intervals to assist fruiting. Repot annually in early spring before the buds break into growth. Follow the repotting procedure described in detail on pages 175-6.

purple-fruited form known to be self-compatible. If only seed-raised plants are available, plant two seedlings about 2 ft apart, and allow the shoots to intermingle after initial training. Hand pollinated flowers usually produce larger fruits than naturally pollinated ones so, where practical, hand pollination is worth while (see page 95). The flowers are short-lived and should be pollinated soon after they open.

Harvesting and storing

For really juicy and good-flavoured fruits, do not pick them until they are fully ripe; they should come off at a touch. When mature the fruit attains a purple colour, and the skin hardens and begins to shrivel. Once gathered the fruit should be used as soon as possible but it can be stored for a few weeks.

Pests and diseases

As a greenhouse plant, the passion fruit is comparatively free of troublesome pests and diseases. The worst problems come from red spider mites, aphids and whitefly, which should be controlled with pesticides or biological controls when seen, as detailed on pages 26–31.

Cultivars

There are no named cultivars available. Purchased fruits are therefore the best source of seed.

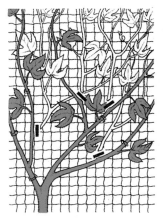

3 In winter, cut back the current season's growth close to other framework stems.

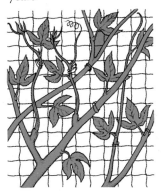

Second and subsequent years

4 In spring, train in new growths on to the support and allow them to develop naturally.

5 During flowering, pollinate with a small brush. Liquid feed every 14 days until the fruits ripen.

Citrus fruits 1

ORANGES AND HYBRIDS
'Blood' (Malta) Delicious flavour. Fruits large with thin skins. Pulp stained deep crimson.
'Embiguo' or 'Navel Orange' Good flavour, sweet and juicy. Large fruits with a nipple-like protrusion at the apex. Pale flesh with few seeds.
'Jaffa' (Jamaica Orange) Excellent

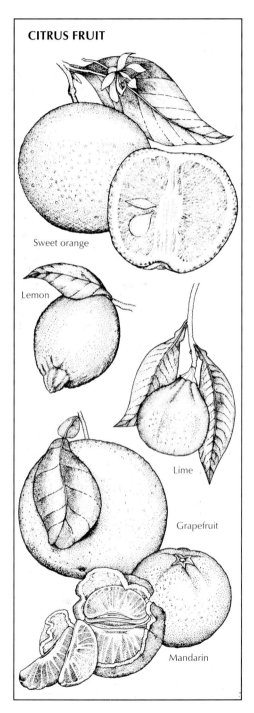

CITRUS FRUIT

Sweet orange

Lemon

Lime

Grapefruit

Mandarin

Citrus fruits (oranges, lemons, limes, mandarins, grapefruits and their hybrids) can be grown in temperate climates, although in most areas they need to be under glass for part of the year at least. They are ornamental trees which have a long history of cultivation in temperate zones.

Climate
Gardeners in temperate climates can cultivate citrus fruits as permanent greenhouse plants, or as container-grown small trees. When grown in containers many citrus trees can be moved into the open in summer, freeing greenhouse space for other plants. There are favoured places, chiefly in zones 9 and 10, where citrus trees can be grown outdoors permanently.

Citrus trees are evergreens and so face severer problems in winter than do deciduous fruit trees, which are dormant when frost strikes. Citrus trees can resist cold and light frosts provided the onset of cold weather is gradual. If temperatures drop steadily, they

1 Plant the two- or three-year-old bush tree in a pot filled with John Innes No. 2.

flavour. Fruits very large.
'Oval' (Malta) Similar to the 'blood' orange in size and form of fruit but without crimson pulp. Flowers profusely.
'Satsuma' A Japanese Tangerine. Fruits small, thin-skinned. Hardy and a good cropper.
'Seville' (*Citrus bigaradia*) Flavour acid – used for marmalade. Fruits medium, thick-skinned, dark orange.
'St. Michael's' Flavour good. Fruits large, thin-skinned. Widely grown commercially. 'Botelha', 'Silver', 'Egg', 'Sustain', 'Dulcissima' and 'Exquisite' are all forms of 'St Michael's'.
'Tangerine' Good flavour. Fruits small, thin-skinned, peel easily. Aromatic flesh. Fairly hardy.
'Tangerine St Michael's' Excellent flavour. Fruits small. Fairly hardy.
'Valencia Late' Good flavour. Fruits large, thin-skinned. Vigorous and heavy cropper.
'Variegated Orange' An ornamental variety with variegated leaves and fruit. Good quality fruits.

---

gradually stop growing and so suffer less from frost but a sudden temperature drop often damages the young wood. The mandarin orange is the toughest, followed in order of increasing tenderness by the sour or Seville orange, the sweet orange, the grapefruit, the lemon and the lime. A temperature of –1°C/30°F will badly damage the wood of a lemon tree, and flowers and young fruits will die at –2°C/29°F. The lime is the tenderest of this group, although it tolerates wetter climates than does the lemon and can thus be the best choice for mild coastal areas with high rainfall.

For ripe fruit, temperature rather than sunshine is the critical factor. Ideally all citrus fruits need six months after flowering when temperatures do not fall below 13°–16°C/55°–61°F at night.

Although all the main citrus species and hybrids tend to flower in spring, some produce sporadic flowers at other times and because the fruits take about 12 months to mature, flowers and fruits can be seen together. The grapefruit can take as long as 17 months to mature, and there are often two crops on the tree at once.

True flavours will not develop if the temperature falls for long periods below 18°C/65°F for oranges, while mandarins of all types are even more demanding.

Cultivation under glass

A well-ventilated greenhouse is required, ideally sited so that it receives a good winter light. A minimum winter temperature of 7°C/45°F should be maintained although the lime tree really needs 10°–13°C/50°–55°F. All the remaining citrus trees mentioned here tolerate short periods of lower temperatures, to a degree above freezing point, but this is best avoided. Citrus trees do not tolerate a stagnant humid atmosphere and on sunny days, even in winter, ventilation should be given. If the plants are grown under glass all year round, light shading from May to September is beneficial, especially if the greenhouse is in a sunny site. In summer, full

2 From spring to autumn, give the container-grown plant a liquid feed at 10–14 day intervals. Do not let the plant dry out. Ventilate the greenhouse on sunny days.

3 During the growing season, remove low shoots as soon as they appear to establish a single-stemmed tree. Cut back short any over-vigorous shoots that mar the symmetry.

Citrus fruits 2

ventilation must be given on all but the coldest days. On hot days damp down the soil and benches daily.

Cultivation without glass

If a shed or outbuilding is available for overwintering, ideally with glass on three sides and sufficient heat to keep out frost, the hardier citrus fruits can be grown in containers without a greenhouse. During mild spells in spring and autumn place the trees outside by day and take them in at night. From early summer to autumn, grow them outside in a sheltered sunny place.

Propagation Citrus fruits can be grown from seed, by budding on to seedling stocks, by layering, or by taking cuttings in summer. However, propagation from seed when fruit production is the object is a waste of time because such seedlings take about 7–8 years to flower and the fruit quality is poor. It is best to buy a named cultivar two- or three-year-old bush tree grafted on to the correct rootstock and prepared for pot culture.

Soil Soil type is not critical; for trees grown in pots a standard compost such as John Innes No. 2 (or for large pots No. 3) is best. Citrus trees grow in soils with a wide pH range (5.0-8.0).

Feeding Plants grown in the greenhouse border should be mulched annually in early autumn with well-rotted manure or garden compost. In addition, in spring apply a general fertilizer containing important trace elements, such as zinc, according to the manufacturer's instructions.

Container-grown plants should be given a liquid feed, also containing trace elements, at 10–14 day intervals from spring to autumn. Plants established for at least one year in their final pots or tubs should be top-dressed annually in early spring, ideally with a good potting soil such as John Innes No. 3, first carefully removing about 1 in of the old soil without damaging the roots.

Pruning Orange trees should be pruned during their growing period, before they reach their fruiting size in about their fourth

4 Cut back to base any vertical stems (water shoots) that grow in the centre of the tree, that are too tall, or that spoil the tree's symmetry.

5 During the first few years, allow only three or four fruits per plant to set. Remove all remaining fruitlets.

or fifth year as grafted plants. If left to themselves they put out multiple stems and end up as straggly bushes, so remove low shoots both below and just above the union as they appear, and cut back short any excessively vigorous shoots that mar the symmetry of the tree. When the tree reaches fruiting size, no further pruning is needed. Excessive growth can be removed, but in general the less citrus trees are pruned the better.

All citrus trees are prone to produce branches known as water shoots. These are vertical stems which grow direct from the main branches, usually during the early life of the tree. Cut out completely those water shoots that grow in the centre of the tree, that are too tall or that spoil the tree's symmetry.

Pollination

Pollination is not a problem because citrus trees are self-fertile. However, with pot-grown trees, the number of flowers that are allowed to set into fruit must be restricted to the number the tree can bear without strain. Start with three or four per plant.

Harvesting

Citrus fruits do not ripen uniformly, so pick fruits as they ripen. Fruits should reach a good size before they start to colour. The fruits should be snipped off with secateurs, taking care not to bruise or break the peel. The best way of storing citrus fruits is to leave them on the tree; they will not deteriorate but are, of course, subject to damage by wind and frost.

Pests and diseases

Areas where citrus fruits are grown commercially, such as Florida and California in the USA, have serious problems with several citrus pests, but these give less trouble elsewhere. Mealybugs, aphids, whitefly and scale insects attack citrus trees. Spray with insecticidal soap in summer when mealybugs, aphids and scale insects are seen. Spray whitefly when seen with permethrin or pyrethrum at four-day intervals or use biological control.

Second and subsequent years

6 Pick each fruit when it ripens by snipping off the fruit with secateurs. Take care not to damage the peel.

7 In early spring, repot annually into a larger pot until the tree is the required size. Thereafter, carefully replace about 1 in of the old soil with a good potting soil.

Index

The RHS and the Publishers can accept no liability either for failure to control pests, diseases or weeds by any crop protection methods or for any consequences of their use. We specifically draw our readers' attention to the necessity of carefully reading and accurately following the manufacturer's instructions on any product.

Acknowledgements
Most of the artwork in this book has been based on photographs specially commissioned from the Harry Smith Horticultural Photographic Collection.

Artists: Arka Cartographics Ltd, Janet Blakeley, Lindsay Blow, Linda Broad, Charles Chambers, Pamela Dowson, Chris Forsey, Tony Graham, Eric Howley, Alan Male, Ed Roberts, Colin Salmon, Mike Saunders, Stonecastle Graphics, Lorna Turpin, West One Arts.

THE R.H.S ENCYCLOPEDIA OF PRACTICAL GARDENING

EDITOR-IN-CHIEF: CHRISTOPHER BRICKELL

A complete range of titles in this series is available from all good bookshops or by mail order direct from the publisher. Payment can be made by credit card or cheque/postal order in the following ways:

BY PHONE Phone through your order on our special credit card hotline on 01903 828503; speak to our customer services team during office hours (9am to 5pm) or leave a message on the answer machine, quoting your full credit card number plus expiry date and your full name, address and contact telephone number.

BY POST Simply fill out the order form below (it can be photocopied) and send together with your payment to LITTLEHAMPTON BOOK SERVICES, FARADAY CLOSE, DURRINGTON, WORTHING, WEST SUSSEX BN13 3RB

ISBN	TITLE	PRICE	QUANTITY	TOTAL
1 84000 160 7	Garden Planning	£8.99		
1 84000 159 3	Water Gardening	£8.99		
1 84000 157 7	Garden Structures	£8.99		
1 84000 151 8	Pruning	£8.99		
1 84000 156 9	Plant Propagation	£8.99		
1 84000 153 4	Growing Fruit	£8.99		
1 84000 152 6	Growing Vegetables	£8.99		
1 84000 154 2	Growing Under Glass	£8.99		
1 84000 158 5	Organic Gardening	£8.99		
1 84000 155 0	Garden Pests and Diseases	£8.99		
			Postage & Packing	£2.50
			Grand Total	

Name...(BLOCK CAPITALS)
Address...
....Postcode.......................

I enclose a cheque/postal order for £...................... made payable to Octopus Publishing Group Ltd.
or:
please debit my: Access ☐   Visa ☐   AmEx ☐   Diners ☐   account
by £.........................   Expiry date...................

Account number ☐☐☐☐☐☐☐☐☐☐☐☐☐☐☐☐

Signature.................................

Whilst every effort is made to keep our prices low, the publisher reserves the right to increase the price at short notice. Your order will be dispatched within 28 days, subject to availability. £2.50 p&p applies to UK only. Please call 01903 828503 for details of export p&p.
Registered office: 2-4 Heron Quays, London, E14 4JP Registered in England no 3597451
This form may be photocopied.